Maurice Hamilton is an award-winning motorsport journalist and broadcaster, who has worked at the *Guardian*, the *Independent* and the *Observer*. He was the F1 summariser for BBC Radio Five Live and has written more than 30 books on the subject, having attended more than 500 Grands Prix in his career.

Hamilton got to know Lauda well during five decades of reporting on Formula One.

Niki Lauda

THE BIOGRAPHY

Maurice Hamilton

SIMON &
SCHUSTER

London · New York · Sydney · Toronto · New Delhi

First published in Great Britain by Simon & Schuster UK Ltd, 2020
This edition published in Great Britain by Simon & Schuster UK Ltd, 2021

1 3 5 7 9 10 8 6 4 2

Simon & Schuster UK Ltd
1st Floor
222 Gray's Inn Road
London WC1X 8HB

www.simonandschuster.co.uk
www.simonandschuster.com.au
www.simonandschuster.co.in

Simon & Schuster Australia, Sydney
Simon & Schuster India, New Delhi

A CIP catalogue record for this book
is available from the British Library

Paperback ISBN: 978-1-4711-9204-3
eBook ISBN: 978-1-4711-9203-6

Typeset in Bembo by M Rules
Printed in the UK by CPI Group (UK) Ltd, Croydon, CR0 4YY

MIX
Paper from
responsible sources
FSC® C020471

In memory of Alan Henry (AH), who introduced me to Niki and remained a dear friend to us both.

CONTENTS

FOREWORD

I still remember when I met Niki for the first time. I must have been about six years old. Niki's family and my parents often spent time on Ibiza and met up there on occasions. I was still quite young, but I remember the moment precisely: how impressed I was to come face to face with this racing legend. I have always been a massive fan of Formula One, and was watching it on TV even as a small kid while playing with racing cars. Formula One was my everything. Never in my wildest dreams could I have imagined that one day I would be a top-class driver, winning a World Championship and that it would be Niki Lauda himself who would congratulate me on my victory. That moment, when I got out of my car and Niki doffed his red cap to show his respect will forever be one of the outstanding memories of my career.

Niki has always been an idol for me. He finished his career in 1985, the year I was born. I never got to experience him racing live. But as a young driver I watched many of his races on video and learnt a lot. Niki was always very considered, took few risks and worked incredibly hard. He was highly intelligent and was always looking to analyse and to understand. Preparation and set-up were everything. He has shown that as a driver you don't always have to win, you don't always have to be the fastest. But you have to be consistent, avoid mistakes and never rest on your laurels. This approach has been a big influence on me and I put it to good use in my own career. Niki's incredible drive and career have impressed many, not least me. If there ever was someone who never gave up, it was Niki. How he fought against setbacks and adversity only to end up at the very top again, that is impressive, that is huge. We should all be grateful for this inspiration and we all have taken something from him on our way and will remember him forever for it.

Niki was a very passionate man – there were three things he loved more than anything else: Formula One, flying and his family. He was very straightforward and a frank guy, sometimes brutally direct, but always fair and honest. If you wanted a straight answer, you got it from him. Even if it hurt. During my time at Mercedes there were a few difficult moments, especially between myself and Lewis [Hamilton]. Niki often acted as mediator and sat down with both of us to talk through our issues. There were moments when tempers were high. But even in those times, Niki was the one who tried to understand all sides. He was always the go-between to reconcile us. He was very good at it, and it was vital for the team's success. He could get angry, too, but always ensured that we came back together and worked as a team. And he never bore a grudge – no matter what happened, Niki and I always sorted it out. Niki had a gift of leaving the door open for all, and all doors always remained open for him. No scorched earth. 'You always meet twice' was not only one of Niki's mottos, but also my father Keke's, and one I've adopted for myself – Niki has been my great inspiration in that respect as well.

When I decided to finish my career as a racing driver Niki wasn't impressed – for him and the team it was a blow: I had just become World Champion, was a strong driver and important for the team. His reaction to my decision was hard to swallow, but I tried to see it his way. Niki simply did everything with an incredible passion. That's why he was also successful outside of racing. He was one of the few drivers who managed to transfer their Formula One success to other areas of life, which is rare. Today, as I have become an entrepreneur myself, I find myself thinking of Niki even more often, despite our different approaches. Niki was passionate about flying and built a successful airline business. In my projects I'm hoping to drive positive change and link business with doing good. I could often do with Niki's advice on the challenges I encounter. His honest feedback always helped me in my Formula One career and today I draw inspiration from his life. Sometimes when I have decisions to make, I ask myself, *what would Niki say?* In such moments, I can still hear his voice, loud and clear, telling it point-blank.

I will always be indebted to Niki for everything he did for me. He played a huge part in my sporting success and has enriched my life forever. That is amazing and I am very, very grateful for his support.

Nico Rosberg

PREFACE

It was never my intention to write a book about Niki Lauda. I had the good fortune to get to know him during four decades of reporting on Formula One. In common with everyone else who had appreciated his incisive and sharp-witted company, I had come to relish experiences that never ceased to surprise or entertain.

But the thought of writing about it never occurred until the week following Niki's death on 20 May 2019. The outpouring of respect; the flood of tributes from around the world; the genuine emotion for a man who, in truth, was not noted for sentiment: all of these things combined to encourage the belief that such a truly remarkable life really ought to be reflected upon in print.

At the same moment, my literary agent, David Luxton, called with exactly the same thought. The enthusiasm of Ian Chapman and Ian Marshall at Simon & Schuster to publish was the final prompt to begin what has turned out to be a wonderful journey (helped, it must be said, by travelling through a period of F1 populated by colourful and frequently controversial characters).

Before making a start, however, it was important to receive the approval of the Lauda family. I am deeply indebted to Lukas and Mathias for their support. I hope the thoughts, memories and love from the host of willing friends and colleagues within these pages has helped sustain the family in the sad aftermath of such a huge loss.

Before going further, I must offer a word of special gratitude to Bradley Lord and Oliver Owen for their invaluable guidance in various ways.

Finally, and not least, sincere thanks to the following (in alphabetical order) for the time taken to help make this book happen: Jean Alesi, Pino Allievi, Daniele Audetto, Gerhard Berger, Mike 'Herbie' Blash, Daniel Brühl, Mathias Brunner, Will Buxton, Tim Collings, Vivien Cullen, Stuart Dent, Bernie Ecclestone, Rita Farmer, Mauro Forghieri, Lewis Hamilton, Mark Hamilton, Thorsten Hans, Darren Heath, John Hogan, Mark Hughes, Mario Illien, Eddie Irvine, Tony Jardine, Eddie Jordan, Linda Keen, Florian König, Gerhard Kuntschik, Lukas Lauda, Mathias Lauda, Otmar Lenz, Paddy Lowe, Max Mosley, Giorgio Piola, Alain Prost, Nico Rosberg, Dave Ryan, Michael Schmidt, Nav Sidhu, Marc Surer, Jean Michel Tibi, Herbert Völker, John Watson, Toto Wolff, Karl-Heinz Zimmermann and Helmut Zwickl.

INTRODUCTION

Niki Lauda's arrival on the international motor-racing scene was hardly indicative of a brilliant future as a three-time World Champion and a global sporting icon. But then Mallory Park, the scene of his debut, was hardly Silverstone, Monaco or Monza.

Mallory Park remains as uncomplicated as its address on the inside cover of the race programme from four decades ago: 'Mallory Park Circuit, Kirby Mallory, Leicester. Earl Shilton 2631.' Telephone callers in early 1971 learned that the circuit was hosting a Formula Two International Race on Sunday 14 March and admission would cost £1.50.

The inside back cover of the programme (15p) carried a circuit map, shaped rather like a section through the head of a golf club with a lake in the middle. It was a simple diagram because there wasn't much to say about Mallory Park. At 1.35 miles in length, this squashed oval with a tight loop at one end was hardly likely to tax a driver's memory or his skill.

Regardless of the venue's foibles, the track would stage what amounted to a warm-up for the 1971 European Formula Two Championship; a prestigious series thanks to up-and-coming drivers having the opportunity to race against many of the big names from Formula One. The Mallory Park event would be no exception with an entry list boasting Ronnie Peterson, Henri Pescarolo, Derek Bell, Graham Hill and Jo Siffert; drivers with Grand Prix experience ready to deal with upstarts such as Carlos

Reutemann, John Watson and Mike Beuttler (all due to move up to the senior level in the coming seasons).

For British race fans, the quality of the field made questions about the track's suitability irrelevant. This event would mark the end of a drab winter without racing. The race programme waxed enthusiastically about the possibility of the latest F2 cars breaking the track record of 42.8 seconds; an absurdly short lap time, particularly when compared with the 8 minutes it would take to get round the fearsome Nürburgring Nordschleife, scene of the third round of the F2 Championship in seven weeks' time. For now, however, Mallory Park would provide a chance for drivers and teams to shake down their cars and get ready for the season ahead.

Buried in the published entry list of thirty-one cars was a March 712M to be driven by Niki Lauda. The name of the entrant 'Team Erste Osterreachsche Spar Casse' was spelt incorrectly and longer than the passing mention of the driver in the programme's preview note. In truth, this 22-year-old was regarded as no more than some Austrian kid who had managed to persuade a bank to lend him money to go racing. Lauda's early competition career had gone some way to forming that dismissive summary.

Enthusiasts in Britain remembered seeing this 'N. Lauda', whoever he was, crashing his McNamara Formula Three car at Brands Hatch the previous July, but they could recall precious little else. It had been typical of a young driver's tenuous effort to gain some sort of foothold on the motorsport scene, Lauda's enthusiastic struggle being mirrored a thousand times over on racetracks around the world.

Lauda had begun competing in 1968, using a Mini Cooper S to take a number of class wins in hill climbs (or 'mountain races' as they were referred to in Austria). With typical restless ambition, he had traded the Mini for a more powerful Porsche

911, juggling the outstanding premiums on the former with a revised financial arrangement for the sports car. The fact that he often could not make the necessary monthly payments meant more borrowing and increased debt. Not that it necessarily bothered a teenager enjoying the security associated with a wealthy family running a paper mill; a public assumption that conveniently disguised his parents' disapproval and refusal to contribute to their son's motorsport aspirations.

A switch to circuit racing and Formula Vee with the Bergmann team in 1969 increased the challenge for Lauda's shoestring operation, particularly when he managed to somersault the Kaimann single-seater when pushing too hard during his second race on an airfield circuit at Aspern. Lauda was unhurt and intent on learning from his mistake rather than feeling sorry for himself.

The absence of any fear factor would be proved later in the season when he became the first driver to lap more than 170 corners of the fearsome Nürburgring Nordschleife in under 10 minutes in a Formula Vee car; a remarkable achievement by any standard. Lauda may have won just one race in Formula Vee, but his attitude made an impression on Kurt Bergmann, his team manager. Speaking to Lauda's biographer, Herbert Völker, Bergmann said:

Lauda knew nothing about the technical side. He had instinct and a very good touch but he couldn't describe it or build up theories about it. His life was totally given to motorsport. He asked me whether he was a good driver, or did I think he would ever be a good racing driver. I had the feeling he might never get enough money; that finance would be his undoing, because money was decisive for getting on. He was up to all the tricks and he was unbelievably obstinate with people he hoped to get something from but, all the same, I simply didn't see any hope for him to get hold of so much money, as was necessary if you were really going to get on quickly. He lived very modestly and always wore the same clothes and got himself nothing except what had to do with motorsport. But it wasn't much help.

Using the aforementioned stubbornness to pull together financial support from a number of small sources, Lauda bought himself a Porsche 908. This may have been one of the most competitive cars in its class, but Lauda quickly assessed that sports car racing was not the way forward if he wished to progress to the top. The route clearly involved F3 and onward to F2 – and then F1.

His power of persuasion, and just enough sponsorship, earned a drive with the McNamara F3 team founded by Francis McNamara, a United States soldier who had raced in Formula Vee while stationed in West Germany.

With an unfortunate irony, Lauda went to war on the very first day of practice in the 1970 season. A collision while trying to slipstream another car at Nogaro in France sent the McNamara airborne and ended its flight on top of a guardrail, minus all four wheels. That would be but a brief prelude to a spectacular accident later in the year at Zolder in Belgium. Lauda, perhaps understandably, remembered it well in later discussion with Völker:

That was the maddest thing of all. Third lap: an accident – Hannelore Werner [a German driver] – somewhere on the track. We hit the crest of the hill at 210 [kph] and that's when we find the crash truck doing barely 50 [kph]. The first three skidded past it to the right. Then another tried to pass on the right, he didn't quite make it and went into a spin. I'm now trying to pass on the left. Meantime, the other car is spinning to the left; we collide. I spin right round and the next car comes straight into me. The whole scene takes place slap in the middle of the track. I'm stranded there with my car in shreds when the next bunch of cars comes flying over the hill towards us. By now the yellow flag is up and there's all manner of signals – but that mob just kept their foot down. All I could do was sit tight and wonder which side I would get shot down from first. One flew right over the nose of my car. I jumped out and got the hell out of there.

Lauda's summary of the season would read eleven races with McNamara, no decent results and a catalogue of collisions that made the crash at Brands Hatch in July an off-course excursion of no consequence.

That incident had occurred during a support race for the British Grand Prix. Lauda may not have been doing much for his country's reputation on the international motorsport scene, but the same could not be said for Jochen Rindt. The charismatic and extremely quick Austrian had won the Grand Prix in a Lotus 72 and increased his chances of becoming F1 World Champion.

At the other end of the scale, one of Lauda's competitors in the F3 race had been James Hunt, another young hopeful high in ambition and low in funds. Little did either of them realise that in six years' time they would engage in a World Championship battle so intense and dramatic, the story would be worthy of a full-length feature film four decades later.

In July 1970, however, the only record of their efforts was a third place for Hunt and a report in *Autosport* that referred to Lauda's penultimate lap denouement as '... an accident [after which] Lauda was unhurt but his McNamara was a very sad sight'.

Lauda's name had figured from time to time in the same British weekly magazine. Covering the F3 race at Karlskoga in Sweden, *Autosport* reported: 'In the first heat, Lauda really got his McNamara motoring and made up a place lap for lap to move from eighth to third.' On the race at Knutstorp a week later on 16 August, *Autosport* noted: 'The big surprise was provided by the young Nicki [sic] Lauda, who went quickly right from the very start of training and claimed pole. Then he spun to last while leading lap 2.'

During that season, Lauda's car may have been dented – severely at times – but not his confidence. That stubborn streak was infused with a belief that, given the right opportunity, he could prove he was quick enough to reach F1. Having done F3, the next logical step in his mind was F2, even if his bank balance made such a step seem totally impossible.

Understanding the need for money, Lauda applied that logic to the requirement of a racing team he knew to be even more desperate than himself. In September 1969, March Engineering had been founded on fast talk, reasonably fast racing cars and a brass neck on a grand scale. Confounding all predictions of impending disaster, March had produced cars mainly for F1, F2 and F3 – and somehow survived their debut season in 1970, helped by a surprise victory in the Spanish Grand Prix.

Now that the novelty of such impudence had receded, the difficult bit would be carrying the momentum through to a second season. An ace card in the British-based company's hand carried the image and reputation of Ronnie Peterson, a young Swede of prodigious talent and about to start his first full season (Peterson having raced for a privateer March owner during a handful of races in 1970).

Peterson would also head the March F2 team in 1971, his drive paid for by Swedish sponsors. As for the remainder of the

March F2 entry, these cars were available to the highest bidder. Or, as Lauda quickly assessed, any bidder with access to reasonable funds that would help keep March afloat.

With his eye on a drive in a brand-new March F2 car (the 712M), Lauda set about finding the 0.5 million schillings (approximately £8,000) required by March to provide him with the opportunity to show how good he was when matched against some of the best drivers in the world. With barely 1,000 schillings to his name, Lauda pulled together support from various sources and topped it off with a bank loan using his life insurance as collateral. In Lauda's view, this would simply be a means to an end. His results would speak for themselves, a works drive would be forthcoming and his earnings as a fully fledged Grand Prix driver would settle all debts eventually. Simple.

That was the plan as Lauda found his way to Mallory Park in March 1971 and his first outing with the brand new F2 car, painted yellow in deference to the bank spelt wrongly in the programme. John Watson had no such difficulty with proper identification since he didn't have a sponsor. This was the Ulsterman's second season in international motorsport as a privateer; the prelude to eventually becoming a Grand Prix driver and F1 teammate to Lauda – not once, but twice. Watson said:

Like everyone else, I read the motorsport magazines every week and checked the race results to see who was doing what. Niki Lauda was not a name I knew; nothing had stood out to say here was a driver who was going to be a triple World Champion. When he rocked up at Mallory Park that weekend, the thing I remember principally was he came in a brand new 911S Porsche and he was accompanied by Mariella Reininghaus, who was like a piece of Dresden porcelain; a classically beautiful girl. I remember thinking: 'Bloody hell! This guy's got his priorities right.'

Lauda qualified tenth, 1.8 seconds slower than Peterson on pole, but not the slowest of six similar March cars on the grid. The race was run in two heats, Lauda retiring from eighth place in the first heat when a fuel line came adrift (probably the result of overworked March mechanics attempting to service such an extensive entry). The second heat had been much more promising until the twenty-ninth lap (of 40) when the Ford-Cosworth engine failed just after Lauda had worked his way into an impressive fourth place.

The story of the day, however, concerned Peterson. While heading for what appeared to be a comfortable and expected win in the first heat, a ball-joint on the left-hand steering arm broke, just as Ronnie swept into a fast right-hander. The March mounted the safety bank before riding up and over the top and landing upside down between the grass bank and a wattle fence separating spectators from the track. A muddied and shocked Peterson emerged from beneath the wreck, leaving officials to contemplate what might have been had the March travelled a few metres further. The only casualty was a small boy whose face received cuts from flying debris. Any immediate distress was quickly forgotten when Peterson autographed a piece of the wrecked bodywork and handed it to the delighted youngster.

Peterson's retirement had robbed the race of much interest for spectators, a fact this writer can vouch for. Keen to see the season started, I had joined the dedicated race fans trekking up the M1 motorway from London. The grass paddock in Mallory Park had been easily accessed, mainly because fencing and gates were deemed unnecessary and, in any case, an unwanted expense.

Savouring the atmosphere on race morning and wandering among the various trucks and paraphernalia, I had come across Lauda quietly settling into the cockpit of his 712M. Apart from one mechanic, there was no else present, the majority of spectators and March personnel crowded around Peterson's car some distance away. With no notion at that stage of a career as a motorsport writer, I had visions of perhaps becoming a photographer. Moving in close, I took a shot of this fresh-faced no-hope kid. I have no idea why.

Forty years, four months and eight days later, I showed the black and white photograph to Niki Lauda for the first time.

CHAPTER 1

Mad March Days

'I'm like a little boy! Where's this?'

'It was Mallory Park, March 1971. Your first F2 race.'

'Could've been ... don't remember. How did you get this?'

'I took it! I was just a fan at the time and in those days it was very easy to get into the paddock. But I don't know why I took a photo of you; you were a nobody at the time!'

'Correct! The thing that interests me is the ring I'm wearing. This was my family's signet ring; look, there's a family crest on it. I don't know how to say in English, but it was handed down from my grandfather and my father ...'

'We would call it an heirloom.'

'Okay. It was given to me and, at this time, I was still thick enough to use it! My family was a kind of – what's the word: aristocrat? These funny people; in England there are a lot of them! In Austria, there are less. Anyway, I was very young – you can see here the way I looked – and I thought that wearing this ring was the right thing to do.'

'It's on your left hand, which suggests you were married.'

'I wasn't married; nothing like that. I didn't even know

how to wear it properly; just shows how stupid I was. This is a very interesting picture; thank you for showing me this. I had completely forgotten I actually had this ring on when I started racing. I remember soon after this, I threw away the ring, left behind the images of my family's upbringing and good manners, and all that, and decided to try to be a proper racing driver!'

Lauda's attempts to be a 'proper racing driver' with the F2 car in 1971 did not, initially at least, impress the owners of March Engineering. And nor did they need to. An amalgam of the initials of the company's founders (Max Mosley, Alan Rees, Graham Coaker and Robin Herd), March was all about survival. The immediate priority was relieving wannabe champions of their money; their prospects were a secondary – if potentially useful – consideration.

Coaker brought administrative and production experience; Rees, a highly rated F2 driver, acted as team manager; Herd, a genius who graduated from Oxford University with first-class degrees in both Physics and Engineering, provided the technical and design input; Mosley, a qualified barrister and former amateur racing driver, was an eloquent, quick-thinking front man with a razor-sharp intellect. Mosley recalled:

March didn't have any money. Niki came and saw Alan Rees, actually; not me. He had £8,000; that was a lot of money then. Everybody liked him; we were all impressed by Niki as an individual. He was clever. I remember he had dinner with my wife [Jean] and I at an Italian restaurant in Bute Street in South Kensington. He was very good company. Jean and I had moved out of London to Oakley, near the March factory in Bicester, and Niki rented our flat in Victoria for a short while. It never occurred to any of us that he was quick [as a driver]; because he wasn't. He wasn't as fast as Ronnie [Peterson] – but, then, I don't think anyone was.

Typically, Lauda saw the presence of Peterson in a similar F2 car as a means of measuring improvement in his own performance. Lauda was sharing a flat with Mike Hailwood, the former world motorcycle champion turned F1 driver, at Heston, near London's Heathrow airport; a convenient base, not least because Peterson and his wife, Barbro, were living in the same building. Lauda recalled:

> Ronnie and Barbro were in the flat below me. I looked upon Ronnie as 'The Master'. I used to go with him in his Mercedes to [March at] Bicester and I remember very well he was always braking with the left foot. I asked him why he was doing that because this car had a manual gearbox and a clutch, so you used your right foot for braking and accelerating in the normal way. He said this was because he was training – I couldn't understand what he was training for. But Ronnie was so flexible, he could brake with either foot and you wouldn't know it sitting beside him. He was so smooth. He impressed me in every way. I knew, when racing against him, what it was all about because Ronnie was the fastest man at the time.

Lauda was also party to other experiments carried out by Peterson on the run to Bicester. Mosley explained:

> There's a corner on the road to Bicester – between Long Crendon and Oakley – where the road goes up a hill and sweeps left and then right. It's an infamous bend. Ronnie had this theory that he could take this flat [without lifting his foot from the accelerator]. On one occasion he had a

Scandinavian journalist with him who told me that Ronnie wanted to know what speed he was doing through this corner. He knew he could take it flat but he wanted to know how fast the car was going. So the journalist had to watch the speedometer while Ronnie concentrated on the driving. If you go round that corner, the idea of taking it flat in a Mercedes is ... well ... he did it apparently. This poor journalist looked quite pale when he spoke about it. And I'm sure Niki would have been witness to similar exploits with Ronnie.

Apart from a notable sixth place on the Nürburgring Nordschleife, Lauda's first half of the season included retirements and one failure to qualify – ironically at Crystal Palace, the parkland track in south London where Lauda's fellow countryman, Jochen Rindt, had first sprung to prominence with a spectacular drive. Then things began to look up for Niki on 27 June at Rouen-Les-Essarts, a challenging road circuit, noted in particular for a series of downhill swoops leading to a long uphill climb on the return leg and a flat-out blast towards the finishing line. Lauda said:

I was faster than Peterson once in an F2 car. That was at Rouen and it was only because March were trying different rear wings. Ronnie had this new, low wing, which was better on the straights. I had the normal wing – and blew him off because I was much faster through the downhill section because of my rear wing. That felt a bit strange because, as I say, Ronnie really was the master.

Lauda finished fourth that day; his best result of the season. Peterson went on to win the 1971 F2 championship with ease; Lauda was placed tenth. John Watson said:

As the season progressed, Niki's qualities had become apparent. Not just as a capable driver but as an intelligent man who was able to communicate with Robin Herd and the team about how he wanted the car set up – and how to make it better. His position grew primarily because of the feedback he was giving. You could see that, increasingly, Niki was the guy the team turned to in terms of where the car was when it came to technical set up. The other noticeable quality was his ability to generate funds. He may have come from a wealthy background, but it was impressive for a guy at that time to have his level of confidence to walk into a bank and come out with sponsorship to go motor racing. It was becoming clear that Lauda was not some rich guy operating on a whim and dabbling in the sport.

Lauda was also changing the opinion of Austrian journalists, among them Helmut Zwickl, motorsport reporter for *Kurier*, a daily newspaper published in Vienna. Zwickl said:

I was very critical of Niki in his early career. He was not a winner right from the beginning in Formula Three and so on. The relationship between us was not very good. We had lost Jochen Rindt the previous year [the Austrian had been killed during qualifying for the 1970 Italian Grand Prix to become the sport's only posthumous World Champion]. Lauda was very different to Jochen in every way. He didn't have Jochen's charisma for a start. I didn't think he would be a great driver – a mistake by me! But it was becoming clear in 1971 that he could be good. Our relationship improved a lot and we were to become very good friends.

In his season survey, *Autosport*'s F2 correspondent Ian Phillips wrote: 'Niki Lauda's experience was somewhat limited by his age but he soon adapted to the March and put in some highly promising drives which went a part of the way to ensuring his enviable contract for next year.' This review was written in November 1971, Phillips having used his contacts and investigative powers to uncover the fact that Lauda would be racing in both F1 and F2 for March in 1972. Lauda had signed a twenty-two-clause contract on 23 September, making it clear he would be the team's second driver in each category (Peterson being number 1).

Clause 11 on the three-page contract stated: 'The Driver will pay the Entrant £50,000 on the signing hereof in return for his place in the Formula 1 and Formula 2 teams. The Entrant will pay the Driver 45% of all start prize and bonus money earned by him in the Entrant's car.' The figure '£50,000' had been stroked out and replaced in handwritten ink with '$2,500,000 (Austrian schillings)'; 'the signing hereof' had been stroked out and replaced with 'as set out in clause 22 hereof'.

Clause 22, handwritten at the bottom of the final page, stated: 'It is a condition of this Agreement that the Driver will either pay the monies due under clause 11 hereof on the 29th September 1971 or will produce an undertaking guaranteed by his father that he will pay before October 31st 1971. Breach of this condition gives the entrant the right to withdraw without prejudice to any other remedy.' Lauda and Mosley had either signed or initialled the changes and additions.

Lauda had every reason to believe he could produce the funding. The Erste Oesterreichische had been pleased with the exposure gained in 1971 and agreed to a further year's backing. Suddenly, and without warning, Lauda was informed by the bank that the deal was off. He discovered that Hans Lauda, his grandfather and never a fan of Niki's racing ambition, had leaned on his old mates in banking and persuaded the Erste Oesterreichische's board of directors to turn the project down and 'bring the boy to his senses'. Lauda's response was typically quick and straight to the point.

> I telephoned my grandfather and asked him if he could please fuck off interfering in my business. But he said he would not and that no Lauda would ever be a racing car driver; that I should be working in the business and not getting involved in a stupid, dangerous sport. I never spoke another word to him for the remainder of his life and, unfortunately, he died before I became World Champion. But now I was in a tricky situation. I had signed a contract and couldn't pay what I had agreed, which was not the way I had been brought up. The way I saw it, I couldn't let March down.

With March's deadline closing in, Lauda immediately switched his attention to the Raiffeisenkasse bank. Lauda said:

> I met a very good guy there, Karlheinz Oertel. He set up an interest-free, five-year loan in exchange for having his bank's branding on my car and crash helmet. Then he asked what would happen if I killed myself. I thought 'Shit, I hadn't thought of that.' We finalised the deal by securing the money against an insurance policy on my life. But assuming I survived, there was still the loan to pay back. I was leaving myself with no cash in hand and enormous debts.

Ian Phillips was soon on the case, *Autosport* reporting:

> The Raiffeisenkasse has announced that Niki Lauda will race the F1 and F2 March in the colours of the bank. The bankers granted Lauda a credit up to an amount of £38,000 and Niki must refund the amount within three years through his income from starting and prize money. £6,000 is declared

as sponsorship of the car. Lauda, son of a very wealthy bank chairman, is not a risk for his financial partner because his family bears the responsibility for the refunding.

Whether or not the family were aware of this responsibility is debatable. Nonetheless, Lauda was not about to be turned away by March Engineering Limited. The company had lost £73,000 and were overdrawn to the tune of £40,000; substantial sums at the end of 1971. Lauda had signed the contract and promised to deliver his financial end of the bargain. Given the figures involved, Mosley had asked for the letter of guarantee from Lauda's father. He said:

I didn't know much about his background initially. I only found out later about the story concerning the grandfather and the money. I didn't realise he came from quite a big Austrian family; Niki was not the type to discuss that sort of thing. He said he would produce this letter with a guarantee from his father. I remember explaining to our bank manager that it's okay: the money's coming. The money didn't come and Niki was saying: 'Don't worry, don't worry; I'll get it fixed.'

He finally produced this letter. It appeared to have been typed on the same typewriter and paper as previous correspondence from Niki and the signature was pretty illegible – and seemed to have traces of Niki's handwriting. We had no money coming from anywhere else, so what were we going to do? I then said to the bank manager that everything's okay because his father is guaranteeing it. Of course, the bank manager didn't want to shut us down. When the money finally arrived, the bank manager said: 'I can't believe this. It's like getting the Trustee Savings Bank to buy Formula One.'

Lauda said:

> It was a huge gamble, quite crazy really. But being young, I
> thought it would be okay. I was not going to get my family
> money to go racing. It seemed to me that this was the right
> way to get myself quickly into the big league; I'd do the
> season, prove I was quick, then be in demand the following
> year when I'd be paid enough to start paying the money back.
> I was confident I could do it. But, of course, it all depended
> on the car being reasonable.

Lauda had been impressed by March's second F1 car. The 711
had taken Peterson to second place at Monaco, Silverstone,
Monza and Mosport in Canada in 1971. There was every reason
to believe the 1972 car would follow this progression and be
better still. In fact, it would turn out to be one of the worst
cars the company ever produced; a design hamstrung by over-
ambition on the part of Robin Herd. Lauda said:

> Robin and Max told me all about the wonderful new car
> I'd be driving in F1, the 721X. It had a transverse Alfa
> Romeo sports-car gearbox positioned between the tub
> [chassis] and the engine. The idea was to have the weight
> as much as possible in the middle to give the car what they
> called a low polar moment of inertia; this would make
> the car more responsive. There was no reason to doubt
> them; Ronnie had finished second in the 1971 World
> Championship.
>
> I started the 1972 season with updates to the '71 car, which
> was okay, but getting a bit old. I finished eleventh at the first
> race in Argentina. In South Africa, I finished seventh, just
> two places behind Ronnie and, of course, he was thought to
> be the big talent of F1 at that time. So that was okay for my

starting point as an F1 driver. But we badly needed the new car – this fantastic 721X.

A test with the new car was arranged on the Jarama track, scheduled to hold the Spanish Grand Prix a week later. Lauda had no complaints when Peterson was entrusted with the 721X – particularly when Ronnie's feedback was positive. Lauda said:

Ronnie was testing it because he was the number 1; I was the schoolboy. Ronnie ran and ran and ran with this car for two days. It all looked good, particularly when the lap times weren't bad compared to Jackie Stewart [the reigning World Champion], who was testing at the same time in the Tyrrell. In the last hour of the second day, they let me in the car.

I did two laps and said: 'This is biggest pile of shit I've ever driven.' Herd was kind of impressed by my words – but he wasn't happy. This car understeered [wanted to go straight on at a corner], it oversteered [attempted to spin], it was slow down the straight and the gear change was terrible. If you pushed it from fifth to fourth, sometimes you would get second or first. It was just pure luck if you got the right gear. But the handling was the worst thing. There was just no margin between driving and sliding.

Ronnie didn't understand what I was talking about because he would use his ability to drive round any problem the car had. He couldn't tell how good or how bad a car was; he had no idea. He just drove flat out and dealt with whatever the car was doing. There was no way I was going to do that – there was no way I *could* do that! When I later said to Robin after some more laps that I just couldn't get on with this car, he said to me: 'When you've got as much experience and you can drive as well as Ronnie Peterson, you'll be able to do it too.' I can remember every word. It made a big impression on me.

Herd doubted Lauda's assessment because of Peterson's positive response, allied to matching the lap times set by Stewart. Such a comparison failed to take into account Tyrrell's testing of various developments that were not working as hoped and, to prove it, the normally consistent and precise World Champion had been off the road a couple of times.

Reality would begin to dawn on 29 April as official practice began for the Spanish Grand Prix. Peterson would qualify ninth (1.4 seconds slower than the pole position Ferrari of Jacky Ickx and half a second off Stewart's fourth-fastest Tyrrell) and a deeply unhappy Lauda was twenty-fifth fastest, on the back row of the grid and a shocking 5 seconds away from Peterson, never mind the favourites at the front. It was a merciful relief when Lauda's car broke early in the race, Peterson also retiring his 721X with mechanical trouble.

March persevered into the next race at Monaco – and probably wished they hadn't. On a track where Peterson had excelled himself in 1971, he struggled to qualify sixteenth. That was some consolation for Lauda, starting from the back row once more before somehow staying away from barriers in a very wet race to be classified sixteenth, albeit six laps down. Peterson had come home eleventh – a 'mere' four laps behind the winning BRM of Jean-Pierre Beltoise. Herd did not need to be told that Lauda's initial colourful assessment of the car looked like being spot on:

Ronnie was one of my best-ever friends; a fabulous driver and a lovely human being. But he could fool himself, just like I could. The 721X was dreadful. Never mind the gearbox being ahead of the rear axle line in the hope that the car would handle better; the first thing you have to do with a racing car is to keep the tyres happy, and the 721X didn't do that. Going into a corner it understeered madly, then it would snap into sudden oversteer. Both Ronnie and I so wanted this car to work. Ronnie tried so hard – then Niki got into it. Niki always spoke as he found and he didn't hold back when talking about the 721X. Even though I didn't want to accept it straightaway, he was absolutely right.

It confirmed an initial impression I'd had. The first time I thought Niki might be any good was when we took Ronnie and him to Thruxton [in Hampshire] for back-to-back testing. Niki had done a couple of F2 races and hadn't shone particularly. He went out for ten laps to set a base time and then Ronnie went out in the same car. I drove with Niki to the very fast section round the back of the circuit to watch Ronnie. He came round on the warming up lap sideways on. The car leapt into the air off a bump; the tyres were smoking; it was the usual Ronnie. Niki took one step back and he literally went pale. He was absolutely quiet and then he said: 'Robin, I could never, ever, drive a racing car like that in my life.' You could see his whole spirit had gone.

Ronnie did his ten laps and, as we headed back to the pits, I asked Niki what time he thought Ronnie had done. Niki thought about it and said: 'I did 1 minute 14 seconds. He must have been two seconds faster – say 1 minute 12.' Ronnie's lap was, in fact, 1 minute 14.3 seconds. I thought then that maybe Niki was going to be good.

If Lauda had been momentarily depressed by what he had seen at the back of the Thruxton circuit, he was to feel utterly dejected by his struggle to make any sense of the 721X: 'I had really doubted myself during the week between that first test and the start of practice for the Spanish Grand Prix,' he said. 'I thought there was no way I could be as fast as "The Master". But then we got into official practice in Spain and suddenly the 721X didn't seem quite so marvellous.' He continued:

After Monaco, they stuck in a Hewland gearbox to replace the Alfa Romeo gearbox, which made the gear change better, but the rest of the car was as hopeless as ever. It got really bad when Ronnie complained that a privateer in a F2 March with a Formula One Ford engine in the back had blasted past him on the straight during the Belgian Grand Prix [at Nivelles]. By the next race [the French Grand Prix at Clermont-Ferrand], we had the same thing: a F2 car with an F1 engine in the back. It wasn't great, but it was a lot better. At least I could attempt to drive it.

Herd recalled: 'We replaced the unloved 721X with an F2-based car. We called this car the 721G – G for Guinness – because, in desperation, we produced it in nine days, which we thought was good enough for *The Guinness Book of Records*.' It was only good enough to allow Lauda to claim a distant ninth in the British Grand Prix, otherwise he either retired with mechanical woes or finished outside the top ten. With no points to his name, he did not figure on the Championship table. Peterson was ninth – which may as well have been ninety-ninth for a man reckoned to be the fastest in F1.

Lauda said:

The 721X could have wrecked my career before it had started. It was a disaster for me at the time. For Ronnie, who'd already made his reputation, it was okay. He could walk away from it – which he did when he went off to join Lotus in 1973. But, for me, it looked like the end. Ronnie was very supportive during this time. He would help and encourage me, particularly when we were in his car going to Bicester. One of the reasons I didn't lose confidence was that whenever we tested, I'd do a time close to Ronnie's, some-times even quicker. As he was one of the top guys I realised

I couldn't be too bad. And when we raced in F2 together, I could be competitive with him.

Lauda claimed three podium finishes in the 1972 European F2 Championship. Coincidentally, there was a British F2 Championship; a series of five races that didn't amount to much. But two in particular would work in Lauda's favour. In pouring rain at Oulton Park on Good Friday 1972, Lauda won in the absence of Peterson and then returned to the Cheshire track in September to finish second between Peterson and James Hunt (racing a privately entered March). 'When Niki won that day at Oulton Park, the writing was on the wall,' said Mosley. 'When somebody was quick in the wet, it would tell you a lot. It was one of the first things I looked for in a driver. If Niki's teammate had been anyone other than Ronnie, his latent talent would have been more obvious sooner.'

But talent, recognised or otherwise, would not be enough when it came selecting drivers for 1973, despite the best intentions of both sides. Lauda felt he had done all he could and the team, appreciating the appalling car he had been presented with at the start of the season, would make allowances.

On 4 November 1972, Lauda shared a March-BMW sports car with Jody Scheckter (soon to win a scholarship to race in Europe and later become World Champion) in a nine-hour race at Kyalami in South Africa. Lauda came away with more than fourth place as his hopes were raised by Herd discussing details of March's F1 plans for the following season. Being motivated completely by the technical challenge of a new F1 car for a new season, Herd was not fully aware of – or did not want to know – the company's dire financial position. The bottom line looked no better than it had twelve months before – as Lauda was about to find out. He said:

I went to Bicester in December and Max told me there was no money for me to drive in F1. He said I could drive in F2 and do testing of the F1 car because they now knew I was good at that – which was a bit late for me. There was nothing more to say. I was in complete despair. I had no money, I owed two million schillings and I had no contract, mainly because of having to drive that shit box 721X.

Just down the road from the March factory was a big wall straight ahead at a stop sign, where you had to turn right or left. I thought for one second I'll drive into the wall and kill myself because there is no solution to pay the money back and I've failed completely proving myself in F1. Thank God it was only a flash and I controlled it quickly. But I remember this moment very well.

I later thought about my options. To pay back that money would be impossible if I got what you would call a 'normal' job; it would take the rest of my life. So, there was no choice; I had to become an established F1 driver. And it had to cost me nothing. Another loan was impossible.

Mosley said:

Niki told me this [the brief thought of ending his life] much later. When you come out of Murdoch Road where our factory was situated and into the main road, there was a point where there was a wall. He thought 'Why don't I just floor it?' Happily, he thought better of it, but it was a moment of complete despair.

Robin had all the dealings with him – I didn't see much of Niki – but Robin hated confrontation. It fell to me to tell Niki the bad news. It was one of those things you remember all your life. I knew that what I was telling Niki was catastrophic for him – but I had no choice. Then he went off and thought about ending it all. We talked about it often in later years. It had been a very bad moment. And for Niki to say such a thing gives you an indication of his complete despair at that point.

By the time he had reached the airport and boarded a flight to Vienna, Lauda had begun hatching another audacious plan. And it would involve an F1 team owner not averse to bold embellishment himself.

CHAPTER 2

A Haughty Helping Hand

Louis Stanley did not actually own BRM, but liked to create the impression that he did. British Racing Motors had been founded in 1945 as a means of restoring the country's engineering and motor-racing pride immediately after the Second World War. The method of financing the project was through a trust fund, but the British motor industry would prove as unwieldy as a complex racing car that failed to perform. As support drained away, it fell to one of the partners in the trust, Sir Alfred Owen, to take control.

BRM became a small cog in the massive Rubery Owen engineering group, Sir Alfred seeing the racing team as a means of proving the firm's competence. That came slowly, BRM winning their first Grand Prix in 1959 and a World Championship with Graham Hill in 1962. Success had finally come about thanks, in part, to the arrival of Louis Stanley – who initially knew little or nothing about motor racing.

Stanley, managing director of London's Dorchester Hotel, had married Jean Owen, sister of Sir Alfred. A chance visit to the 1959 Monaco Grand Prix had sparked the Stanleys' interest in the sport, encouraged further by BRM breaking their duck at the very next race. Sensing simmering unrest within the team, Stanley used his considerable organisational skills to shift the power base and place key engineers in the right places. The accompanying increase in competitiveness in the early 1960s made BRM a highly respected team – a fact Stanley was only too happy to capitalise on.

With Sir Alfred, a deeply religious man, declining to attend races on Sundays, Stanley became BRM's figurehead. An imposing individual with a regal air, Stanley fell into the role with practised aplomb, particularly when abroad. He was not averse to being mistakenly introduced – particularly among the more gullible members of America's racing society – as 'Lord Stanley', an elevation he chose to carry with pompous pride rather than politely refute.

Supporting the efforts of Jackie Stewart, Stanley did good work with the introduction of much-needed medical back-up at the races, but it was his team that, ultimately, would be in need of resuscitation. When Sir Alfred suffered a heart attack in 1969, Stanley was unchecked. Elaborate plans with new-found sponsor, Marlboro, led to the expansion of BRM into a four-car team and a roster of drivers, with as many as nine during 1972.

This had not gone unnoticed by Lauda. Suspecting Stanley would be susceptible to a flattering approach enriched by the prospect of money, Lauda made contact and arranged an appointment. He said:

I knew Stanley was looking for sponsorship. I called him up and said: 'Sir, I would like to drive your racing car, blah, blah, blah.' I convinced him that I had a sponsor – which I didn't have. He told me he would come to Vienna immediately in order to negotiate terms. We met at the airport and he was negotiating with me and a bank manager who I brought along. I had borrowed some money from this man and I was trying to convince him he could be my new sponsor. The bank manager didn't speak English very well and I was translating – let's say in a way that favoured me. I got Stanley to agree to his 'sponsorship' coming later than scheduled, in May at around the time of the Monaco Grand Prix.

BRM already had [Jean-Pierre] Beltoise and [Clay] Regazzoni as drivers with [Vern] Schuppan as maybe a third driver. I convinced Stanley to let me have the third car. I made a deal there and then that I have to pay my first amount of sponsorship to BRM in May. Then Stanley said I could do the first three races only [Argentina in January; Brazil in February; South Africa in March; all alongside Regazzoni] and then Schuppan would take over. I said I wanted more than that, but I knew I would have to make those first races really count.

In the first two races of 1973, Lauda retired with engine problems in Buenos Aires and finished eighth in São Paulo; in each case, the slowest BRM driver. The picture would change dramatically in South Africa when Regazzoni crashed and was rescued from his burning car by Mike Hailwood. Beltoise retired after a few laps, leaving Lauda as the sole BRM runner and holding an impressive sixth place when the engine failed. Had this been enough to ensure future Grands Prix with BRM? Lauda recalled:

> Schuppan drove the car in a non-championship race at Brands Hatch and I don't think he did that well [Schuppan qualified third but crashed in the race]. Whatever the story, they could see I had been quick right away – particularly in South Africa – so I kept the drive. Then I scored my first championship points by finishing fifth in Belgium. The problem was, of course, that Mr Stanley would be waiting for his money in Monaco – and I didn't have any. None at all.

Lauda's pragmatism allowed his driving to overrule financial concerns as he tackled the famous street circuit, the layout of which had received a major change along the harbour front for the first time since the introduction of the Monaco Grand Prix in 1929. Lauda adapted quickly and was the fastest of the three BRM drivers in two of the three practice sessions, the red and white car earning sixth place on the grid, directly ahead of Regazzoni.

Lauda made the most of his starting position and soon found himself in third place, behind the Tyrrell of Stewart and Emerson Fittipaldi's Lotus. Not only was Lauda the leading BRM, he was also ahead of the Ferraris, a fact that did not go unnoticed at Maranello in Italy as Enzo Ferrari followed the progress of his cars. Lauda's place in the sun lasted for 24 laps before the BRM's gearbox broke. A point had been made. But not the dollars needed to satisfy Stanley's contractual requirements. When Lauda received an invitation to dinner in the Hotel de Paris, he knew his host would want more than compliments for his choice of expensive wine:

When Stanley asked: 'Where's the money?' I couldn't really answer him. And he knew that. Then he said: 'I know that you have difficulties but you impressed me so much with this drive [in Monaco] and everywhere else that I'm going to give you the drive to the end of the year without sponsorship. But I need you to sign with BRM for another two years. I will pay you £30,000 a year.' I signed the contract that evening and returned to Austria the next day.

Niki was living in Salzburg, where he had use of a small office belonging to his cousin. Lauda said:

There was a standing joke with my cousin's secretary, who did some work for me. Whenever I left the office, I'd say:

'When Ferrari calls, then tell me straightaway.' As soon as I returned, I'd ask: 'Ferrari? Did they call?' and she would say: 'No, not today', or 'No, the telephone is out of order', or something. On the Monday I got back from Monte Carlo, she said: 'Ferrari called.' I gave a rude reply and she said: 'No, no! Ferrari called. Look! Here is the number.' I said: 'Are you being serious? Who should I speak to?' When she said it was 'Monte-something [Luca di Montezemolo, Ferrari's team manager]', I knew it had to be true.

So, I called Montezemolo and he said Mr Ferrari has been impressed with what I did in Monaco and he wants to speak to you. The next day, I went down to Italy, spoke to [Enzo] Ferrari and he said: 'I saw you at Monaco driving ahead of our fabulous Ferrari. I want you to drive for us.' I said I had made a deal two days before with Mr Stanley to drive for him. Ferrari said: 'Leave it to me. I take care of all this. I just want you to sign for us.'

I had seen everything Ferrari had in Maranello: a private test track with automatic timekeeping; closed circuit television and computers; technical resources with lots of people. When I thought about the facilities I'd experienced with my previous F1 teams, March and BRM, I just could not believe what was available at Ferrari. My first impression? 'Why don't they win all the races?' Immediately I wanted to go there and not even think about if it will work or if it won't. They were having a bad time [in 1973], but I had the feeling they were going to do something and get on with the programme. I was pretty sure something would happen at Ferrari.

Ferrari's intuition would also be proved correct at Silverstone when Lauda, the fastest of the BRMs, briefly held second place in the British Grand Prix (on the restart following a multi-car collision on the first lap) and was thinking about challenging

Peterson's leading Lotus. The effort took too much from his tyres and Lauda gradually dropped back. But another point had been made. Lauda remembered:

> I liked the old circuit at Silverstone. I'll never forget, when I was an idiot driver in F3 in 1969, I was watching the F1 cars practise for some race [the non-championship International Trophy] at Woodcote, the corner before the pits. Jochen Rindt came round that corner, in the wet, sideways. I still have this picture in my mind. It was unbelievable. And I do remember the Grand Prix there in 1973 when [Jody] Scheckter crashed and caused the big mess at the end of the first lap. I had broken the driveshaft on my BRM on the start-line so I didn't get away as a result. This was lucky for two reasons. I was therefore not involved in the crash and, when I saw Beltoise's car had been damaged and would not be able to take the restart, I got my mechanic to take the driveshaft off and put it on my car. This was good because I was able to take the restart and go really well until the tyres gave up – which I knew they would, so I had to do what I could when the conditions were right.

Tyre trouble would once again bring retirement from the Dutch Grand Prix at Zandvoort, but not before Lauda experienced what he later described as one of motorsport's darkest days. On the eighth lap, Roger Williamson's March left the road due to a suspected front suspension or tyre failure. The car hit the barrier, which bent back as the March ran along it, ripping off a fuel tank on the right-hand side. When the car came to rest, it was upside down and alight.

David Purley, a British driver who happened to be following Williamson, stopped immediately and ran back to assist his friend. It was to a heartbreaking and hopeless task, the inverted angle of the March being so severe – and in the absence of help from marshals who stood helplessly by not knowing what to do – Purley could not right the car as the fire took hold. All the while, the race continued; unthinkable by today's standards.

Drivers were signalling to officials as they passed the pits but, in the absence of proper telephone communication with the marshals' post near the scene of the accident, no one in control knew what to make of it. The drivers were also confused, Lauda later explaining that they thought they could see the driver out of his car attempting to put out the flames, when in fact it was Purley trying desperately to save his friend from being burned alive. (Purley's car was out of direct vision on the other side of the track and then shrouded in smoke from the burning March.) Williamson was twenty-five and taking part in only his second Grand Prix. Lauda later told his friend, the journalist Herbert Völker:

> Roger wasn't just another driver. He was one of the nicest people around. I liked him as a person and I was close to his sponsor, Tom Wheatcroft, a gentle and intelligent man. Our friendship went back to Formula Three days and our relationship was close, not just a casual Grand Prix familiarity. When we discovered later what had really happened, we were all devastated. I will never forget the sight of Tom Wheatcroft's crumpled figure, tears streaming down his cheeks. I look back on Zandvoort 1973 as one of the darkest days of my entire professional career.

Lauda's remarks take on added poignancy considering the similarity between Williamson's crash and Lauda's near-fatal accident three years later. Before then, however, he had to finalise details of his Ferrari deal and hope the breaking of the BRM contract would not present a problem. Enzo Ferrari, in turn, would have noted that Lauda had been fastest of all in a wet practice session at Zandvoort; a significant indication of a driver's true potential, as mentioned by Max Mosley when recalling Lauda's F2 victory in the rain at Oulton Park in 1972.

Lauda's notable efforts would come to a painful halt at the Nürburgring Nordschleife when he left the road on the fast climb from Bergwerk (not far beyond the scene of that much more serious crash to come in 1976). Lauda lost a very impressive fifth place when the BRM destroyed itself against the guardrail. Reporting for *Motor Sport* magazine, the respected journalist Denis Jenkinson wrote:

> On the second lap as Lauda took the tight climbing right-hander at Bergwerk he felt there was something odd about the feel of his BRM, and while he was thinking about it and taking the flat-out swerves at Kesselchen he flew off the road and in a long accident completely demolished his BRM and broke his wrist. It all pointed to a deflating rear tyre, for BRMs have not been prone to breaking suspension members, wheels, or steering parts, like some cars.

The timing of this accident was bad for a number of reasons, not least that Lauda would have to miss his home race, which came next. He was behind the wheel again for the Italian Grand Prix, a return compromised by the engine's shortfall in power being exposed by Monza's long straights. Since the V12 engine was proudly designed and built by BRM themselves, Stanley never felt comfortable in the face of complaints from his drivers. Lauda said:

> I had been telling him about this all the time. To speak about these things with Stanley, you would be invited to the Dorchester Hotel in London to have afternoon tea with him.

You can imagine what that was like; it was like he owned the place. One time I was telling him that his great twelve-cylinder engine was not delivering enough horsepower and he was listening very politely and drinking his tea. Then he says he will find a solution right away. He gets up and goes to the bathroom. He's away for about ten minutes and, when he comes back, he says in that very formal and grand way he had of speaking: 'I have just spoken to the engine test bench. We have found another twenty horsepower in the exhaust system.' Of course, you go to the next race and the engine is exactly the same.

Engine power was never going to be so critical on the twists and turns of Mosport, particularly when the Canadian Grand Prix began on a wet track. If Lauda had failed to catch the eye of the F1 cognoscenti with his previous efforts at significant moments, he truly made his mark by immediately storming through from eighth on the grid to snatch third place. Covering the race for *Motor Sport*, Andrew Marriott wrote:

> The man to watch was definitely Lauda, his bright red helmet proving easy to spot amidst all the spray and, at the start of lap three he squeezed by [Jody] Scheckter going into turn one to grab second place and, a lap later, he was in the lead of a Grand Prix for the first time in his career. Two laps later he had an eight-second advantage and, by lap ten, he was over a quarter of a minute in the lead and had lapped the last eight runners. His superiority in the wet was remarkable and, while we all know that BRM and the Firestone tyres suited the conditions, Lauda deserves a great deal of praise too.

Ferrari, having already seen more than enough, had formalised his deal with Lauda for 1974. Lauda recalled:

When I signed for Ferrari, it was another big risk because I knew I would have to fend off legal action from BRM as a result. But, really, it was obvious by then that BRM was going nowhere and that if I wanted to have a chance of making it as a professional driver, I had to accept that Ferrari deal. If I'd turned it down, I don't think it would have been offered again. But, of course, I was new to it all and didn't understand the subtleties of working with the Italians. That was yet to come.

CHAPTER 3

Oiling the Ferrari Machine

Lauda immediately got down to work at Ferrari in his inimitable way. He told them their F1 car was rubbish.

In the absence of the contractual restraints that today prevent drivers from barely speaking to their new team before the existing season with their present employer has finished, Lauda was invited by Luca Montezemolo to the Ferrari headquarters in Maranello – specifically, the company's Fiorano test track – in the autumn of 1973. There he would be reacquainted with Enzo Ferrari, meet Mauro Forghieri, Ferrari's technical director, and Piero Lardi (Enzo Ferrari's illegitimate son, who would not be formally recognised until the death of Ferrari's wife, Laura, in 1978 and allowed to add 'Ferrari' to his name).

Lauda was asked to try the Ferrari 312 B3 which, along with the B2 early in the season, had not won a single race and would contribute to sixth place in the 1973 Constructors' Championship, Ferrari's worst result since the advent of the championship fifteen years before. According to Lauda:

This car was so bad, it made me realise just what a good chassis the BRM had been, even if its engine lacked power.

I have to say, that Ferrari was very bad. Because I spoke no Italian and Mr Ferrari spoke no English, Piero Lardi – poor guy – had to translate. So, I got out of this car after maybe half a dozen laps at Fiorano and said to Piero: 'Tell him that the car is a piece of shit.' Piero was horrified. 'No, no! There's no way I can do that.' So I said: 'Okay, then tell him it's got terminal understeer; whatever you like. There is something wrong with the front suspension. If we don't get on and fix it, this will be a total waste of time.'

It is important to fill in the background to two key Ferrari associates who would play an influential part in Lauda's success in helping turn the team around.

Luca Cordero di Montezemolo, aged twenty-six, was already on his way to becoming the equivalent of Italian royalty. Of noble blood and a member of the Agnelli dynasty that controlled Fiat, Montezemolo had gained a Masters degree in International Commercial Law at La Sapienza University in Rome before spending time at Columbia University, New York. When Fiat became associated with Ferrari in 1973, Montezemolo was drafted in to look after the auto manufacturer's interests at Maranello, acting as an unobtrusive liaison between the racing team, Enzo Ferrari himself and the Fiat board of directors. Having competed in Italian club racing, Montezemolo had a feel for motor racing and understood the significance of the sport – specifically Formula One – to Enzo Ferrari.

With the 'Old Man' (as he was affectionately known) refusing to attend races – and perpetuating the Ferrari 'legend' in the process – the team manager was Ferrari's eyes and ears. Montezemolo was following a line of famous (and occasionally infamous) names carrying out a role that often created more havoc than it prevented. The difference this time was that, rather than play politics and tell Ferrari what he wanted to hear, the urbane Montezemolo would gently state the facts, no matter how unpalatable they might be. It was an asset Lauda quickly realised he would need to depend on in order to get things done properly.

According to racing drivers who had benefited from his work at Ferrari, the bespectacled Mauro Forghieri was a design genius with a passion for the sport that occasionally spilled over in dramatic – and frequently entertaining – fashion. Having been with the company since he was a trainee engineer, Forghieri became technical director overnight in 1961 when Enzo Ferrari fired his entire management team following a major disagreement. Forghieri had more than proved his worth with racing cars that would become Ferrari classics. But his boss's penchant for sudden and dramatic change was never far from the surface – as Forghieri had recently discovered when he took the blame for a disappointing season in 1972 and was shunted off to a special projects department within Ferrari's road car division. When the 1973 season proved to be even worse, Forghieri was quickly forgiven, his return to the racing team coming shortly before Lauda's test of the current car and a damning summary that did not surprise Forghieri in the slightest. Lauda said:

You couldn't help but notice the potential of this team. It was unbelievable. And yet they were producing these terrible cars. I quickly came to the conclusion that a major problem had been politics inside the team. It was just a question of organising these good people properly. Once I got to know Luca, I could see how valuable his contribution was. He was starting to get everybody together, persuading them, in the way he can, to pull in the same direction. Forghieri was obviously a tremendous engineer and Luca was very good at telling the Old Man about what was happening. He did it with a totally impartial mind, which was very good. In the past, the communication had maybe been not too good . . .

A final and important part of the racing team was Lauda's driving partner for 1974. Clay Regazzoni had raced with Ferrari for three years (winning the 1970 Italian Grand Prix) before tiring of the slump in 1972 and moving to BRM – which was where he got to know Lauda. Niki enjoyed Clay's roguish company, his love of racing and a complete absence of political guile. 'I'd never say we were close friends,' said Lauda. 'But I liked him and valued him. He was the perfect team partner. In many ways Regazzoni was what people expected a racing driver to be; he was stocky, rough, moustache and a big smile. Women loved him.'

It said much about Regazzoni's qualities as a team player that Ferrari should reconsider the Swiss and also take heed of his complimentary assessment of Lauda as a driver worth watching.

What Ferrari truly made of this confident young Austrian's criticism of his car after a few laps of Fiorano will never be known. But his response was indicative of how he would handle such cutting analysis of the Ferrari's front suspension. Ferrari immediately asked Forghieri how long it would take to make the changes Lauda had suggested. When the engineer said it would take a week, Ferrari turned to Lauda and asked how much quicker he could go. 'I replied half a second,' recalled Lauda. 'I probably should have said three-tenths, but I had already discussed this with Forghieri and knew the time was there if we made the changes to the suspension.'

This particular car was, in fact, a heavily modified version of the one raced with such little success, Forghieri using lessons learned as a basis for the 1974 car. Lauda spent the week in the company of the technical guru, looking and learning. 'When I got back in the car,' said Lauda, 'I found eight-tenths and from that moment I had Mr Ferrari's respect.'

Fiorano would become Lauda's second home that winter. Enzo Ferrari frequently visited the test track to check on progress. When he didn't show up, Lauda would make a point of finishing his day's work by driving the short distance to the company's office and speaking directly to the boss. That was a good way of gradually fostering a relationship with someone possessing a prickly reputation; it was also convenient for the rest of the team to be aware that Niki increasingly had the Old Man's ear.

The continual quest for improvement meant Forghieri had instigated almost thirty alterations to his original concept of the 1974 car, the Ferrari 312 B3. Apart from detail changes, the car had received a fundamental revision with the fuel carried more centrally and the cockpit moved forward. The success of this major rethink brought a new experience for Lauda as he was fastest in a practice session for the first race in Argentina and went on to score his first podium by finishing second. The novelty value would continue into the third race in South Africa, where Lauda claimed his first pole position – only to face a less enjoyable phenomenon: the disappointment of likely success being denied by a mechanical problem beyond his control.

Lauda's first win seemed only a matter of time. It came at the next race in Spain. Lauda remembered:

The conditions were slippery and difficult. I could see Montezemolo standing next to the race director for the final three laps and wondered what the hell he was doing. He was apparently trying to get the race stopped while I was still ahead! That evening, I received a phone call in my hotel room from Emerson Fittipaldi, whom I didn't know well at that stage. He told me that the first win was always the most difficult and the rest would come easily – and he was right. But saying that, there were a few things that got in the way.

It would be particularly irritating at Monaco where a certain win in such prestigious and demanding surroundings was lost because of an obscure electrical failure. Two months later, annoyance of a different kind appeared unexpectedly at Brands Hatch as Ferrari prepared for the British Grand Prix, only to be informed that the team's transporters were likely to be impounded because of Lauda's 'ongoing' contractual dispute with BRM. Lauda said:

As far as I was concerned, this had been taken care of by Ferrari's lawyer. In any case, BRM had gone down; finished. Mr Stanley, in fact, owed me money; I hadn't received anything despite his promise at Monaco in 1973. So, Ferrari got information from British lawyers that they're going to impound Ferrari's equipment because of my fight with BRM. I called Bernie [Ecclestone – de facto leader of the F1 teams] and told him this was partly my fault, but I thought Ferrari would have a problem at Brands Hatch and I explained why. Straightaway, Bernie said don't worry, he would sort it out. I don't know what he did, but we heard no more about it!

Nonetheless, it was to be a bad omen for Lauda's weekend, even though he enjoyed the undulating circuit in Kent. Leading comfortably with about 20 laps to go, Lauda felt the rear of the Ferrari lose some of its stability. An eagle-eyed Jackie Stewart, commentating for BBC Television, spotted a slight dip in the profile of Lauda's right-rear tyre, indicating a slow puncture. The Ferrari crew noticed the deflating tyre as well and prepared for their man to make a pit stop. But when Lauda pressed on, determined to try to reach the finish, not even an agitated Mauro Forghieri waving frantically from the pit wall could convince him to come in. When Scheckter's Tyrrell took the lead with four laps remaining, Lauda continued to stay out.

On the penultimate lap, the tyre failed completely, leaving Lauda with no option but to head for the pit lane. The Ferrari mechanics changed the wheel in less than 15 seconds (impressive in 1974) and sent Lauda on his way to what should have been fifth place and two championship points. But he got no further than the pit lane exit where, unforgivably, the organisers had parked a Ford course car. As Scheckter crossed the line to take the chequered flag, the Ferrari and its furious driver were engulfed by a hoard of photographers and onlookers, keen to witness the winning moment. As if to rub salt into the wound, an official stood in front of Lauda, holding a red flag to indicate the blindingly obvious that the Ferrari should go no further.

Forghieri was fit to be tied, but no amount of ranting and raving at officials could undo the ridiculous folly. Lauda was classified ninth and out of the points. Not even the eloquence of Montezemolo could persuade the race stewards to change their minds. Ferrari then lodged an official protest, which was rejected by the Royal Automobile Club, Britain's motoring authority. A subsequent appeal to the CSI (Commission Sportive Internationale), motorsport's world governing body, saw the RAC's judgment overturned two months later. Lauda was awarded fifth place. But, as events unfolded, the additional two points would make no difference to his championship; despite heading the points table, he had already begun to lose that through inexperience and basic errors.

Lauda had qualified on pole for the German Grand Prix at the Nürburgring Nordschleife but fumbled his start. Regazzoni swept into the lead, followed by Scheckter. When Lauda tried to dive down the inside of the Tyrrell at the second corner, he lost control of the Ferrari and spun off. As ever, Lauda had immediately formed a critical mental analysis of his driving:

Obviously, I couldn't expect Jody to give me much room, but I still tried to get through. As I went on the brakes I realised that they were pulling me to the right, towards the Tyrrell. I tapped his car, spun across his front wheels and went smashing into the catch-fencing. I made a complete idiot of myself by trying to pull a manoeuvre that I could have managed at any other time round that fourteen-mile lap. I didn't want Regazzoni to get away at the start because I knew on that circuit it would be difficult to catch him unless I quickly got past Scheckter. It was just stupid.

As far as Brands Hatch was concerned, it was a gamble, a real 50–50 situation. The tyre might well have lasted, and who's to say that the wheel nut wouldn't have jammed if I had to come into the pits earlier? I honestly didn't feel I made a mistake at Brands. It was a gamble that didn't come off. Very simple.

There was no question about where the fault lay in Canada, Lauda sliding off the road while defending his lead from the McLaren of Emerson Fittipaldi. The subsequent win for Fittipaldi would put him back in the front of the title fight and set up a championship showdown between the Brazilian and Regazzoni at the final race in the United States. These two had dominated the championship, Lauda leading mid-season thanks to wins in Spain and Holland.

Since Marlboro sponsored McLaren as a team and had personal deals with both Ferrari drivers, this arrangement tested the diplomatic skills of John Hogan, the head of motorsport for Philip Morris and its Marlboro tobacco brand. Hogan said:

I had joined Philip Morris on 1 September 1973. So, I came in at the end of Marlboro's association with BRM. You could already see that Niki was the man of the moment – and that really came home to me when he was in the BRM and chasing better cars and better drivers during the wet Canadian Grand Prix.

We had a thing at that point called the Marlboro World Championship Team, which was all about personal sponsorships, and this included Niki and Clay. Niki's contract was up for renewal at the end of that year, 1973. I was commanded to go and renew it. Fortunately for me, I had got to know Niki when he was driving that horrible McNamara F3 car and he was friendly with James [Hunt]. I was sort of a hanger-on; that's how I got into that.

When it came to doing the deal with Ferrari, Luca was key to this. He was confident, dynamic and very street smart. He could see that Niki was the man of the future. So, 1974 was turning out to be a real development year for Niki – and for me as I learned a lot about contract negotiation in that year.

Dealing with Niki was totally straightforward. His opening gambit would be: 'I want more money. Yah?' You'd start from there, kick it around until you had a deal that worked – and shook hands. That's how it was done then: on a handshake.

By securing his second world title at the final race, Fittipaldi triggered criticism that Ferrari had lost out thanks to their drivers fighting each other rather than working as a team. According to Hogan:

That had something to do with it. By his own admission, Niki made mistakes on the track although I think the main reason for losing the championship was that he and Ferrari underestimated Emerson; he was such a smart guy. He weighed up everybody and he knew just how far he could push his competitors. Niki was still learning at this stage and I know he got a bit irritated by the suggestion that the only reason he had lost the title was because of in-fighting with Clay.

Lauda said:

I got tired with those people who said that if Clay and I had run as a team we would have done better in 1974. There was just no way we would have improved. There were even some idiots who said that if I hadn't won two Grands Prix that year, then Regazzoni would have been champion. They were almost blaming me for winning races! To be honest, I didn't care whether I was number 1 in the team or number 15, so long as I was happy and getting the equipment to do the job. And I was happy because the team was brilliant. If I'd asked for a square wheel to be fitted on one corner, they would have done it without question. The co-operation between the team and drivers was fantastic. It was a hundred per cent effort.

I knew we could only get better – and I had to stop making stupid mistakes. I have to say, I had not been ready to become World Champion. I had screwed up. But I knew what I needed to do for 1975.

There was no question that Lauda had 'screwed up'. In fact, his occasional impetuosity – the Nürburgring first-lap incident being a good example – begged questions about dealing with the inevitable pressure that comes with trying to win a world title while driving for Ferrari. But that took no account of an exceptional ability not only to learn from mistakes but also to ensure they did not occur again. The forthcoming season was about to provide proof of that.

CHAPTER 4

A Championship Made Easy

There was a completely new car for 1975, the Ferrari 312T. After its first race, Lauda knew he had a problem – not with the car, but with gloomy predictions by the Italian media that the 312T with its supposedly clever gearbox did not work and Ferrari would be in trouble.

Mauro Forghieri had heeded his drivers' complaints that the 1974 car had an annoying tendency to understeer, thus reducing the sharpness and precision Lauda and Regazzoni needed when turning into a corner. In a wholesale revision of his thinking, Forghieri had introduced a transverse gearbox by effectively turning it through 90 degrees and mounting the transmission across the back of the car rather than in the traditional longitudinal position. This, coupled with a redesign of the suspension and other features, had cured the understeer but made the car feel more nervous; not necessarily a bad thing if the driver could keep such edgy mechanical energy under control.

A car that was 'alive' had the potential to go faster. Lauda could cope with that. But he found it more difficult to deal with the ill-informed views of sports writers who were fashioning opinion, particularly across the Ferrari workshop floor. With

Italian national newspapers devoting entire broadsheet pages to Ferrari, the need to create stories on a daily basis often subjugated facts that were boring but annoyingly correct. The first race for the Ferrari 312T had been a case in point.

Development progress with the new car during the winter had been badly disrupted when Regazzoni wrote off the first 312T during a test session on the Vallelunga track to the north of Rome. Preferring to play safe, Forghieri had decided to take a pair of 1974 cars to the opening races in Argentina and Brazil in January. Ferrari returned from South America with no decent results to speak of because, as Lauda summed up succinctly, the 312 B3 'had completely used all its potential and was slow'.

The Ferrari 312T was taken to the third round at Kyalami and both drivers would come away even lower on the championship table than they had been on arrival in South Africa. Lauda's weekend had started badly. Caught out by oil dropped seconds before by Fittipaldi's failing McLaren, he had spun into the banking. The car was repaired in time for the race but a slow start dropped Lauda down the order, from which he never recovered thanks to the engine feeling gutless, particularly on the long straight that characterised Kyalami. Unable to make any impression, he finished fifth, half a minute behind Scheckter's winning Tyrrell. To compound Ferrari's disappointment, Regazzoni, having run behind Lauda, retired with a broken throttle linkage.

When the team later examined Lauda's flat-twelve engine in the workshop, it was discovered that a drive belt had been slipping badly and lost some of its teeth. By which stage the media, unaware that Lauda had been attempting to race with an estimated four-fifths of his engine power, had sharpened their particular teeth. Rising speculation that the new car was a dud had already begun to have a deleterious effect on the workforce.

Alan Henry, a British journalist who had known Lauda since his international debut at Mallory Park four years before, was one of a handful of F1 writers Lauda liked and trusted outside his associates in the Austrian media. Reflecting some years later on this potential loss of faith at Maranello, Lauda told Henry:

As I went round the factory various people would sidle up to me and ask if this new car was any good. I was really quite shocked that all this stupid criticism had sapped their spirit completely. There was only so much I could say. So I suggested to Luca and Mauro that we take a B3 and a 312T over to Fiorano and I do a back-to-back test. Which is what we did. First I set a time with the B3 and then followed that up by breaking all the lap records with the new car – and I hadn't been going deliberately slow with the B3, as the lap times showed. When I came in, all the mechanics were laughing and everybody in the factory was happy again.

The Ferrari workforce may have been reassured but the criticism would continue even after Lauda had narrowly won a non-championship race at Silverstone with the 312T at the end of an entertaining battle with Fittipaldi's McLaren. Lauda told Henry:

You wouldn't believe it. I made the mistake of saying to somebody that I switched off the [engine's] rev limiter and gave it a good burst to 12,800 rpm as I tried to pass [James] Hunt [in a Hesketh] in the early stages. When I found it made no difference, I switched the limiter back on again. So one Italian paper said: 'Lauda was lucky to win the race because he over-revved his engine and he wouldn't have won if it had been a full-length Grand Prix.' I mean, what do you say to idiots like that?

Such idle comment may have been part and parcel of everyday racing, particularly in Italy, but events at the next Grand Prix in Spain would create headlines of a more worrying and serious nature.

Montjuïc, overlooking the city of Barcelona, provided a breathtaking racetrack on public roads sweeping through the municipal park. An already high element of risk became unacceptable in April 1975 when the Grand Prix teams turned up to find that the crash barriers had not been installed properly. Led by Lauda, Fittipaldi and Scheckter, the drivers refused to take part in the first practice session; an unheard of militant action. A reluctant compromise was reached when the organisers threatened to impound the teams and their cars. Lauda then came in for criticism when he put the worries behind him, climbed into the Ferrari and claimed pole position. Lauda explained a few weeks later:

> Some people find it hard to realise if you are driving a racing car, you are driving on the limit. If you drive on the limit all the time, if something goes wrong with the car, you will have a big accident. The problem we faced in Barcelona took me back to when I started racing and I had asked myself: 'Do you want to drive? Do you want to take the risk?' At that time, I looked very carefully at the problems and for me that was the end of them. It's the way I decided for myself – and I can go on this way. Which is why I did what I did at Barcelona even though we were unhappy about the way the barriers had been installed.

Speaking many years later to the journalist Mark Hughes, Lauda recalled a lighter moment during practice at Barcelona:

> The 1975 Ferrari was a fantastic car. The '74 car had given us a strong base, but this one had a better balance. It understeered

less, and, though it was more twitchy, I soon adjusted my driving style and had the feeling it would do exactly what I wanted it to do. It was just better than everybody else's car; better engine, chassis and gearbox.

Forghieri was a genius, but you needed to control him. I remember in Barcelona, I came in and told him I had understeer. He said, 'You're taking the wrong lines.' I asked where and he said, 'Round the back of the circuit.' 'How do you know?' 'Because I have a friend out there who tells me.' 'Who's your friend?' 'It's the lady friend of my doctor.' I said, 'Fix my fucking understeer!' He did, and I put it on pole.

That would turn out to be the easy bit as tension cranked up even further on race day. The start/finish straight reached a crest, which led steeply downhill to a hairpin. As the field, led by the two Ferraris, crested the rise, Lauda's car was tapped from behind and slewed sideways into Regazzoni. That triggered other collisions and resulted in Lauda's immediate retirement against the barrier. Fittipaldi completed one slow lap with his arm in the air in protest and the stressful weekend would reach a terrible conclusion when the rear wing failed on Rolf Stommelen's Hill-Cosworth, the car flying over the barrier and killing four bystanders. The race was stopped, Regazzoni being classified ninth after a pit stop for damage repairs.

Regazzoni would be in the wars again at Monaco where, on a wet but drying track, he brushed the barriers several times before doing terminal damage to the Ferrari's suspension. For Lauda, however, this was the beginning of a golden period. Starting from pole, he led all the way to finish just under three seconds ahead of Fittipaldi; another win from pole two weeks later in Belgium put Niki at the top of the championship standings for the first time.

It did little to stem the adverse comments about his car. Instead of being too slow, now it was too fast, Lauda's detractors claiming his success was due to Ferrari's twelve-cylinder engine being more powerful than the V8 Ford-Cosworths used by the majority of the field. Lauda told Henry:

It was unbelievable. I tried to take no notice of all those remarks but I have to be honest and say they began to infuriate me. If I'd had the twenty or thirty horsepower over my rivals, as these people said, I'd have been walking away with races using only one hand. I'd have been doing that because the 312T chassis was so good that any power advantage like they were saying would've left me with a huge advantage. That chassis was perfect. It was totally neutral and totally progressive. But I promise you, we didn't have that much extra power over the Cosworths. No way.

Monaco was a good example. In final practice, I had done a 1 minute 27.3 seconds, or something like that, and came into the pits to find Luca dancing around saying: '[Tom] Pryce has done a 1 minute 27.09 seconds [in a Shadow-Ford V8]! What are you going to do about it?' At times like this, you must produce a ten-tenths effort and when you do, particularly at a place like Monaco, you've got a good chance of hitting the wall or going off the road. I went out and did a 1 minute 26.4. I can tell you, I was terrified. I was absolutely on the limit with nothing left. When I got out of the car I found myself trembling. And people thought I'd be carrying on like that if I'd got more power over everybody else? No fucking way.

As it turned out, the next race in Sweden would provide Lauda with a perfect, if unwanted, opportunity to prove where his lap times were coming from on a circuit where a horsepower advantage, imagined or otherwise, would have little effect. A troubled practice on the Anderstorp track saw Lauda start from fifth on the grid, gradually move forward and eventually close in on Carlos Reutemann's leading Brabham-Ford, Lauda taking the lead with ten laps remaining. Lauda had needed to work hard, the pay-off being his championship lead over Reutemann had extended to ten points.

That advantage would grow by another three points in Holland but that would be the end of the good news as far as Lauda was concerned. He had been beaten fair and square on the day by James Hunt, the man who was to become his greatest and most memorable rival in twelve months' time when racing for McLaren. In 1975, however, Hunt was driving for Hesketh, a privately owned team that partied as hard as it raced. Hesketh had been going from strength to strength since their debut with a customer March at Monaco two years before. Now boasting their own car, Hunt was making increasingly good use of it. Although starting from the second row of the grid behind the Ferraris, a damp but drying track would be perfect territory for the enterprising Englishman and his willingness to take an informed gamble.

Lauda made a perfect getaway, with Hunt fourth behind Scheckter and a slow-starting Regazzoni. Rooster-tails of spray emphasised that grooved wet-weather tyres were indeed the right option. But not for long. The rain stopped as quickly as it had started and the stiff breeze produced a drying racing line. Working on the adage that it's often better to make the change sooner rather than later, Hunt was the first to head for the pits for slick tyres at the end of the seventh lap. He rejoined in twentieth place, buried among the backmarkers.

Hunt's move triggered a chain reaction throughout the field over the next few laps. Critically – and an indication of just how slippery the track remained – Lauda stayed out for another six laps. As the Ferrari headed for the pit exit, Hunt steamed by at top speed – and into the lead. At the end of the next lap, he was 10 seconds ahead. There were 60 laps remaining.

The key would be how the cars were set up for the latest conditions. Ferrari had gone for a compromise between wet and dry whereas Hesketh had gambled on completely dry settings. The race was now going their way while, at the same time, Ferrari's inherent speed advantage had been lost. On the other hand, Lauda had experienced winning five times before whereas Hunt was unaccustomed to running at the front. First, though, Lauda had to fight his way past the Shadow of Jean-Pierre Jarier. It would be another 30 laps before the red car was ahead of the black one.

For several laps, Hunt maintained a lead of around six seconds. But then, inexorably, the gap began to close with 20 laps to go. The pressure was on. But the Ferrari wasn't quicker where it really mattered. Despite the Ferrari filling his mirrors, Hunt stayed calm, particularly when dealing with backmarkers as the Hesketh gave first warning of the leaders' arrival and, in the process, helped smooth the path for Lauda. Hunt did not put a wheel out of place; did not allow Lauda the break he needed and took his maiden victory, a car's length ahead of the Ferrari. It was not the last time these two would engage in combat, Lauda having had a close view of what his rival was made of.

Lauda would remain at the head of the championship despite the disappointment of not winning at home, nor across the border at the Nürburgring Nordschleife where he had produced a very impressive sub-seven-minute lap to take pole at an average speed of 122 mph, a truly startling speed for such a potentially lethal place. Having worked that hard, a certain win in the German Grand Prix would be denied by a puncture relegating Lauda to third.

With just two races remaining, Lauda went into Ferrari's

home race knowing there could be no better place to clinch the title for himself and Ferrari than at Monza. Both Ferraris on the front row (Lauda on pole) guaranteed a full house, the passionate fans beside themselves with joy when Regazzoni won the race and Lauda, thinking of the bigger picture, eased back to third and earned enough points to become World Champion. Lauda said many years later:

> It was relatively easy. I had the best car in every respect. The chassis was good, the engine was good – and the transverse gearbox, too. All good. But what was important was the co-operation between the mechanics and engineers; everything. Even better than before. In 1975, it was perfect.
>
> I had screwed up the previous year but in 1975 I was quick. I had learned to think about everything. Winning a race was very nice; some sense of emotion. But as soon as it was over I was already thinking ahead to the next event. I always said to myself: 'This is why I'm paid and this is what I have to deliver.' I only worried if I didn't deliver. I didn't waste time thinking about how well I'd driven – even on the podium I'd be thinking: 'What could I have done better today and what can I do in the next race?' I never looked back at the past, just drew on the experiences I'd gained if I thought they'd serve me well in the future.
>
> When I was in that shit box March [721X], for example, I was very worried and I just couldn't understand it. But I must tell you that I learned a lot from this car. Having all those problems, I learned all the important things I was able to use when I got to Ferrari. Sitting in that 1975 car – a fantastic car – I had known exactly what to do.

Lauda was made number one in the Top Ten driver assessment published in *Autocourse*. The annual was not alone in recognising how the Austrian had learned from mistakes made in 1974. It seemed more than reasonable to assume that Lauda would become the first driver since Jack Brabham in 1959 and 1960 to win back-to-back titles. But that did not allow for either the appearance of a doughty rival or the effect of a fearsome accident that would come close to costing Lauda his life.

CHAPTER 5

Along Came James

Political turmoil in Argentina brought the cancellation of their Grand Prix scheduled for January 1976. It would presage a season of controversy and intrigue even if the opening two races suggested nothing had changed at all. Niki Lauda won them both.

There had been one significant move behind the scenes at Maranello following the promotion of Luca di Montezemolo to other duties high in the Fiat managerial chain. This was a blow for Lauda, who had established an effective working relationship with the charismatic team manager. They were close in age and ambition; Montezemolo possessing the same pragmatic view on how things should be done, but perhaps using a more temperate and diplomatic manner to achieve it. Enzo Ferrari would listen when Montezemolo went in to bat on Lauda's behalf: Niki was not so sure Luca's successor would gain quite the same respect from the Old Man.

Daniele Audetto was a Fiat man insofar as he had managed the Lancia rally team and possessed a charm to accompany a strong professional ethic and a wish to progress within the organisation. Whether running the Ferrari F1 team would help or hinder that goal remained to be seen. Certainly, victories in Brazil and South Africa had been a handy start. He said:

I was not completely new to the Ferrari F1 team. In 1975, I had done some races with Luca because he broke his arm in an accident. So I went to help, and that was when I first met Niki Lauda. I really understood that he was a special guy. I saw also how close Niki and Luca were. They were like brothers; both young and thinking alike. In 1975, I gained experience representing Ferrari in meetings with the Formula One Constructors' Association [FOCA]. So I had some knowledge of F1 in 1976 when we went to the first Grand Prix in Brazil.

Once again, Ferrari had chosen to take the previous year's car to the opening long-haul (so-called 'flyaway') races, the 312T serving them well as development continued with the 312T2 for 1976. Lauda had a feeling he would need the new car sooner rather than later, judging by the emergence of potentially serious competition at Interlagos and Kyalami.

The winter months had been hectic for McLaren. Emerson Fittipaldi had sprung a surprise by announcing his intention to join his brother in the establishment of Copersucar-Fittipaldi, the first Brazilian F1 team. The eleventh-hour decision had left McLaren in the lurch since the leading drivers had long since signed and sealed their deals for 1976. McLaren's only hope lay with James Hunt, made redundant by Hesketh after the champagne and money had run out for the jaunty British team. Hunt's record was chequered, to say the least, but his flashes of brilliance were enough to prompt his signing by a former championship team that, in truth, had little choice.

It would be the start of a dynamic partnership – as Lauda discovered in Brazil. Hunt had hustled the McLaren M23 onto pole position and challenged for the lead until the throttle slides jammed on the Ford-Cosworth V8 engine and sent the red and white car into the catch-fencing. Lauda was already familiar with Hunt thanks to time spent together in the junior ranks, particularly in 1971 when they both lived in London. Their first proper chat as mates had come during the previous season following an energetic duel during a F3 race in Sweden. Hunt had later explained:

> Racing drivers never talk among themselves about death. But that night in Sweden, I did discuss it with Niki. We came to a practical rather than some philosophical conclusion. We both realised, because of the game we had chosen, there really was no point in leaving the celebrations until later. It was quite a simple realisation. The chances were pretty high that we'd both get killed. So we decided, there and then, that we'd celebrate as we went along.

Their paths would diverge slightly in 1971 as Niki made the step up to F2 and James had to be content with a year driving a works F3 March. In August of that year, however, they appeared on the same entry list when Hunt managed a one-off deal for a vacant F2 March in a non-championship event at Brands Hatch. They shared the same sharp sense of humour and cheek, Lauda recalling an incident that weekend:

> We were both more or less racing with March, me with my car sponsored by the bank and James had somehow managed to find the money for this one race. We both have engine trouble during practice and, typical March with no budget, they only have one spare engine. I was talking to [Robin] Herd and [Max] Mosley about what they're going to do about this and how I should have this engine, and James walks in

and immediately says – in that very British way he had – that he should have the engine, no question. When I asked him why, he said: 'Because, my dear chap, I blew mine up first!' Bloody typical James! He had this air of confidence and you couldn't help but like him. That's why I would always think of him as an open, honest-to-God pal. He was my kind of guy. We would become cast as rivals in 1976, but we would always be good friends.

Lauda would have a ringside view of Hunt's impetuosity at the third Grand Prix of 1976 during the first-ever F1 race on the streets of Long Beach, California. Challenging the Tyrrell of Patrick Depailler for second place, Hunt found himself being eased into the wall. The McLaren may have come to a halt, but not James as he instantly sprang from the cockpit, stood on the edge of the track and gesticulated furiously each time Depailler came by. Not satisfied with that, Hunt later marched unannounced into the press conference for the top three finishers (Depailler had claimed third behind the Ferraris) and began ranting at the hapless Frenchman – much to Lauda's amusement.

Even though Ferrari were continuing with the 1975 car, the United States Grand Prix (West) had been dominated by Regazzoni at the end of one of those weekends when the Swiss had been in his element. Clay loved California. And California – well, most of it – loved him. Regazzoni had been in trouble a few days before when he had taken a ride in a police patrol car. The only problem was, neither of the policemen were present and did not take kindly to having their car taken for a drive. It required all of the organisers' contacts and powers of persuasion to have their star driver released in time to claim pole and win the race.

Ferrari had revealed their 1976 challenger to the media a few months before, the 312T2 being distinctive thanks to two

nostril–like openings either side of the cockpit in order to help
channel cool air to the engine. This was a result of a ban on
the air box previously carried high behind the driver's head
and forced the introduction of the T2. Nonetheless, Ferrari felt
the car was fit to race in Spain – unlike their lead driver. 'I had
borrowed a tractor to work on a bank by the swimming pool
at my house,' said Lauda. 'The thing tipped over and buried
me underneath it. I was lucky because a couple of inches either
way and I would have been killed. But I had broken two ribs,
the pain was unbelievable and I couldn't get up without help.'

Lauda had commissioned an architect to design a house
on land overlooking Fuschlsee, a lake to the east of Salzburg.
The original intention had been to settle there with Mariella
Reininghaus, his girlfriend for several years. When Mariella,
who was not interested in racing despite having offered loyal
support, felt Niki ought to retire from such a hazardous sport
once he had won the championship, the relationship developed
an edge. It ended suddenly, not long after Lauda met Marlene
Knaus in the autumn of 1975. They hit it off immediately,
Lauda attracted by Marlene's ability to relax in a way he never
could; an attribute underlined by the demeanour of her Spanish
mother, sister and brother when Niki met the family at their
home in Ibiza. Within months, they had moved into the new
house and got married in a register office in Vienna – but only
after a flight to England and a visit to Reading in Berkshire.
John Hogan said:

> Marlene rang me in the office one day. She said she wanted to
> get married, she wanted to do it straight away and she under-
> stood that this could be done quickly in England. Since that's
> where I was living and she realised Niki seemed to trust me
> to deal with such private matters, that's why I got the call. I
> wasn't sure about this but, by coincidence, I was living near

Reading at that time and I knew where the Reading register office was. I said to come over and we'd have a look.

So, Marlene and Niki turned up. I picked them up in a Ford Granada with Marlboro plastered all over it and we went to the register office. It was a typical squeaky old town hall, and this very nice man came out and asked if he could help. When I said my friends wanted to get married, he was very apologetic and said the law had changed and you needed to get a licence and other bits and pieces. It was no longer possible just to turn up. So, Niki simply said: 'Okay, we'll find another way.' We got back in the car and returned to the airport. The next thing I know, he's got married in Austria.

If Niki was scarcely one of the world's great romantics, Marlene was equally ambivalent about racing. But she was happy to accompany him to Grands Prix and sit calmly on one side without making unnecessary demands – which perfectly suited her new husband. With his broken ribs, Niki needed help from his new wife. It was immediately obvious to Lauda that the damage went beyond his injured ribs and he would need to inform Daniele Audetto at Ferrari. Audetto recalled: 'I phoned Mr Ferrari – and he was immediately looking for an alternative driver. We called Maurizio Flammini, an Italian who was very competitive in Formula Two at the time and he was supported by the Automobile Club of Italy. We told him to be ready for testing at Fiorano. When Niki heard this he said he was fit to race. We could only say: "If you say you're fit, then okay."'

The rapacious Italian media were not so accommodating with their derisory headlines about Ferrari's World Champion being unfit to drive a tractor, never mind a Formula One car. Within days, Lauda was receiving reports of Italian newspapermen camped out in a nearby village, with rumours of one equipped with a telephoto lens stationed on the opposite side of the lake.

Hogan said: 'Marlboro heard all about this and I was immediately expected to deal with it. Obviously, there wasn't much I could do – the silly bugger had broken his ribs, and that was it. I mean, what did he expect? He'd built this house on the side of a bloody hill, he's on a tractor mower, driving along the side of the hill and the thing topples over. So I sent him a telegram, just to cheer him up.' Hogan's message read:

WORLD LAWN MOWER CHAMPION. SORRY TO HEAR
THAT YOU LOST CONTROL. MAYBE MODEL WITH
REDUCED POWER WOULD BE BETTER IN FUTURE – CSI
[motorsport's governing body] SERIOUSLY CONSIDERING
ADAPTING NEW FORMULA FOR NEXT SEASON –
MANDATORY REQUIREMENTS WILL BE ROLLOVER
BAR, SEATBELTS, EXPERIENCED DRIVER AND POWER
LIMITED TO 10 HORSEPOWER – ALL SWIMMING POOLS
AND POOL-SIDE TREES TO BE SURROUNDED WITH
ARMCO. SEE YOU ON POLE IN SPAIN. HOGAN

'The thing was,' said Hogan, 'no one had ever confronted him in this way about being unprofessional. Niki loved it. He thought I was a "good guy" and this was a sort of breakthrough in my relationship with him.'

Lauda found the telegram light relief in the midst of media criticism. The gist of stories being filed centred on Lauda's possible absence giving Ferrari the chance to employ an Italian driver – as seemed right and proper to many of the fanatical readers. Painfully (literally) aware of this Lauda knew a speedy recovery was needed for the Spanish race in a fortnight's time. His local doctor reckoned it would be six weeks minimum before the cracked ribs would have healed sufficiently. And Lauda knew this did not take into account the physician's lack of knowledge of the g-forces exerted within a F1 car.

One man who might understand was Willi Dungl, a masseur and health guru who worked with Austria's ski-jumping team and was recommended by a local radio reporter. Lauda immediately recognised a like mind when, on his first visit, the monosyllabic Dungl offered no sympathy but laid down a tough regime for recovery – of sorts.

Lauda duly turned up in Spain, the tight corners and bumps of the Jarama track causing great discomfort. 'The problem was,' said Audetto, 'that with broken ribs, you're supposed to rest because the ribs can damage the lungs, and that becomes dangerous. So, to do a F1 race with broken ribs was a very bad idea. But . . . Niki is Niki and he wanted to race.'

Lauda qualified on the front row, alongside Hunt's McLaren, and jumped into an immediate lead. Hunt bided his time, waiting for the twists and turns to take their toll. With less than half of the 75 laps completed, Hunt sensed his rival was tiring, took the lead and finished half a minute ahead. 'When he got out of the car, he collapsed,' said Audetto. 'I had to go on the podium with Hunt and Gunnar Nilsson [who finished third] to receive the trophy presented by King Juan Carlos of Spain.'

Hunt had reduced Lauda's championship lead from 18 to 15 points – for the time being. Post-race scrutineering found the dimensions of the winning McLaren to be 1.8cm too wide. The victory was thrown out, a verdict that, according to the McLaren team boss, Teddy Mayer, was akin to being hanged for a parking offence. An extreme comparison, perhaps, but an indication of Mayer's determination to use his training as a lawyer to appeal.

Lauda extended his total to 55 points thanks to wins in Belgium and Monaco, followed by third in Sweden. Hunt was languishing on eight points. In the space of two days, however, the face of the championship would change dramatically. Hunt would win in France and, twenty-four hours later, a tribunal would reinstate his victory in Spain. Lauda (who had retired from the French race with a seized engine) now dropped to 53 points whereas Hunt had rocketed to 26.

Meanwhile, Lauda's relationship with the Italian media had come under further pressure thanks to undertones that the spectre of him continually winning was boring. That received the expected short shrift from the championship leader, all of which heaped more problems onto Audetto's plate. Fortunately – or unfortunately, depending on the point of view – the Ferrari team manager would have more serious matters to contend with when his drivers collided at the start of the next race at Brands Hatch.

Lauda, having claimed pole for the British Grand Prix, started from the front row alongside Hunt. Regazzoni was on row two, directly behind the McLaren. Lauda made a clean getaway, but Regazzoni made an even better one, overtaking Hunt and aiming for the inside line and the lead as the Ferraris reached the downhill and tricky Paddock Hill Bend. Realising his speed was exceeding his ambition, Regazzoni locked his brakes, which pitched the Ferrari sideways and into his teammate, causing mayhem with the following 24 cars pouring over the crest.

Hunt was among the victims, the McLaren becoming airborne briefly after making contact with one of Regazzoni's rear wheels before crashing back onto the track. Hunt knew immediately that his steering was damaged and thought his race was over. Even more annoying was the sight of Lauda escaping unscathed.

Given that the preference in those less safety-conscious days was to allow a race to carry on if at all possible, it says much about the extent of debris scattered beyond the blind brow that officials decided to show a red flag, bringing the race to a halt. It was such a rare decision that the race stewards, not helped by a grey area in the rule book, did not know how to deal with the restart. Should this be a completely new race, in which case spare cars would be allowed to replace those damaged in the chaos? Or should this be a continuation of the existing race, in which case spare cars would not be allowed? Officials eventually chose the latter – and covered all bases by permitting the use of spare cars. But this would not allow for another point of debate raised by Ferrari.

Having examined the rule book, Audetto pointed out that only cars that had completed the opening lap would be allowed to take part; a condition that appeared to rule out Hunt since he had limped through a back entrance to the pits and, unlike Lauda, not completed the lap. To which the astute Teddy Mayer quoted another clause stating that all runners 'at the time of stopping' will be allowed to take the restart, Mayer's contention being that Hunt was actually running – albeit slowly – when the red flag was shown and the race officially stopped.

While all this was going on, Lauda remained in his car in the pit lane. Angered by the 'stupidity' of his teammate and ordered by officials to go to the grid, Lauda, without waiting for a signal from his mechanics, booted his throttle and stormed out of the pits – dragging a slave starting-battery behind the Ferrari.

Meanwhile, the 77,000 spectators, sweltering on an exceptionally hot summer's day, were becoming restless. When loudspeakers broke the news that Hunt might not be allowed to take the restart, the reaction was instantaneous. Booing and slow-handclapping gave way to a hail of beer cans clattering onto the track. Whipped up by the media, the British fans had come to see their man defeat the allegedly arrogant Austrian in the red Ferrari, and now James was apparently being prevented from starting because of some footling regulation.

Over an hour had passed since the original start, during which time feverish activity by the McLaren mechanics had seen Hunt's original car repaired and made ready for its place on the front row. This time the field negotiated the first corner without incident, Lauda leading Hunt. Almost immediately, Niki felt his gearbox begin to tighten – possibly the unseen legacy of his teammate's overenthusiasm at the original start.

As the race went on, the problem became worse. Uncertain which gear he might find when looking for fifth, Lauda resorted to staying in fourth. Hunt closed in. On the 45th lap, the McLaren dived inside the Ferrari to take the lead. Brands Hatch went crazy.

The euphoria reached a climax 30 laps later when James Hunt became the first Englishman to win his home Grand Prix in eighteen years. Lauda managed to bring his car home in second place. That may have been the end of action on the track but a different kind of combat was reigniting in the pit lane.

Speaking to Peter Windsor of *Autocar* magazine, Mauro Forghieri made his team's displeasure known. 'I tell the stewards that we are going to protest,' said the Ferrari technical director. '"Protest about what?" they ask. Look, Niki drives the whole race fighting with a damaged gearbox – probably damaged in the accident – and Hunt wins in a car that was repaired. And he didn't complete the first lap of the race. I think,' continued Forghieri, perhaps remembering the shambles in this very pit lane two years before, 'it is disgusting, this race in England. Disgusting.'

By now they had been joined by Lauda. 'And why did they stop the race at all?' asked Niki. 'All right, there was a lot of stuff on the track and someone might have been injured. But when I came round on the second lap of the real race, there was just as much stuff on the road [caused by a collision between the March-Fords of Ronnie Peterson and Hans-Joachim Stuck]. Why didn't they stop it then? Because Hunt wasn't involved?'

Hunt and Lauda were separated by 23 points with the threat of a Ferrari protest hanging in the air. The totting up of championship points may have been the lead story as the teams left Brands Hatch that night but such details were about to seem insignificant when swept aside by a shocking and graphic reminder of motorsport's ever-present peril.

CHAPTER 6

Ring of Fire

'I've mixed feelings about this place. While it's a tremendous challenge, it's dangerous; very dangerous. See those trees over there? They look like small trees, don't they? They're actually the tops of very tall trees. If you go over there, they'll have difficulty finding the car, never mind the driver.' Jackie Stewart was at the wheel of a BMW 633CSi touring car on the afternoon of Thursday, 29 July 1976. The three-time World Champion was describing the unique challenge of the Nürburgring Nordschleife and pointing out the seemingly endless hazards throughout its fourteen-mile lap. Stewart may have retired from the cockpit three years before, but he was more than adequately qualified to speak about the scene of that weekend's German Grand Prix. In 1968, the Scotsman had produced a drive of epic proportions on the same circuit as he raced through rain and mist, rivers of water invading a track surface that changed with every lap. He won by four minutes. No one could come close that day to such virtuosity, commitment and bravery.

Stewart said: 'On this downhill plunge [Fuchsröhre or 'Foxhole'] you're doing about 170 mph, and the dip you can see at the bottom is so severe at these speeds, your feet can fly from the pedals if you're not ready.' Several miles further on, Stewart's commentary continued as he reached Pflanzgarten. 'This is where I'd change up to fifth gear just before the jump – there's no point in landing at peak revs in fourth; it doesn't do the transmission any good.'

He was asked if the long, undulating straight at Tiergarten would offer a degree of respite during the final miles. 'Not at all. You're absolutely flat out in top gear. There's a gap in the trees and you can get caught out by a gust of wind. If anything happens here, you're a passenger; just a passenger. That's the problem with the 'Ring. It's so long, with the best will in the world, they can never marshal it properly. If you go off in certain places, you're in the lap of the gods.' Those words would become eerily prophetic three days later.

The Nürburgring project had been instigated in 1925 to alleviate unemployment in the Koblenz-Cologne region and would later be seen as the perfect proving ground for the might of a German automobile industry led by Mercedes-Benz and Auto Union. The Nürburgring in its entirety measured 17.58 miles, made up of two circuits, the South (Sudschleife) and the North (Nordschleife), each using the same start/finish line and paddock complex. There were more than 170 corners as this giant of a track dipped and climbed through the Eifel mountains.

The Nordschleife had become the preferred choice as a venue for all classes of motor racing and Niki Lauda was familiar with it. In fact, in his youth, he had enjoyed competing there. He said:

In the beginning I even loved the 'Ring because I was the ideal type of driver for it. It was a racetrack I could work on, examining every detail and trying to get everything perfect. I was actually pretty good on the 'Ring because I knew it so well. I used to practise for a whole week: you really had to know which way it went. I even took part in a twenty-four-hour marathon – can you imagine going round there in the dark? Completely mad!

I was young and didn't really worry about safety in those days. For me, danger was part of race driving. My attitude began to change, because the longer I had been racing, the more people I knew who had been killed there. When someone was killed, your attitude was they probably made a mistake and I wouldn't make a mistake like that. But then when drivers you know to be good lose their life, you begin to think about it. Roger Williamson's accident [1973 Dutch Grand Prix, see page 34] had a big effect on me because it could have been prevented. So, when we continued to race at the Nürburgring, it seemed to me that we were adding unnecessary risk.

In 1976, the drivers had a meeting and I proposed that we boycott the 'Ring. Of course, as soon as I mentioned these things, people [outside the drivers] starting saying I was the bad guy and a coward. It was very simple; the Nürburgring was unnecessarily dangerous. But then the contradiction would come when I'd do things like in 1975 when I took pole position [for the Grand Prix] with a lap under seven minutes. I was in a mind to do it that day – but thinking about it, not just many years later, but soon afterwards, it was complete madness.

Lauda's motion to boycott was voted down, largely on the grounds that the track's owners had invested in improvements to safety precautions. This amounted to no more than a sticking plaster over a festering wound, a shortcoming that Lauda and Stewart were among the few willing to speak about in public. Thus far in 1976 alone, three drivers had been killed on the Nordschleife.

On 2 April, Alex Wittwer had crashed at Fuchsröhre during the first lap of practice for a round of the European F3 Championship. This may have been the 22-year-old Swiss driver's first visit to the Nürburgring but it was thought that his car had suffered a mechanical failure. A report in *Autosport* said: 'The suspected failure caused his car to vault a ridiculously low barrier and crash into the trees some way below.' Wittwer died of a broken neck.

Ernst Raetz had been the most recent fatality when the East German driver's Formula Vee had become airborne and crashed at Flugplatz on 9 July.

A week before the Grand Prix, Lauda had given an interview to Dieter Stappert, highly respected editor of the Swiss magazine *Powerslide*. Lauda said of the forthcoming Grand Prix: 'I dread the weekend; so boring. The important thing is to get through it alive, in my opinion. I don't know what the others think, but that's what I think.' When questioned about whether or not he could avoid driving flat-out and reduce the risk, Lauda said:

That's it, you must [go flat out] otherwise there's no point and I know that now. I must, but I don't want to. If the crowd hiss when I appear, I don't give a damn, let them hiss. If nothing happens this weekend it will be a miracle, I can tell you that. And then on Monday we shall all say thank God; all of us. But the only people who understand this are those who've driven there. What other people say doesn't count.

Just take what happened a little while ago; that last accident. The death of Herr Raetz, or whatever he was called, wasn't thought important. But just imagine what would have happened if [Emerson] Fittipaldi had got burnt, if you see what I mean. It's madness; they take no notice of the other poor devil. If you [Stappert] hadn't written about it, nobody would have, and that's murder. After the accident, the race should have been stopped. As for the 'Ring – thank you very much, goodbye, I've had enough.

Lauda had also not held back when talking to *Autosport* a few days before:

> My personal opinion is that the Nürburgring is too dangerous to drive on nowadays. Because, if I go to Paul Ricard or any other permanent circuit and something breaks on my car, the wing falls off, the suspension fails, I have a 70/30 per cent chance that I will be all right, or I will be dead because of the circumstances of the circuit. We're not discussing if I make a mistake. If I make a mistake and I kill myself, then tough shit. If I have been so stupid to make a mistake, this is my risk in motor racing. I have to be fit. I have to be mentally free to drive my car, concentrated on not making mistakes. So at the Nürburgring, if you have any failure on the car, [it's] one hundred per cent death.

Strong words to back an earnest belief. Lauda's sincerity would also be evident in his professionalism on the first morning of practice when he went out and set the fastest time. A lap of 7 minutes 8.2 seconds may have been slightly slower than the previous year (due to technical regulations designed to reduce performance), but a lap average of 119 mph was proof that 'flat-out' was indeed his creed – backed by unspoken courage. In the afternoon, Lauda went faster still, but was narrowly beaten by Hunt. Given less favourable conditions on the second day of practice, these times would establish the grid positions.

Race morning was dry but a stiff breeze from the north-west brought clouds that threatened rain. As the cars completed a warm-up lap of the entire circuit (as opposed to a short loop around the pits sometimes used for this purpose), reports of rain began to come in from various parts of the track. By the time the cars had returned to the grid, the question of whether or not to fit wet-weather grooved tyres was being answered by increasing spots of rain prompting umbrellas to appear throughout the spectator enclosures in the start/finish area. When officials declared a 'Wet Race', the matter was decided for all 26 starters – except one.

Jochen Mass, Hunt's teammate, was a local man with knowledge of the Nordschleife and good contacts among the officials. Herbert Linge, an experienced endurance racer charged with driving the official pace car, had a quiet word in Mass's ear and informed his fellow countryman that word was coming through that much of the track was drying quickly. Starting from ninth on the grid, Mass felt it was worth the gamble of staying on slicks.

It seemed a foolhardy decision as the field disappeared into a haze of spray during the charge to the first corner. By the time they got nine miles out and reached Hohe Acht, the highest part of the circuit, it had become apparent that Mass had made the right call; he was already up to third place.

There had been much swapping of positions at the front, but Lauda was not among them. A poor start had dropped the Ferrari down the order, Lauda being among the vast majority to dive into the pits for slick tyres at the end of the first lap, the Ferrari rejoining somewhere in the mid-field after quick work by his mechanics. Applying caution, watching out for remaining wet patches, Lauda worked though the curves of Hatzenbach, climbed Flugplatz and charged along the open high ground towards the right-hander at Aremberg. Then downhill, flat out between the trees, thumping the dip at Fuchsröhre before immediately shooting uphill and into the bends at Adenauer-Forst.

From there, on towards Kallenhard and, eventually, the tight left at Wehrseifen. (Jackie Stewart: 'I'd change straight from first to third, coming out of here. It's downhill and helps ease the load [on the transmission] and keeps the car calm. Then we come to what I regard as the most difficult part of the Nürburgring; the descent to Adenau. Look at it; one bend after another, with adverse camber in places. And all of it in fifth gear. Very, very fast.')

At the bottom, the cars would sweep left and across the bridge straddling the road between the village of Breidscheid and the small town of Adenau. Climbing once more to a long fast right before levelling out through a series of quick curves in preparation for Bergwerk, six miles from the start. (Stewart: 'Bergwerk is a long right-hander, taken in third gear. The temptation is to turn in too early – but it's a long, long corner. You don't begin to head for the apex until you get to see the small house – wait for it . . . just there . . . on the outside.')

Lauda never got to see the house for a third time on that Sunday afternoon. He had dealt with the potential hazards of Fuchsröhre, the descent to Adenau and the rest. Reaching 130 mph through a left-hand bend – so innocuous it was one of many Stewart had never mentioned – the rear of the Ferrari suddenly twitched right and then left. It immediately speared through catch fencing and into an earth bank on the right before rebounding and spinning into the middle of the track with one side of the car on fire, the left-hand fuel cell having been ripped off by the impact.

The flames became an instant inferno when the Ferrari was rammed amidships and sent 100 metres further on by the Surtees of Brett Lunger after the American slammed on his brakes and desperately tried to avoid the wreck; the tangled mess was compounded by the arrival of Harald Ertl's Hesketh. At some point during this shocking sequence, Lauda's helmet had been ripped off, fracturing a cheekbone in the process. That injury would be the least of his worries.

Lunger and Ertl were joined by Guy Edwards (who had squeaked past the wayward Ferrari as it came away from the grass bank) and Arturo Merzario, who had just managed to stop short in his Williams. They found Lauda partly conscious in the cockpit in the middle of this blaze.

With just one hopelessly equipped and inadequately dressed marshal on hand, the drivers knew they had to act quickly. Ertl found an extinguisher, thumped it into life and began spraying the cockpit area. Lunger, a veteran of the Vietnam War, straddled the middle of the car, but it was impossible to make progress until Merzario, a former Ferrari driver and familiar with the seat belts, dived into the intense heat and released the buckle on Lauda's six-point harness. 'It wasn't easy,' recalled the little Italian. 'Niki was obviously in agony, straining hard against the belts, trying to get away from the flames. Thank God he eventually lost consciousness; it was only when he relaxed that I could free the buckle ... ' The release of body weight caused Lunger to topple over, taking Lauda with him.

They helped Lauda to the side of the track as other drivers, including John Watson, arrived on the scene. Now in his third full season of F1, Watson was driving for the American Penske team. Watson said:

I pulled up just as they were getting Niki out of the car. I had no idea what had happened, but it was clearly a mess with the Ferrari on fire. The racetrack around the car was soaking. I didn't know whether it was something from an extinguisher or whether it was fuel, but the best thing was to move him away. Niki needed a bit of help, but he was able to walk the twenty yards or so before we got him to lie down.

I kneeled down and got him to put his head on my thighs, which meant I was looking down on his head and his face. He was conscious, obviously in shock, but he was able to talk and ask what his face looked like. I told him it was fine. I could see his forehead and the right side of his face had been burned and his skin had peeled off. The worst injury I could see was his scalp, which was charred in places.

So, my immediate thought was: 'Okay, he was going to get treatment for the burns. He has some other fractures but they're not particularly significant.' It was a matter of waiting for an ambulance to come. That took maybe three or four minutes; I can't be sure. But it didn't seem that long because, in all likelihood, there would have been access at Adenau Bridge, which wasn't far away and that was the most likely place for an ambulance to be stationed. Other drivers had stopped; some had driven slowly by and gone on to the pits. Once the ambulance had picked him up, I got back in the car and drove back to the pits.

After a while, the grid reformed and they restarted the race. It seems surreal to say that, having been with the guy who had just had a very big accident and seen the extent of his injuries – or at least, the ones that were visible. But to then blank it out, anaesthetise yourself, get back in the car and go racing again; a contemporary driver could never conceive of doing something like that.

The burns Watson referred to were bad enough, but the potentially lethal damage was out of sight. Lauda's windpipe and lungs had been seared by the combination of fumes from the burning petrol, bodywork, deformable crash structure and the well-intentioned but caustic contents spewed by the fire extinguisher.

At the time of the accident, Hunt had been pressing on, intent on winning this race. He said:

I knew nothing about the accident. I was into the third lap when I saw the 'race stopped' flag signals. I eased up and there it was, with all the cars stopped. Niki had gone by this time and I chatted around with the other drivers to find out what had happened. I was told the car had been on fire. They said Niki was burned a little around his face and wrists but it didn't look serious and everything was fine. Niki was off to hospital and obviously wouldn't be racing again that day, but he'd have his burns patched up and we'd see him at the next race in Austria; that was the story we had then. It was still the story when we were getting ready for the restart. There was a suggestion that he had broken a cheekbone from a smack on the face and then it was said his helmet had come off and that was how he had come to be burned. But there were no alarm stories and, at that time, it was evidently not serious at all.

The race was eventually won by Hunt, with Mass finishing third. Hunt said: 'I was very pleased with that win – and then we started to find out a bit more about what had happened to Niki. It began to appear he might be very bad indeed.'

The mood in the paddock was sombre. There had not been an official statement regarding Lauda's condition and the teams were as much in the dark as everyone else. Max Mosley, looking after an entry of two cars, had followed Lauda's progress with interest since he had left March at the end of 1972. Even though fluent in German, Mosley had been unable to establish little in the way of hard fact. He recalled:

Neither of our drivers [Ronnie Peterson and Vittorio Brambilla] could add much. The thing that sticks in my mind is Huschke von Hanstein [65-year-old former racing driver and president of the Automobilclub von Deutschland, organisers of the German Grand Prix] saying everything was going to be fine; that Niki was okay; that he had been talking to people and they'd taken him to hospital for treatment to his burns. I hadn't seen the footage of the accident but, from what we'd heard, that didn't sound altogether right. There was always that tendency with what you might call 'old school' people like Huschke to play down things like this. He was also probably being defensive because of the previous strong criticism of the 'Ring being unsuitable for racing.

As word of Lauda's injuries began to spread, drivers' opinion about racing on the Nürburgring Nordschleife was hardening exponentially. For one, Chris Amon, this was the final straw. He had raced here in eight Grands Prix, finished third when driving for Ferrari in 1967 but, more often than not, suffered retirement through mechanical failure. That was more typical of the New Zealander's atrocious luck, Amon being considered one of the greatest natural talents never to have won a Grand Prix. In 1976, he was coming to the end of a career stretching across fourteen seasons. Having driven with top teams, he was racing with Ensign, a small British outfit with more promise than money. John Hogan said:

I was in the Marlboro caravan. Chris Amon came in, sat down and said: 'That's it. I'm not doing this any more, I've had enough of this shit.' He actually refused to take the restart. While I understood why he had reached that decision to quit racing, it was such a complete waste of talent. He'd taken that little Ensign and put it third on the grid a few weeks before in Sweden. But he'd had enough. Even as we were sitting there, the reports on Niki were getting progressively worse.

John Watson said:

> Having seen what I had seen, these reports were hard to take
> on board. Usually, if a driver dies in a motor-racing accident,
> he dies at the scene because it is such a big accident. I couldn't
> put into context the fact that he had been able to walk away,
> with assistance, from the car; he was able to lie down, have a
> conversation, look to all intents and purposes that he would
> be okay because the burns, while being unfortunate, were
> not life-threatening burns. It was only when you began to
> think about what he might have inhaled that it started to
> make terrible sense – and, suddenly, this was a very different
> scenario. Now we were wondering if he was going to survive.

Helmut Zwickl, the Austrian F1 journalist and pilot who had
flown with Lauda on several occasions, was shocked by what
had happened – but for reasons beyond the obvious:

> Three days before the race, I drove with Niki in a Fiat
> road car around the Nordschleife. He was talking about the
> dangers of racing there and pointing out various things and
> saying it was not safe to race on this track. At one point, he
> stopped the car and said: 'Take this place, for example. If you
> have a crash here, you have no chance.' This was the exact
> place, just before Bergwerk, where he would crash three
> days later. I could not believe it when I found out. As I drove
> back to Vienna that night, me and my photographer friend
> agreed that, if Niki died, we would finish with Formula One
> immediately. After the loss of Jochen [Rindt, at Monza in
> 1970], this would be too much.

As evening began to draw in at the Nürburgring, a group of
British journalists gathered for a glass of wine by a camper

van parked among the trees nearby. Each news bulletin being received from their passing Austrian and German colleagues seemed worse than the previous one; apart from extensive burns, Lauda had inhaled toxic fumes; he was in a very bad way indeed. As the reporters headed for home, they began mentally preparing obituaries for the following morning.

CHAPTER 7

Force of Nature

On the day he had arrived in the Nürburgring paddock, Lauda had proudly been shown a photograph of Jochen Rindt's grave by a well-meaning if curiously motivated fan. Lauda possessed no more interest at that moment in his fellow countryman's resting place than he had in considering this to be a macabre omen. But it was to be a bizarre start to a weekend that had ended with the terrible possibility of Lauda joining the 1970 World Champion as another of motorsport's sorrowful statistics. Of the time in between, Lauda could remember nothing beyond accelerating out of the pits to rejoin the race following his pit stop. Daniele Audetto recalled:

> Our pit stop had been a little slow. Also, the tyres at this time were very cold, and the weather was cold. So Niki didn't rejoin in a good position. He left the pits with lots of revs and immediately began to overtake cars. Then, of course, he didn't appear at the end of that lap.
>
> Huschke von Hanstein came to me and he said: 'Daniele, there has been an accident; come with me in my Porsche.' We went to the hospital in Adenau. We heard that, when

they were waiting for the ambulance at the scene of the accident, Niki had been talking. But when I saw him in the hospital, he was losing consciousness. The problem was not the superficial burns that he had; it was that he had inhaled the fumes and so on, and this was blocking his lungs. The doctor in Adenau said they could do nothing there. Von Hanstein called a doctor at Ludwigshafen Hospital because he knew they also took care of the American Forces based near there, and they specialised in burns. They said they would get a clean room ready and to get him there as soon as possible.

While we were waiting for the helicopter, Niki told me to go to the Bilstein [shock absorbers] motorhome at the circuit, which was where he had left his briefcase with his documents. I was also to call Marlene and tell her to come to the hospital. I could tell at this stage that he was already having trouble breathing.

I went back to the paddock, picked up his things and got to the hospital in time to speak to the doctor. He said Niki had a respiratory block and, for the moment, he was all right, but they didn't know if he would last twenty-four hours. He was in a critical condition with his lungs.

All Lauda could vaguely remember was the clatter of a helicopter's blades, followed by an overwhelming wish to sink into the soft comfort of sleep. In various interviews, later that year and in 1980, Lauda recalled the moments that followed once he had reached the burns unit in Ludwigshafen, about 150 kms southeast of the Nürburgring as the helicopter flies:

I had been lucky in some ways. They'd taken me at first to the hospital in Adenau where they said I was too critical for them to touch. So they sent me to the best hospital in Germany.

When I got to Ludwigshafen, the boss of the whole place just happened to be there. Don't forget, this was a Sunday, so I was lucky he was there. He took one look at me and immediately decided that the burns on my face were secondary to the burns in my lungs. So he sent me to the Intensive Care Unit in Mannheim. There my luck was still good. The youngest professor in Germany just happened to be working that Sunday. His name is Professor Peter and I owe him my life. He did everything absolutely right and never made a wrong move.

You must realise that the medical knowledge about treating lung damage is not as great as in some other areas. If, for example, I had been given oxygen – which would seem logical for someone with damaged lungs – I would have been dead immediately. The lungs were in bad condition and when they X-rayed me on the Tuesday they were getting worse. The thing they were worried about most was the oxygen count in my blood, which was below the life-maintaining level of a figure of 8. It went down to the figure of 6.8 – so in theory there was no more life. The doctor said, and told my wife, that there was no hope that I would survive.

On the Sunday night they had put a tube down my throat into the lungs and connected it to a vacuum pump to drain off the liquid and the infections. This was critical because if the pump was used too much it would destroy the lungs. From the Sunday night my brain was always functioning but I felt that my body was giving up.

I can't remember the exact times because you get mixed up. You don't know whether it was day or night. I remember at one stage feeling that the end is coming. You just feel that everything is so weak and ... it's not the pain; the feeling you have is that everything is so complicated and difficult that you want to let go and then you feel like going to sleep. I was very frightened at that feeling. It was like you were falling into a big hole, a black hole, and you just let go of everything.

At the same moment, the fear comes into you, and I said: 'Shit! This is not the right way to go.' And then you tell yourself: 'Do something!' But you can't do anything because you lie there and can't move or anything. So, I just tried to listen to the doctors, to what they said and to concentrate. The only thing I could do was hear; I couldn't see anything. I was just listening to them all the time, trying to interpret the meaning, and why, and so on.

I remember the nurse asked me if I wanted a priest. I couldn't say anything. I thought a priest can't be bad. I heard nothing and didn't know what was going on. I thought that maybe he comes later or in two hours or the next day; I don't know. I still heard nothing, felt nothing until suddenly he must have touched my shoulder. I thought at first the nurse had just touched me. Then I thought: 'Shit! It must be the priest.'

He didn't say one word to me; he just came and gave me the last rites and left. I think that is the worst thing you can do to anybody. At least he should come and say: 'Here my son, here you are. You're a bit screwed up but, don't worry, with the help of God you will be all right again.' Just tell you anything. But he didn't do anything. He came, gave me the last rites and turned away. I remember my heart started beating hard again when I realised because again, you can't do anything; just lie there and things happen you don't like, but you can't react.

Then I got a bit better and I thought the only way is to co-operate with the doctors as much as possible with the treatment I get. The more co-operation they get, the better it must be because it's all in their hands if I help them to do it better. It must help me, and that's what I basically did.

For example, they could only use the vacuum pump to my lungs for about an hour at a time. But when I felt the lungs filling up then I called for them to switch it on – even though the pain was enormous. The doctors told me that was the first time that anyone had asked for the pump to be switched on themselves. But I knew I could only survive if I followed every instruction of the doctors.

Marlene was marvellous. It was very shocking for her, but never once did I feel what she was going through when she was with me at the hospital. She would hold my hand and keep on telling me that I was going to get well again. She must have been terrified by my face but she only made me feel I was a great man and gave me the will to get well again. So many women would have cried or have become hysterical. I discovered that there was much greater depth to Marlene than even I had realised.

I do not believe in a personal God, but I believe that there is something more than this life. And I live by the rules. My strength to live after the accident came from this, from my mind and from my wife.

Three days after the accident the lungs began to get better. My blood count was still bad, with the oxygen at the 6.8 level. Nobody knew if my system would start working again and produce enough oxygen for the blood. If it didn't restart, then they could have changed my blood every so often but they knew that I would then only have one or two years in which to live. So they put a new blood into me and waited to see the reactions. After four days it slowly improved and they changed the blood again. Soon it was working and I was back to normal with the right amount of oxygen in my blood.

On the Thursday after the accident, they took the tubes out and, for the first time, I could speak. The nurse came and said: 'Do you want to have a look in the mirror?' I said: 'Okay, let's have a look.' They opened my eyelids, because they were all swollen and I had two little slots there. I looked like a huge pig, all swollen up. The nurse said that's what happens in a temperature of 800 degrees C. I thought ... 'You look a bit funny, my friend.' That is the only thing you can say and think because, if you think about it too much, you know you look pretty sad. They said it would all go away. Fluid comes into this part of you and the neck swells straight up like this. A couple of days later it got less and less and less.

As soon as Lauda was considered to be out of immediate danger, work began on the surgery to his face. The most significant operation involved skin grafts from the upper right thigh to his forehead. Lauda continued:

How I looked was a problem in the beginning. I was under no illusions; I knew I was not handsome when my thigh is on my face. On the first day it was completely blue when the blood came. But then I looked at the thing and said: 'What can you do?' You will look like this for the rest of your life but if I start worrying about it now then I am worried for the rest of my life. So I finished the discussion with myself on the way I look.

The only thing I did afterwards was start watching people because I had no problem with myself. I just walked into some place and looked at them. One looks at you and then looks away. Then the other, he just talks to you normally. You could divide the people. There were those who only go on how people look. If someone looks ugly or bad, then they don't want to talk to them. I think that's bad because it's not the way you look, it's the way you think and the way you are.

After my skin graft everything was getting a little better. Suddenly, I went absolutely mad because I had a little bit of power back in my body and they couldn't make me sleep or anything. So I said let me go home because as soon as I am there, it's a different air and it's my own house. So let me go home. One of the doctors was clever and he let me go home. I had only been sleeping one or two hours in the hospital; at home, I slept for six hours right away.

As soon as I was home everything was better – except the people who turned up. I had been smuggled out of the hospital and flown to Salzburg. It was only a few people who knew I was home. But then the word got out. Once we had to call the police because it was a joke. People wanted to come and look. The other thing was newspapers who wanted to take pictures of the way I look. When I was in hospital a guy came into the room, took pictures – click, click, click – and ran off.

Lauda's biographer, Herbert Völker, was present in the house not long after Niki's return. He said:

I was more or less the only one who got access to his house when he came back from the hospital. We had known each other since 1969 and worked together on various books and columns. I was also very close to Willi Dungl. I stayed there four or five days and it was just the four of us; Niki, Marlene, Willi and me. I could see straightaway that he was absolutely determined to come back to racing. Even knowing him as I did, this was completely beyond my imagination.

Lauda was keen to see images of the accident that had caused all of this. The only footage ever recorded came from a teenage boy, standing with an 8mm camera on the banking high above where the blazing Ferrari came to rest. Lauda felt absolutely no involvement as he watched the blurry pictures of a Ferrari twitching one way and then the other for no obvious reason, disappearing briefly out of sight and reappearing on fire, with much of the left-hand side missing. As he watched Lunger's car suddenly appear and change the scene from a fiery crash to blazing carnage, Lauda could not relate to the driver eventually being pulled free.

He was none the wiser why this had happened. The Ferrari's sudden flick to the right was not in line with losing control in the normal way. While he could not rule out driver error, the movement of the car suggested something in the rear suspension might have broken. He reasoned that little could be proven, given the state of the subsequent wreckage.

The absence of any obvious mistake on his part was some consolation. However, unofficial briefings from Ferrari, while not suggesting it was the driver's fault, failed to rule that out as categorically as they denied a failure on the car. Audetto said:

No one will know what happened. Ferrari made an inves-tigation because Mr Ferrari wanted to be sure there was no technical problem with the car because people were sug-gesting something may have broken with the suspension. It looked like Niki came a little bit too much on the kerb. It was not wet, but let's say, still damp, the tyres were cold, and he lost control of the car. We saw it was not a technical problem because there were marks from the four wheels [tyres] as you would expect to see them going into the barrier, which means there was nothing broken at that stage.

As far as Lauda was concerned, Ferrari should have reiterated that no one was ever likely to know the precise reason for the accident. He had drawn a line under it in his own mind. Time to move on. He said: 'Being home made the difference. I was walking around to try and get the physical side back up. I could only walk for five steps – so I wasn't going anywhere because I was so weak. Training was a joke. But I had [Willi] Dungl with me all the time, working me very hard. I wanted to get back to racing. I had decided myself that I wanted to do it. Simple.'

Interviewed many years later, Dungl would reveal part of his remedy:

When I see him after the accident, his head is swelling out like a balloon. Physically and mentally he is down, his hands burnt. And so you have to start like a baby. He has much pain and needs much massage with oils. Every oil that we tried, it did not work.

And then I remembered a herb from the sea – comfrey – and I find it in the sea near Niki's home and I cook it. I put it on Niki's head and after ten hours the swelling had gone down and he slept like a baby. When he woke up, he has no pain, nothing. We go to Ibiza and I put the burning Niki in the sea water and after five days he is much better. Later, he comes to me and says: 'Look, about racing ... do you think it's possible I make a comeback?' I said: 'Listen, first you need a good condition and character training.' And so, we start.

Apart from this intensive work at home and in Ibiza, Lauda's extraordinary recovery was also helped by the response from his fans. 'The effect was very big; very encouraging and often touching,' said Lauda. 'People were writing, offering their skin, or their ears; telling me of their experiences of burns and skin grafts and so on. One little boy sent me his toy Ferrari because he heard mine was burnt.'

The Nürburgring car (chassis number 028) had been destroyed but, as far as Lauda was concerned, they would either build another in readiness for his return or he could use the spare car (chassis number 26), which had been taken to the races as a backup. Enzo Ferrari had other ideas. Audetto said:

When I was at the hospital, I was calling Mr Ferrari to keep him informed. He said to me: 'What are you doing at the hospital? There are doctors there; they will take care of him. Come back and phone Emerson Fittipaldi and ask if he wants to drive my car in the next Grand Prix.'

Emerson said he was very sorry but he had a contract with Copersucar and if he went back to Brazil and said he was leaving, they would kill him! I went back to Mr Ferrari, told him this, and he said to contact Ronnie Peterson. We knew Niki was out of hospital but no one honestly thought he could drive again. We started negotiation with Peterson but it was a little complicated because he was under contract with March – and we knew Max Mosley would want money if he were to lose his star driver. I contacted Count 'Gughi' Zanon, a wealthy friend and supporter of Ronnie. Gughi came to see Mr Ferrari and he said he would resolve the problem because he wanted Ronnie to drive for Ferrari. We started preparing the car for Ronnie because he was taller than Niki and adjustments would need to be made to have everything ready for a test at Fiorano.

When Niki heard about this, he became mad. He called Luca Montezemolo and said he would be able to drive again. Luca Montezemolo called Gianni Agnelli [head of Fiat, which owned 50 per cent of Ferrari] and he called Enzo Ferrari. Mr Ferrari asked me to come to his office and he told me to call Ronnie Peterson and tell him the test is cancelled; we don't want him. But he did not explain the reason why and I was trying to convince Mr Ferrari that this was a good solution. Mr Ferrari became so upset with me, he started shouting: 'I am the boss; I make the decisions; I do what I want!' He was shouting and screaming so much that his secretary came in to see what was happening. 'Get out! Get out!' he shouted. 'And you, Audetto – Goooo!'

Lauda had begun to get a sense of Ferrari's feelings when his friend, Emerson Fittipaldi, had revealed that the Old Man had approached him with a view to signing a two-year contract – with immediate effect. If Lauda was bemused by that and angered by the negotiation with Peterson, he was incensed by news of Carlos Reutemann having been signed. Enzo Ferrari may have been trying to send an unsubtle message to his reigning champion about his fitness to race, but it had got lost in translation. Lauda's dislike of the Argentine driver was so intense that he was determined to return at all costs. An original plan to make a comeback at the Canadian Grand Prix on 3 October was immediately brought forward by one race to the Italian Grand Prix on 12 September.

Lauda announced his intention at a press conference in Salzburg. Gerhard Kuntschik, motorsport writer for *Salzburger Nachrichten*, was in the audience on behalf of the German language paper. Kuntschik said:

I hadn't been at the Nürburgring. On the first of August, I was at a European rallycross near Vienna. That was the morning when the Reichsbrucke, a major bridge over the Danube, had collapsed. Fortunately, it was five o'clock in the morning and just one person was killed; it would have been a tragedy had this been at a busy time during the day. Then, in the afternoon, we heard that Niki Lauda had crashed and then that he was severely injured; we couldn't believe this either; two big shocks in one day.

I was at the press conference at Schlosswirt zu Anif near Salzburg when he announced his planned comeback in Monza. He had all the bandages around his head and the press conference was run by Römerquelle, the mineral water company that sponsored him. Everybody thought he's mad. This won't work.

'Nobody believed that Niki would be racing in Monza. It went against all logic,' said Audetto. 'We were preparing a car for Carlos Reutemann at Monza and for the rest of the season; he was under contract also for 1977, to join Clay Regazzoni. When I told Mr Ferrari that Niki wanted to race, he said that, contractually, Lauda had to show him that he is fit and fast.'

Thirty-eight days after the accident, Lauda reported back to Maranello as a means of showing Ferrari and the world that he was ready to drive a F1 car again. Audetto said:

It is one of the most incredible days of my life. He came in his plane with his pilot – but he also flew himself. We picked him up from Bologna airport. We were ready and waiting at Fiorano. I saw this guy come in wearing overalls that looked two sizes too big; very pale, head bandages with encrusted blood. Everybody, including [Ermanno] Cuoghi [Lauda's chief mechanic], was shocked. It was like seeing a ghost walking in, like in a movie.

He got into the car and did two laps, quite slowly. Everybody is thinking 'poor guy'. He came in and said he wanted to adjust the seat belts as he wasn't comfortable. He goes back out and after five, six, seven laps he goes faster and faster. After about ten laps he comes in and asks for adjustments to the car. He goes back out for a long run; again, going faster and faster. I don't remember what the lap record was, but he was close to it.

I went to Mr Ferrari and he asked about the lap time and how many laps Lauda had done. Then he said: 'We have to send him to Monza; contractually that's what we have to do because he's shown us that he's fit and he's fast.' So we then had to call Monza and to call Bernie [Ecclestone] and say we would be entering three cars. That was a big effort for us; more mechanics; more parts to be made ready for three cars. But we had to do it.

Ferrari had not taken part in the Austrian Grand Prix on 15 August. The official reason was out of respect for their fellow-countryman. Few – including Lauda – believed it. More likely was a cynical move to have the race cancelled and thus deny Hunt and McLaren at least one opportunity to make up ground. The merry-go-round continued – as the hard-nosed Enzo Ferrari, of all people, should have known it would – and the Scuderia made a single entry for Clay Regazzoni in the Dutch Grand Prix on 29 August.

Audetto said: 'Not going to Austria was a mistake. Ferrari said it was a protest over the decision to reinstate James Hunt's points from Spain. And also, he said, to respect Niki Lauda. We should have gone and Clay Regazzoni could have scored points. Also, going only with Clay to Zandvoort was a mistake. The car was not being developed.'

James Hunt finished fourth in Austria and won the Dutch Grand Prix to move to within two points of Lauda at the top of the championship. James had been keeping a close watch on his friend and rival's progress. He said:

When I heard he was thinking about coming back, I was not surprised. I could understand why Niki wanted to get back and race. You have a lot of time to think in hospital and, once he had decided to come back, he had to get on with it. He had a terrific amount of motivation, too, because he was still leading the championship and he really wanted to win it. It was a massive stimulus to get back and get stuck in. Here was a challenge and he accepted it.

Whatever Ferrari might think about either the Austrian's fitness to take part or having Regazzoni and Reutemann primed and ready, Lauda was determined to go racing before Hunt made further inroads into the championship.

The fight between these two was being covered with increasing interest by the British press. David Benson, writing for the *Daily Express*, had got to know both drivers, his relationship with Lauda helped by the fact that he had assisted with arrangements for the restoration of Niki's Bentley in England. During one of their telephone discussions about progress with this classic car, Benson asked if Lauda would agree to tell the story of his recovery – for a suitable fee. An agreement was reached and, as good as his word, Lauda invited Benson to join him on a private flight from Salzburg to Milan for the Italian Grand Prix. The bulk of Niki's recall earlier in this chapter of his days in hospital comes from Benson's interview. The writer would later relate in his book on the 1976 championship: 'This [interview] was the most remarkable narrative of indomitable human courage that I have ever heard.' Here, Lauda talks of the forthcoming race at Monza:

A lot of people have said they think I am crazy to go back to racing so quickly. They say that a man with a face that is not like that of a human being but like a dead man's skull should want to give up immediately. People who think like that would probably be very happy to be ill and stay at home and not have to go out to work. This is not my attitude to life. I do not enjoy life unless I am active and have something to do and look forward to. I must work. If I have an accident in my work then my aim must be to recover as soon as possible with all the help of modern medicine. Once I had decided to go on then I had to make a comeback as soon as possible. This is why I'm going to Monza.

My lungs and my physical fitness have been certified as being 100 per cent. In fact, I feel better now than I was before. My training programme is entirely up to me and my own willpower. That was when I took the decision to go to Monza. I've been running day and night and have been taking physical exercises for twelve hours a day. Fortunately, I have with me twenty-four hours a day Willi Dungl who is a world expert on the treatment of athletes after they are broken. He also brought me on with massage and exercise every day, until we have built my body up to a point where I can complete a full sixty-five minutes physical training session. He is a practical expert who works with a doctor and looks after every detail of my day including my times of rest, the food I eat and how much exercise I can stand.

The doctors checked me yesterday and said I was in perfect condition. I've tried my Ferrari and my attitude to racing has not changed. I like being back in the car, I love driving it. And I feel very happy. I love my sport and I love my job. One thing about the test [at Fiorano] I needed to know was if the helmet [specially adapted by AGV] would fit because of my [right] ear. It hurt like hell. Apart from that, everything was good. The accident was a bad thing to have happened but now I just look forward to getting back into racing again.

Motor racing is dangerous, we all know that, and when my accident happened I was not that surprised it should have happened to me. This may surprise people who don't understand racing but it's true. In the kind of job I have, it is the risk I must take.

The problem I have had to face since the accident is whether I would enjoy my motor racing again and what effect it would have on me. No one can discover this until they have been through an experience like mine. I have found that I love the positive side of motor racing. So why should I give it up?

I have not raced for over a month and when I climb into my car there will be enormous pressure on me because it is in Italy and Ferrari is the king and we have three cars entered for the race. But I will not let this pressure affect me. I may only finish in fifteenth place, but then I know that I am ahead of my programme and we can go to Canada and North America. I will be in a position to win and to keep my World Championship. Ferrari has been trying not to make me race at Monza. Mr Ferrari told me: 'Don't go to Monza because if you lose the championship, it's better like this.' I said: 'Commendatore, if I'm ready to race, I race.'

There can be no better definition of Lauda's icy pragmatism than all of the foregoing rationale. It also revealed a voracious desire to not merely compete but also to overcome any obstacles that might stand in the way of winning. As if the pressure was not extreme as it was, Monza, Ferrari's home track, was the worst possible place for Lauda's comeback, particularly as he hoped to keep as low-key as possible. The ancient circuit within the crumbling walls of a royal park on Milan's northern fringe had regularly generated weekends frothing with crazy emotion. This one would be no exception thanks to the presence of a disfigured man many had not expected to see again, never mind take the controls of a Ferrari F1 car and go racing in this passionate cauldron of sporting endeavour. It would be one of the most remarkable comebacks in the history of sport, never mind motor racing.

CHAPTER 8

Fighting Fear

'Monza? A crazy place,' said Lauda. 'I remember walking out of the paddock and there was a woman at the fence with a little baby. I had the police around me to protect me and she was holding the baby towards me and I'm thinking: "What's going on here?" It was like she was treating me as if I was God. I'll never forget this sight . . . Completely crazy!'

Lauda had enough distractions to deal with. Rather than make him feel welcome and ease his path given all that he had been through, the organisers of the Italian Grand Prix seemed to go out of their way to make life difficult. Lauda suspected the influential hand of Enzo Ferrari, still keen not to have him race and force the team to run three cars. Lauda said:

So, I get to Monza on the Thursday, and they say I have to go to the hospital and do this medical check – to prove I'm fit to race. I hated this and felt it was so unnecessary. There was no regulation requiring this; no one from Formula One was saying I had to do it. It was just the Italians. They really drove me crazy, with their mafia-like organisation. They said it was to improve my racing! Unbelievable. So [Willi] Dungl came with me and they checked me and didn't find anything. I was mad with them. I said: 'What the hell are you doing? I'm fit. It's my decision.'

That obstacle having been overcome, Lauda faced another on the first day of practice. Rain was the last thing he needed, particularly on a very fast track where spray and mist tended not to disperse quickly thanks to the surrounding trees. Very few cars went out during the morning practice session but, when the rain continued, Lauda knew he would have no choice. It was a moment many had been waiting for – including Michael Schmidt, a young German fan, many years later to become a highly respected F1 writer. Schmidt recalled:

I had been following all the Grands Prix as best I could. Strangely enough – and I don't know why – the German Grand Prix at the Nürburgring had not been televised. I had listened on the radio and heard there was a big accident and then fire. But they said it was okay because Niki was out of the car. He had some burns, and that was it. It was only in later news reports on television that they said he was fighting for his life. Over three or four days, there were big stories in the tabloids and I thought this guy's never going to come back; he'll be happy to survive.

I had never actually been to a racetrack before but, in September, because my father had to do something in the Monza area, I asked if I could come with him. I knew I wasn't going to see the race because my father had to go back on the Saturday. But at least we could watch first practice. It was raining like hell. We went in the main grandstand, because it was the only grandstand which was covered – and this was full, obviously. You could see the pit lane. It was empty because of the rain; people didn't want to stand out. But outside the Ferrari pit was crowded with people. Everybody with umbrellas standing there, waiting for Niki to come out. But very few cars went on the track.

· There was a break before afternoon practice and I was a bit nervous that I wouldn't see any cars at all, as it was continuing to pour with rain. But then they started to come out and, as always happens at Monza, anyone who is not a Ferrari driver but in contention for the championship – someone like James Hunt – people were booing. But when a Ferrari appeared, they were cheering!

Reutemann came out first and then a lot of cheering for Regazzoni. Finally, Lauda appeared – and it was like Jesus coming back. It was unbelievable. Everybody stood up. There was absolutely no cheering – just applause. It was respect. I was stunned. It was as if everyone knew that it was an outstanding and historic moment. A guy who was almost dead is, forty-two days later, back in a racing car. I'll never forget that.

John Watson was among many of Lauda's colleagues keen to see how such a return was possible. Apart from natural concerns about Lauda's well-being, they were curious to discover how any driver would cope with such a situation. Watson said:

I saw Niki in the paddock. It was the most courageous thing I have ever seen from a racing driver, or any sportsman, making a comeback like this. Frankly, he looked a mess and you wondered what goes through your mind as a driver. There was a bit of a backstory prior to him doing this. While Niki was working with Willi Dungl on his comeback, Willi had devised one particular test – probably among others – to cover his concern about how Niki would react if there was, say, another accident. Willi said he rolled up a ball of newspaper, lit it and suddenly threw it at Niki. Willi wanted to see if Niki was able to deal with it rationally, or lose it completely. Apparently, he dealt with it rationally and, at that point, Willi knew that Niki's mind was okay. The body, of course, was a different story and they had a fair bit of work to go through prior to Monza.

But your mind does play tricks when you have had a big accident. You wonder what's going to happen when I get into the car; will I freeze? When you get in the car, all your feelings and emotions come back; it's almost instant. All I knew was it took tremendous courage to do what he did.

Getting into the car was one thing; driving it competitively – or, expecting to be able to drive it competitively – was quite another. At the end of the first day, Lauda was nineteenth, slowest of the three Ferraris. He said:

On the Friday, I could not drive. I got out of the car after a few laps because I was frightened. I was worried that everything happens again. The reason I went to Monza was because the quicker you get back, the better. But the fear, it was there. You tell yourself you can take the corner flat and there's no problem. Mentally, you tell yourself this and then you come to the corner – and lift off [the throttle]. It's a mental brake, which you can't adjust. It's something which is in you. I realised it was going to take time to get confidence in the car. I went to the hotel and thought about it. I more or less said to myself, either you want to race properly or you stop.

At this stage, Mauro Forghieri felt that his initial fears as technical director were being vindicated. He said:

When he had the accident and we heard how bad the injuries were, I didn't think that would be the end of him. No. For me, he was a man deeply convinced in this life and the life for him was racing. It was impossible to say that was the end because, for Niki, the end did not exist. He saw coming back as another start! But I suggested that he should try and avoid Monza because, in my opinion, he was not ready. The blood on his bandages and so on was nothing. The important thing for me was that he was not so well prepared – or as well prepared as he usually liked to be – for the race. I thought that the way he was thinking and looking at the problems was not the same as before. And he had the press everywhere. It was very difficult for him; for us.

Given that the usual close attention from the media would be multiplied ten times by circumstance and the fact that this was Monza, Lauda and Marlene had chosen to stay in a small hotel, some distance from the track and hidden away. The precaution worked well – with one exception.

Ian Wooldridge was an outstanding sports writer. A man for the big occasion, Wooldridge had covered Olympic Games, football World Cups, golf majors and boxing world-title bouts, his prose invariably providing an elegant and entertaining angle in his main outlet, the *Daily Mail* newspaper. In the eyes of the sports editor, Tom Clarke, Lauda's extraordinary comeback was a story worthy of Wooldridge's attention.

The Englishman's expertise may have been in absorbing the scene being played out before him and relaying the moment with captivating eloquence, but first, if he was to fill the allocated double-page spread, Wooldridge would need to find his away around the specialised and unfamiliar surroundings of a Formula One paddock. It was immediately apparent to Wooldridge that a useful interview with Lauda – assuming he even got close enough – would be out of the question. Which was when guile and experience came into play. Calling upon one of his many local contacts, Wooldridge discovered the location of Lauda's hotel; the only journalist to do so. Writing about the experience many years later, Wooldridge described the scene:

> If there was one thing he [Lauda] didn't need at this point in his life, it was to be hounded by the press. Understandably, he, his wife and small entourage had hidden themselves away in a no-star hotel deep in the hinterland. Journalistically, luck was in. One tip-off and a dozen telephone calls by a tactful Milan lady switchboard operator who enjoyed the intrigue, and we were on our way thirty kilometres out into the country.
>
> Lauda was visible through the narrow glass panels of the hotel's dining room door. He was eating painfully, methodically. The only justification for such an intrusion was that the world's admiration matched its curiosity. But it wasn't as easy as door-stopping a mass adulterer or a tetchy trades unionist living it up in the sun. This man commanded ultimate respect. One sat and waited until he came out.
>
> 'Mr Lauda,' I said. 'I have been sent from London to talk to you.' He was furious. He was entitled to shove past, swear, have me thrown out. Instead, he glared through lashless eyes and said: 'You haff exactly two minutes.'
>
> Basically, of course, I haven't been sent to *talk* to him. I've been sent to *look* at him. And what I looked upon was not a pretty sight. It was like interviewing a roasted chicken. One ear was gone. The eyelids, let alone lashes, had been burned away. The lips were puckered. The cheeks looked like mediaeval parchment stretched taut down like a living death mask. A makeshift skullcap hid the loss of hair.
>
> He was brusque, vividly articulate and brief. 'Death,' he said, 'did not interest me. My fear was that my spine was broken. When I knew it was not, I knew I would live. Yes, they sent a priest. So what? There was nothing I could do

about it. To live, I had to stay awake. I stayed awake. I shall drive on Sunday.'

There were other words, but I do not remember them. I was mesmerised. Terminally strong, savagely polite, Son of Richtofen turned on his heel and marched up the stairs. The hotel was too small to have a lift.

Lauda had given the matter some thought in his usual pragmatic way and reasoned that he had tried too hard, too soon. By attempting to immediately go at the pace he had been accustomed to, he had not made enough allowance for either his physical condition or the atrocious weather. He had overreacted, instead of letting his driving flow.

With that in mind, Lauda returned to Monza on an overcast Saturday morning. Having three cars did not help an already cramped Ferrari pit area that was overrun with onlookers and the press. Officials and team members made a desultory effort to control photographers but, this being Ferrari and Italy, it was like trying to herd a bunch of fevered tomcats.

Lauda barely noticed the chaos, such was his focus on getting into the car and dealing with a track that was damp, but drying. Times set in this 60-minute practice session would determine grid positions, the afternoon being given over to a test session (a new timetable that had been tried for the first time at the previous race). With Friday's practice having been badly affected by rain, this promised to be a hectic and important hour.

Lauda decided to go at his own pace initially, Monza at least having the benefit of a wide track that would rule out the Ferrari unnecessarily holding up others in a hurry. With lap times tumbling and Lauda appearing to go nowhere, those who had predicted a difficult comeback – which was the majority of motorsport writers – felt their guarded previews had, sadly, been justified. But that did not account for an extraordinarily calm mindset in this frenetic and noisy place.

'There was huge pressure and mess everywhere I went,' said Lauda. 'But when you get into your car, you are in your own world. This is you, your car and the racetrack. I knew what I had to do. I took it easy at first and then, finally, got going again. It wasn't easy, but it was better. I had no idea about the lap times; just wait until it's over and see where I am.'

He was fifth quickest, a performance made even more remarkable by Lauda being the fastest of the three Ferraris. Reutemann was seventh, almost three-tenths of a second behind, with Regazzoni a further half a second adrift in eleventh. Even better from a championship point of view, Hunt had been having a troubled few days, as ninth fastest proved.

Hunt's weekend started badly when he spun during the opening lap of Friday's practice and damaged the nose of his McLaren, a mishap that engendered zero sympathy from the partisan crowd. Now things were about to get even worse.

During the previous weeks, there had been increasing rumours about McLaren's fuel being beyond the legal limit. It had never been proven, but that did not deter officials at Monza from taking samples from various teams – among them, McLaren. Nothing further was heard until race morning, when the organisers called a conference in the press room and announced that the fuel being used by the McLaren and Penske teams was above the permitted octane level. The lap times set by these teams during Saturday's practice were disallowed. With Friday's times more than 20 seconds slower because of a wet track, Hunt (and two others) would be starting from the back of the grid. And just to rattle McLaren even more, the Italian Automobile Club announced their intention to back Ferrari's appeal against Hunt's victory in the British Grand Prix.

Lauda let all of this go over his bandaged head as he prepared for the race start at 3.30 p.m. on Sunday. It had been a long wait for the 80,000 spectators as the 26 cars made their way to the grid; Lauda on the third row; Hunt at the back. Under a grey sky, the field set off on the formation lap before reforming on the wide expanse of the start/finish line. Lauda looked towards the starter's rostrum high on his left, waiting for an official to drop the Italian national flag. 'I didn't know they had changed the start system to lights,' said Lauda. 'I'm looking for the man with the flag, waiting for something to happen. I'm out of gear – and this green light comes on. There's no countdown; nothing. Ferrari forgot to tell me the fucking system had changed. I was twelfth at the end of the first lap. I was frightened in traffic again. I hated this.'

As during practice, however, Lauda settled down, found his rhythm, gradually climbing up the order; tenth on lap three; eighth on lap seven; sixth on lap 14, each move cheered to the echo by his passionate audience. He overtook the Tyrrells of Scheckter and Depailler between laps 42 and 48; Monza was on its feet four laps later as Ferrari number 1 swept across the line in fourth place. Peterson's unexpected win for March seemed irrelevant as, to a lesser degree, did second place for Regazzoni. Poor Reutemann had long since fallen victim to the man he was supposed to be replacing.

Hunt, meanwhile, was a spectator in the pits after a collision with another car had brought retirement. Despite this disappointment and being five points behind Lauda, James fully appreciated and respected what he had just seen. He said:

Niki's race really spoke for itself. To virtually step out of the grave and six weeks later come fourth in a Grand Prix was a truly amazing achievement, especially as there wasn't much practice time. He just got in the car and had a go. It was bloody good. And he drove a typical Niki race, well contained within himself and within his new limitations, loosening up for the big battles later. He knew I was out of that race so there was no pressure on him from that point of view. He was just putting a few more points in the bag before he went into battle in earnest. He did a super job ... A super job.

An hour and 31 minutes after the race had started, Lauda was completely drained as the Ferrari rolled to a halt in the scrutineering bay. Levering himself slowly from the cockpit, he made his away, accompanied by a police escort with dogs, to the back of the Ferrari pit and began to gingerly remove his crash helmet. Most of his cream flameproof balaclava was soaked in blood and adhering to livid wounds around the skin grafts, some of which had reopened; graphic evidence, if it were needed, of a truly heroic performance. Giorgio Piola, an Italian journalist, was among those who witnessed the post-race scene:

For me, the most shocking thing was the moment when he took off his helmet and you could see the blood on his balaclava. In some ways, he looked like a monster. It was scary and you wondered: how could he possibly drive like this? I had received various injuries and the thing that struck me at that moment was the type of injury he had. When you break a bone, there is pain, but then it is fixed. But when you have a bad cut or a wound, it can be much more severe than breaking a bone. Every time you move, the wound opens and closes. You lose blood and this can create a lot of pain. You could see that's what had happened and yet he drove somehow. That was incredible; quite fantastic.

'Niki had no right to be driving, because he was nowhere near healed,' said Jackie Stewart, a former winner at Monza. 'It's the most courageous thing I have ever witnessed in sport.'

Audetto said:

It was just incredible, the whole weekend. On the first day, he was under a lot of pressure; all the people; journalists came from all over the world. It was a big stress for all the team as well as Niki. We knew he had problems on the Friday. But, typical Lauda, that night he thought about it and decided he had to forget this chaos and concentrate on driving. On the Saturday, he was a new man; a completely different driver. We did what we could but it was Niki alone who found the strength to drive well.

You can't describe what he looked like when he came back after the race and took the helmet off. And because of a problem with his eyelids, he could not close his eyes. He had to wear a mask when trying to sleep at night. But you can imagine the effect that would have when trying to race. To finish fourth – forty-four days after he was dying? Incredible. Just incredible.

The scene was surreal. Racing for Ferrari at Monza is one thing. Having their lead driver – and reigning World Champion, to boot – defying such outrageous odds while looking like an extra from a war movie, elevated the sense of emotion onto a level never experienced before. Never in the haunting history of a race redolent with death and terrible injuries had motorsport – or any sport – witnessed such remarkable fortitude and bravery. Lauda, of course, did not see it that way. There was a job to be done. And he had done it.

CHAPTER 9

Game On

Formula 1 is the most exasperating expression of motor racing where passion, speed, fear, egotism and selfishness combine to give life to that magical non-Italian word: Sport. There is a world contained in that word – a world with all the virtues and the vices that, in turn, represent the facets of our lives. I have always thought that the ratio was even – a simple 50/50. But I'm even more convinced that the driver's desire to win, the anxiety of will, remains the mainspring of racing. Lauda's return is a demonstration of an innate passion for racing cars. Money might have been a consideration, but it was certainly not the determining one. My feelings for him are ones of admiration for a capable and scrupulous professional. I never doubted his recovery.

Enzo Ferrari may have said those words in an interview with *Newsweek* some months after the Italian Grand Prix but, at the time, Lauda had every reason to doubt them. He said:

After Monza, I found out Ferrari were going to Paul Ricard

and I asked them what were the plans for the test. But they just told me that Reutemann was doing all three days; that he would be in charge of testing. I was told that I could bed in brake pads at Fiorano, and rubbish like this.

So, I waved my contract in front of them and pointed out that I had priority for testing as the number 1 driver. I told them I was leaving to drive for McLaren – which I just made up! They told me to wait outside before asking me back in. 'Okay, okay,' they said. 'You can do the third day.' This is to the guy who is leading the championship for Ferrari with just three races to go.

So I turned up at Paul Ricard, everybody was talking Spanish (Reutemann was Argentinian), and I sat around for two days. The mechanics hadn't been told that I was running on the third day. I had to stop them packing up and they had to check to make sure it was okay. I did a few laps on old tyres in a car with a worn-out engine, came in and made a few adjustments, fitted a set of fresh tyres and, bang, four-tenths faster than my friend [Reutemann]. Then I pulled in and parked it. Test over. Let's get on with the racing.

There was a three-week break between Monza and the Canadian Grand Prix at Mosport, Ontario. During that time, the governing body of motorsport (now known as the FIA) sat in session in Paris to hear Ferrari's appeal against Hunt's victory in the British Grand Prix. McLaren, believing they had nothing to fear, had dispatched Hunt to Canada and sent Teddy Mayer and another lawyer to state their case. Ferrari arrived en masse, Daniele Audetto accompanied by their lawyer and one from the Italian Automobile Club, who was also president of the FIA Historic Car Commission – plus Niki Lauda, the heavily swathed star of Monza. Never one to miss an opportunity for gamesmanship, Lauda played the downtrodden hero to a tee.

What effect such melodrama had on the eminent judges from France, Germany, Spain, Brazil and Switzerland will never be known but their verdict was unequivocal: Hunt's win was thrown out and awarded to Lauda.

In the space of an afternoon, Hunt had lost nine points and his rival had gained three. The gap between the two was now 17 points in Lauda's favour.

Such a devastating turn of events would galvanise Hunt, a relentless competitor, whether at backgammon, tennis or motor racing. The British media was on their man's side, the story of Lauda's bravery having been subjugated by reports of McLaren's outrage over the court's decision. Forget the emotion of Monza; the gloves were off again. This was back to the upstanding Englishman against the arrogant Austrian.

Throwing fuel on the fire, one press agency reported Lauda as saying the court outcome had been 'a correct decision' that was 'for the good of the sport'. Another quoted Lauda as being 'madly delighted'. Hunt was not slow in coming forward with an angry retort.

The simmering hostility bubbled over as soon as the teams gathered in the rural community of Bowmanville, close by the Mosport circuit. Lauda and Hunt had been at the forefront of a driver-inspired safety campaign, one that had increased in tempo following Niki's accident in Germany. It had been agreed previously that Mosport, first used for the Grand Prix in 1967, had become excessively bumpy and needed looking at. But in the days leading up to the race, James declared his intention to stand down from the unofficial committee and showed no inclination to attend a meeting at Mosport. In the light of the setback over the British Grand Prix, he said he needed to focus on the championship. Unfortunately, such an understandable motive would develop a cutting edge when Hunt was also reported as saying: 'To hell with safety. All I want to do is race.'

Lauda did not hold back when interviewed by BBC radio: 'Hunt is a member of the safety committee and has a responsibility to the other drivers. He should not refuse to accept the responsibility. I can understand his disappointment over the disqualification, but the responsibility for the safety of all the drivers is a different matter and James must put the disqualification behind him and think of the future of the sport.'

John Hogan, as the Marlboro man with a foot in both camps, found himself torn between the two as soon as he arrived in Bowmanville. He said:

My flight was delayed and I arrived late at the hotel. I go into the dining room – I'm starving – to find James sitting on one side of the room and Niki on the other. They're clearly not talking. Immediately, I hear a shout from James: 'Hogie! Come and sit down over here!' And Niki is pointing at a chair and saying: 'Hogan! Here!' So, I'm caught between the two. James says: 'Tell Niki to stop behaving like a cunt!' Then I get from Niki: 'Why is that arsehole being such a prick?' I obviously knew about James having lost his British Grand Prix points but I didn't know much of the detail about what had been going on in Canada. I couldn't help but think: 'What the hell has got into you two?'

Verbal swordplay aside, Hunt knew he had absolutely no choice but to go for broke – a tactic helped by claiming pole at Mosport while Lauda, struggling with the handling of his Ferrari on the bumps, could do no better than sixth on the grid.

Lauda's sense of unease over the lack of relentless testing to which he had become accustomed was not helped by an argument with officials over the Ferrari's oil-coolers. When these were repositioned overnight, it may have appeared to be matter of little consequence to the outside world. But Lauda was aware that a small move of the oil-cooler on Hunt's McLaren earlier in the year had caused havoc with the car's handling until the reason was discovered a month later. This had happened because of the fuss over changes needed to make the rear of the McLaren legal. This latest oil-cooler dispute was because of a tiny but similar breach of the regulations. Adjustments made; cars declared legal; harsh words spoken; it was time to get down to business on the track.

Hunt drove the race of his life, dealing first with the fast-starting March of Peterson and then withstanding huge pressure from Depailler's Tyrrell in the closing stages. Lauda held fifth until a rear suspension link worked loose, the unpredictable handling forcing him to back off and finish out of the points. His championship lead had been reduced to eight points. There were two races remaining, starting with the United States Grand Prix at Watkins Glen seven days later.

The F1 teams were glad of the opportunity to stay in the Glen Motor Inn, a comparatively small family-run motel overlooking Seneca Lake in the picturesque Finger Lake district of upper New York State. David Benson caught up with Hunt when writing a piece for the *Daily Express*. Hunt said:

All my life, I will feel aggrieved about the British Grand Prix decision. I had adjusted to the disqualification in Spain – which I got back – but then they threw the British disqualification at me. It was really heavy. It seemed to me that, from Spain onwards, the Ferrari team made up their minds that they were going to win the championship on the track or off and they would use every loophole in the rule-book to do so. McLaren made a bad and expensive mistake with the width of the car in Spain and that triggered off the Ferrari attitude; this became apparent when we appealed and got our result back.

Ferrari took the view – and a perfectly reasonable one – that rules are rules and if you are outside the rules you are disqualified and that's the end of it. There is another perspective that says you can take a reasonable attitude about a technical infringement and ask a court to decide the degree of guilt. In favour of the first view is the fact that the FIA is too badly equipped to deal with interpretation of their antiquated rulebook. If you accept the point of view that a rule is a rule and must not be broken, then I get hopping mad about what happened in Canada. The Ferrari was discovered to be illegal and that it had been illegal all season. Their gearbox oil-cooler was in the wrong position. It infringed the regulations in exactly the same way our extra width at the back of the McLaren had done in Spain. But they have been running it all year in that way.

We didn't protest then because we at McLaren knew it did not give them an advantage – but neither did our wide car give us an advantage. Ferrari were acutely embarrassed in Canada when officials pointed out the irregularity and I've never seen a team change anything as fast as Ferrari with their oil-coolers on that Friday night. If McLaren operated like Ferrari, we should not only have had them disqualified from the practice times in Canada for the first day but for the whole season since the rule became effective in Spain.

But we know that the rules are so complicated that it is virtually impossible to build a car that is completely legal. I know that Ferrari do try very hard to build their cars to the legal requirements of the regulations because they are terrified that McLaren will find something wrong and protest.

What is done is done. I desperately want to win the drivers' World Championship this year but, on the day of the race, I won't even be thinking about the championship. I will just concentrate on winning. I will start examining the championship position only when the race is over. I will need a lot of luck to win and a lot depends on Niki's result. So there is nothing I can do but win or finish as high up as I can on the day. Even though Niki is desperate to keep his title, I'm determined to take it from him.

Having got that off his chest, Hunt was at pains to mention that the legal and technical issues would not impact personal relationships, despite the recent deterioration. Alastair Caldwell, as team manager of McLaren, had watched the relationship go through its various phases:

> When it came to Lauda's performance at Monza, I'd never seen bravery like it, not in any sport. You could see Niki was in a lot of pain after the race; that fourth place was unbelievable. James was pleased to see him back. They were good friends and enjoyed each other's company.
>
> The only time they fell out was in Canada, just after Lauda went to the FIA hearing about the British Grand Prix. It was a political thing, probably under pressure from Enzo Ferrari, and Niki wore a bandage with blood on – but I doubt it was blood; probably tomato ketchup used to good effect when the FIA took James's nine points away. He definitely wasn't happy about that. But they made up and they were back to chasing girls together, having the banter and the repartee. They just wanted to fight each other for the championship, never mind all the bloody politics.

Time may have been running out with just two chances remaining to score points but, coincidentally, James and Niki each remembered the pact made during their discussion as new-found mates in Sweden six years before. Recalled Hunt many years later:

The press was winding us both up badly and we both got irritated. For a few hours we hated each other but we got it sorted out by shaking hands after the race in Canada and our good relationship continued. For example, we had these adjoining rooms in the Glen Motor Inn and, in the evenings, we had the door open and we socialised together.

I'll never forget Niki's attempt to psyche me out on race day. I always got up at eight o'clock to be at the circuit at nine. Knowing full well what time I had my call booked, Niki barged into my room at seven o'clock. He was fully bedecked in his overalls and stood to attention over my bed and said: 'Today I vin ze championship!' And then he marched out again. I thought that was hilarious.

'I cannot remember that exactly,' said Lauda, when told the story four decades later. 'But I believe it because we were always doing things like this, making jokes about each other and him being so bloody British! I would have enjoyed that.'

Lauda was hard-pressed to see the funny side once practice began at Watkins Glen and Hunt took pole position with the Ferrari driver half a second behind in fifth place. Lauda had to hope that Jody Scheckter, sharing the front row in a Tyrrell with Hunt's McLaren, would at least keep James busy and, at best, deny him the nine points he desperately needed by finishing first.

Sure enough, Scheckter jumped into an immediate lead. By the time Lauda had worked his way into third place on lap five, he was 5.8 seconds behind Hunt, who was 2.8 seconds adrift of Scheckter. For the next 20 laps, the gaps see-sawed as all three drivers made small errors on the tricky, undulating track.

By half distance, however, Lauda knew he was in trouble as the Ferrari gradually developed a handling problem similar to the one that had dogged him during practice. Rather than think about attacking the leaders, Lauda had to go on the defensive as he came under pressure from Jochen Mass, Hunt's teammate being urged on by the McLaren pit to deny Lauda as many points as possible.

Lauda clung to third place but the news up front was not good as Hunt ended a steely battle with Scheckter by taking his second win in succession. James was now just three points behind. He had done all he could. One race remaining. It was game on.

CHAPTER 10

Fuji

Fuji was never intended to be a Grand Prix track when planned in 1963. On 24 October 1976, those present at the Japanese circuit did not consider it fit for racing of any description. The venue, in the shadow of Mount Fuji, was the last place anyone wanted to be as rain and grey cloud made the country's highest peak completely invisible. The conditions were so appalling that the 2.7-mile track was in danger of lying idle instead of settling the outcome of the World Championship. The original plan had been to make the Fuji International Speedway a high-speed, high-banked oval, suitable for American-style racing. A shortage of funds meant that project was never fulfilled, the final form in 1965 taking the shape of a traditional road course – and an uninspiring one at that. After many years of lobbying and gradual improvements, Fuji was deemed suitable to hold a Grand Prix. It was F1's bad luck that the final race of the season should coincide with a bout of inclement weather.

Practice, though, was in the dry. At the end of the first day, Hunt edged Lauda by a mere one-hundredth of a second. The expected confrontation between these two was to be upset on the final day of practice when Mario Andretti stole pole position with a Lotus that had been improving as the season went on. Hunt would join the American on the outside of the front row with Lauda on row two, 0.28 seconds slower than his championship rival.

The question that evening was whether James could score three more points than Niki and take the title. Twelve hours later, that discussion was almost irrelevant. The element of doubt was whether there would be a race at all. A weather front that had been building up in China finally arrived on race morning, cloaking Mount Fuji and everything around it in unremitting gloom.

A 30-minute warm-up, scheduled for 11 a.m., proved to be a portent of things to come as several cars spun off a track that, in many places, was awash. 'It was ridiculous,' recalled Hunt many years later. 'Approaching the first corner, there was a huge puddle and you had to brake before the actual braking area. But the main concern was the spray. That, combined with the mist, meant you couldn't see a thing. It was madness.'

The race was scheduled to start at 1.30 p.m. but, as the time drew near, the majority of drivers said the conditions were completely impossible. Race officials agreed to wait in the hope that the rain might ease. Ninety minutes passed and there was no let-up. Lauda said:

James, Ronnie [Peterson] and I were all sitting together in Bernie Ecclestone's office. The Japanese race director came in and said: 'Okay, we're going to start the race now.' I was leader of the pack and got up and said: 'What the fuck's going on? The rain is the same as before!' The weather was completely unacceptable – even the biggest idiot could see it was impossible to race. He told us that it would be dark by six so we had to start because of the television deal.

Televising a Grand Prix in 1976 had been a rare event. But the increasingly tense fight between Hunt and Lauda – coupled with the shocking drama of Niki's accident and his remarkable comeback – had moved F1 high in the list of sports editors' priorities, particularly the final race when this battle would be decided one way or the other. The astute Ecclestone was alert to the financial opportunities presented by the sale of television rights. The downside was expensive satellite links – particularly if there was nothing to show. Daniele Audetto recalled:

> The sky had opened, it was a monsoon; typical of the season in Japan. The organisers wanted to start. But it was impossible to race; the drivers didn't want to go out. When the organisers said they were determined to run the race, Bernie called together Emerson Fittipaldi, president of the GPDA [Grand Prix Drivers' Association], James and Niki. He said they had a problem because if they didn't start soon, it would be dark and there would be no race. If that happened, he would lose the money from television and from the promoter. 'We all lose,' he said. 'What I ask is for you to start the race so that we comply with the contract. Then you can stop. D'you agree?'
>
> The three drivers agreed to start the race and stop after two or three laps. Niki was happy because the conditions were catastrophic. Even the paddock was awash. The track was like a river; it was incredible.

The thought of going racing – of simply keeping an F1 car pointing straight – brought an unspoken air of trepidation, particularly for Hunt, at the best of times so wound up that he was regularly sick in a bucket before stepping into his car. Jochen Mass could not help but notice the taut demeanour of his teammate. 'James was definitely more keyed up than usual,' said Mass. 'He was so absent-minded, he walked out of the back of the pits and took a pee against a fence post. He was totally oblivious to the crowd of spectators on the other side of the fence. All the Japanese girls were very shy and turned away. James would never normally do that but, on that day, his mind was somewhere else. No one wanted to race in these conditions.'

McLaren team manager Alastair Caldwell said:

It was pretty spooky. The weather was terrible. Everyone was a bit tense and the race was delayed until the last possible moment because most of them didn't want to race at all, including James. He came back from his meeting with Bernie and some of the drivers and said it was too dangerous. They were going to do a couple of laps and then stop. I told him: 'Don't be a prick! No race; no world championship. Let's go racing. C'mon; we can win this!' I had given one of our mechanics an Acme Thunderer whistle and he was standing on the pit wall, using it to encourage the crowd and ramp up the boos and jeers so that we could get this race started. We fired up our engine, and that got the other teams going. I knew, once a driver gets into the car, he forgets everything else.

Pete Lyons, an eloquent F1 reporter, watched the scene unfold:

Everything balances out in life. Anyone who chokes with envy for a Grand Prix driver's style of life ought to have been in the pits as James Hunt pulled his helmet on one more time. He had to step across to his car on a sort of plank bridge constructed by his thoughtful mechanics to keep his feet out of the water on the ground. He had to settle down into a wet seat despite an umbrella that had been covering it. He had to pause while a mechanic with a drill pierced ventilation holes in his visor. Either side of his hips was a bath of forty gallons of fuel. Behind his shoulders was 485 horsepower. Ahead of him was a road covered in many places by water inches deep. Above him the air was heavy with mist. Steady rain fell out of it. Behind him on the grid, his rivals ...

Hunt knew he could not let those rivals get ahead for fear of having their spray exacerbate the already poor visibility. Having made poor starts more often than not, James, when it really mattered, managed the synchronisation of clutch and throttle as perfectly as anyone could wish for in such slippery conditions. Hunt surged ahead of Mario Andretti, a vastly experienced driver who thought he had seen it all. 'They were the worst conditions I'd ever seen at the start of a motor race,' recalled the American. 'There was so much standing water, it was terrible. I was moving the steering wheel more on the straight than in the corners.'

As Hunt's McLaren poked its nose through the leading edge of a swirling ball of spray, Lauda's Ferrari was lost somewhere in the middle. After two laps of this, Lauda stopped at his pit and climbed from the car. He walked over to the pit wall and watched as Emerson Fittipaldi in the Copersucar and the Brabhams of Carlos Pace and Larry Perkins followed suit. But not the McLaren of James Hunt. Audetto said:

Many people said afterwards that Niki and James had a disagreement about whether or not to race. That was not true. Both had agreed to stop but James was persuaded to race and by the time that had been decided, he didn't have a chance to tell Niki.

So, when Niki stopped I suggested that we say there was something wrong with the car; maybe the engine or something electrical because it was so wet. He said: 'No, no; you say I stopped because it's too dangerous. Period.' Niki is Niki ...

It was my mistake. I did not have the guts to say: 'You continue until James stops, and then you stop.' I saw this guy almost dead two months before. I felt a responsibility if he had an accident. Professionally, I should have said to him to go on. But what if something happened? What would I have said to Marlene?

From the technical director's standpoint, Mauro Forghieri still stood by his original assessment prior to the comeback at Monza. 'In my personal opinion,' said Forghieri, 'by racing at Monza, Niki lost the possibility to find in himself the opportunity to be ready to race in Japan. When you have a certain type of crash, you need to make a reconstruction of your feelings – and this takes time. I think he might have been able to deal with this race; these conditions, if he had allowed himself more time.'

McLaren, meanwhile, were having more immediate dramas. When the breeze stiffened and the rain eased enough to allow the racing line to dry, the wet weather tyres began to overheat and discard small chunks of rubber. A breakdown in communications between the McLaren crew and their driver meant Hunt was dithering over whether or not to stop and change tyres. He was lying second; the six points would be more than enough to win the championship. Should he stop and lose places? Could he make it to the finish on these tyres? After a season of hard racing and high drama, the championship – win or lose – was boiling down to this one decision.

With five laps remaining, Hunt's mind was made up for him when the front-left tyre began to fail. He got back to the pits, where the stop to change the tyre took 27 seconds. He rejoined in fifth place – and out of the championship. Using his fresh wet-weather tyres to the maximum while the rest of the field laboured with well-worn rubber, Hunt quickly worked his way back to third place – and the four points he needed to become 1976 World Champion. The final tally was James Hunt, 69 points; Niki Lauda, 68.

Lauda had long since left the track. He said:

> Since the accident at the Nürburgring, I just didn't have the reserves to take any crazy chances. I decided to do just two laps and go home. I was driven back to the airport with the race still going on. I told the driver to keep the radio on, but we drove through a tunnel and lost the signal. It was only when we finally stopped at the terminal and I saw the Japanese Ferrari importer's face that I immediately knew I'd lost the championship. The point is, I didn't lose the championship in Japan – I lost it at the Nürburgring and by missing two races. Anyway, I was happy that James had won it. He was my mate.

Hunt said:

> I felt really sorry for Niki. I felt sorry for everybody that the race had to be run in such ridiculous circumstances because the conditions were dangerous and I fully appreciated Niki's decision. After an accident like he'd had, what else could he do? Quite honestly, I wanted to win the championship and I felt that I deserved to win the championship. But I also felt that Niki deserved to win the championship – and I just wish we could have shared it.

John Watson, having recovered from an early trip down an escape road and hauled himself up to sixth place, had been forced to retire with engine trouble. The Penske driver had a perfect understanding of the conditions and an informed view on Lauda's decision. He said:

After choosing to come back at Monza, I'd say the second most courageous decision Niki made in his life was to retire in Japan. It wasn't widely known that the burns from the Nürburgring accident had damaged one of his tear ducts and he never had proper control over it. The conditions that day were dire; absolutely atrocious. I suspect what was happening was that with visibility being diabolical, combined with a tear duct that was maybe watering a lot, he couldn't see sufficiently well. The pragmatic side of Niki would have taken over and he made some stark choices: 'I don't want to do this. I want to win the World Championship, but I don't want to drive in these conditions.'

So, he rolled the dice because James had to finish third or better to win the championship, assuming Niki did not score. So Niki rationalised that he didn't feel it was safe in these conditions and what are the chances of James finishing third or higher? Of course, nobody knew what was going to happen, so that led to Lauda's typically pragmatic view. But it took a lot of courage to do that in view of his position in the championship, his role as Ferrari team leader and what Ferrari were going to say.

The thought of Enzo Ferrari's reaction also occurred to Max Mosley as he accepted a lift back to his hotel with Daniele Audetto. Emotions had been mixed for Mosley since he knew and liked both Lauda and Hunt. His March team had a dismal day, Ronnie Peterson failing to complete a single lap after the engine had cut out, and Vittorio Brambilla, after a dubious claim to fame by spinning and almost taking out Hunt's McLaren, eventually stopping with engine trouble. March had ended the season seventh in the Constructors' Championship, Ferrari and McLaren having scored four times as many points at the top of the table. 'Audetto had a Rolls-Royce which had been supplied by the Ferrari dealer in Japan,' said Mosley. 'It had been such a terrible day; everyone was wet and bedraggled. He offered me a lift and we were all squashed up; Daniele and I were sharing the front seat. He'd always been a good friend and I felt really sorry for him because, of course, I knew he had to ring [Enzo] Ferrari. That wouldn't have been easy.'

Audetto said:

I had to call Mr Ferrari as usual. He was speechless. Apart from the championship, we also had to discuss another problem – which was Clay Regazzoni. It was his last race with us and he was very upset with Ferrari. He had been told he would be continuing with Ferrari, along with Reutemann, for 1977 because nobody thought Lauda would be coming back. Then it was to be Reutemann and Lauda, and Clay was told this before the Japanese race. Clay could have finished in front of James. He was running ahead of him after James made his pit stop but, let's say, Clay was not trying hard to help us and he let James through very easily. You can imagine Mr Ferrari's feelings about that.

So, in the end we lost the Driver's World Championship by one point, but we won the Constructors', which was more important for the money. Niki had a bad feeling with me because of what had happened over my approach to other drivers. He thought it wasn't fair that, when he was fighting for his life, I was speaking to Emerson. Plus, he was not happy that I had made a declaration on German TV that we did not have any facts to suggest his car at the Nürburgring had a failure or a technical problem because we had checked everything. It sounded like I was saying the accident had been his fault; his mistake. That's not what I was saying. We didn't know then the reason for his crash and we don't know now. But, for a period of time, I was not Niki's best friend.

The championship finale had been dramatic – but for the wrong reasons. After such a theatrical season of collisions, close racing, disqualifications, shocking accidents and an incredible comeback, to have one championship contender leave long before the finish was anticlimactic, despite the perfectly valid reason behind it. The tension running rife throughout that afternoon in Fuji was, in one way, typical of the 1976 World Championship. But, in another, it had ultimately created a sense of disappointment. It was as if the final page of a thriller had been ripped out and flushed away.

When interviewed by *Newsweek* a few months later, Enzo Ferrari's anger had died down – in public at least. Ferrari said:

> When Lauda pulled out of the Japanese Grand Prix, the criticism was harsh. I was the first to justify his decision. I did so remembering back to 1924 when I had a similar crisis of doubt and finally decided, seven years later, to abandon motor racing as a driver altogether. But now Lauda's own actions have discredited whatever shadows one may have cast on him. He has told me repeatedly that he will stay with Ferrari as long as I'm here. There is nothing that makes me doubt his loyalty. The loose talk comes from newspapers whose only interest is selling headlines.

La Gazzetta dello Sport, as Italy's leading sports journal, had more than a passing interest in Ferrari's future with Lauda. The daily paper's F1 reporter, Pino Allievi, had not been in Japan and was keen to make up lost ground. He would be waiting for Lauda's return to Europe.

CHAPTER 11

Winning Again

Pino Allievi said:

I heard that Lauda's plane was sitting at Zurich airport, so I went there on the Monday after Fuji. Having come off an international flight, I knew he would have to come through customs at Zurich before getting to his private plane. I was sure I would catch him and be the first to talk to him on his return. But the Swiss police helped him go directly from the flight from Japan to his plane. I found out from the police that he was flying to Innsbruck. I managed to get on a flight that was leaving half an hour later and I got to Innsbruck not long after he arrived. I phoned his home and was told to meet him at a water industry business run by his cousin. I took a taxi and he was waiting.

He immediately said: 'You bastard! What do you want?' Of course, he knew very well what I wanted and I did a long interview. Then I rang Enzo Ferrari that night from a hotel and said I had spoken to Niki. He was a bit surprised! He wanted to know how Lauda was. I said he was perfect and that he had the courage to say that he was scared to race in

Japan. Niki had said it was the logical decision as far as he was concerned. He had no regrets. He would say all this to the press the next day but, by then, *La Gazzetta dello Sport* had run the story in that day's paper.

Allievi's diligence had not only delivered an impressive scoop for his newspaper, it had also confirmed that Lauda, as expected, was not looking back in anguish. What was done, was done. Those thoughts would be confirmed when Max Mosley met Lauda at the first Grand Prix in 1977. Mosley said:

I remember having a big talk to him about various things, including his decision to pull out in Japan. I asked: 'Why did you do that? All you had to do was keep going.' He said, because he had been through all those terrible things in 1976, there comes a certain point with stress where – in his words 'The rats get in your head.' That was his actual phrase. 'You just don't think properly,' he said. 'The rats get in your head.' We talked about our time together and the difficult way it had ended in 1972, with his fleeting thought about ending it all. I found – presumably after all he had been through in 1976 – that he seemed able and willing to talk more openly than one otherwise might have expected of Niki.

Elaborating further on Fuji during a subsequent discussion with the British journalist Alan Henry, Lauda said:

Look, at the time in Japan, I reckon I was right. I still do. You know very well that you thought we were all mad during the first few laps. All right, everything dried [on the track] and James was World Champion. But people forget how the conditions were. Hunt was champion and Lauda the idiot pulled out. But think for a moment if something had happened; if, say, something had gone wrong with James's pit stop and he had lost a few more seconds. If, say, somebody had been killed. What if I had been champion even though I had pulled out? Then they'd all have been dancing around saying: 'Lauda, he's fantastic, what a tactician.' But this would have been bullshit because I'm not. It's just not reality to think like that.

Lauda's acute sense of realism left him in little doubt that life at Ferrari had not improved since the edgy days of his comeback at Monza. There was an unspoken feeling that he had returned too soon; that it would have been better to lie low for the rest of the season and at least have a decent excuse for losing the title. Instead, he had raised doubts about his capability as a racing driver by pulling out of the final race.

There was little support and no stability within the team. Daniele Audetto had moved on to other aspects of the motor-racing programme inside the Fiat organisation and, in his place came, not one, but two individuals responsible for team management: Sante Ghedini, looking after administration, and Roberto Nosetto, dealing with the ever-present politics.

Lauda may have been indifferent to them both, but he was definitely bothered about the continuing presence of Carlos Reutemann. The Argentinian's main faults were that he wasn't Clay Regazzoni and, on his day, he could be blindingly quick. And just to aggravate the relationship further, Reutemann had carried out the bulk of pre-season testing.

The cars brought to the opening races in Argentina and Brazil were much as before, apart from a different type of tyre as Ferrari's supplier, Goodyear, reacted to news that Michelin would be arriving with Renault in F1 later in the season. Gone was Lauda's trademark smooth style as he worked hard at the wheel and spun more than once. Retirement with a mechanical problem at least brought respite from the struggle in Buenos Aires. Third in São Paulo looked good on paper, the only problem being that Lauda was nearly two minutes behind Reutemann's winning car after Carlos had driven brilliantly and made the most of other drivers' problems. Lauda was also annoyed by Reutemann having been given a revised rear wing, one that brought an improvement in performance, whereas Niki had been left with the older specification.

Lauda's last win on the road (Monaco in May 1976) suddenly seemed a long time ago. This, coupled with seeing Reutemann's name at the top of the championship table, was all that was necessary to have Lauda march into Enzo Ferrari's office on his return to Maranello and demand that he do all of the testing in future. This would involve time at Fiorano and, more important, the best part of a week spent pounding round the Kyalami circuit in preparation for the South African Grand Prix. At the end of it, the Ferrari 312T2 was finally more to his liking. For the first time since the accident, Lauda felt ready to race on his terms. This was timely since he was becoming anxious about his old sparring partner James Hunt having started from pole in both races in South America and finishing second in Brazil. John Hogan noted:

Niki didn't want James to get on top. No one else had come into the fray at that point. Niki had never really seen Regazzoni as a threat; he saw him as dangerous – which was not quite the same thing – ever since Clay had got them both embroiled in that kerfuffle at the start of the British Grand Prix. Niki had got Clay's number and he had known how to handle him. But it wasn't quite the same with Reutemann, even though Niki knew he could do a better job. From a Philip Morris [Marlboro] standpoint, Lauda was definitely our man.

Part of the clever promotion included a direct reference to Lauda's prominent front teeth and the adoption of his nickname 'The Rat'. Hogan said:

I'd just seen the film *King Rat*, based on the novel by James Clavell about American prisoners of war in the notorious Changi jail in Singapore. I was talking to Niki and the subject came up about the piss-take – started by James [Hunt], of course – over his buckteeth. I told him not to worry about that. 'It makes you look like a rat,' I said. 'Let me tell you about rats. They are survivors, no matter what happens.' Niki liked that. He was instinctively a bit of a rat; a survivor in every possible way. So I thought a bit more about it and, in 1977, had a strip made up to go across the top of his helmet visor, with 'SUPER RAT' in the middle. We were quids-in because everyone took pictures of the helmet and you couldn't miss the Marlboro logo on either side of 'SUPER RAT'. We later added another, with 'KING RAT' in the middle.

In South Africa, Hunt immediately recognised the return to competitiveness of the rival he liked and feared the most. 'The Rat was back,' said Hunt:

That much was obvious when I heard he'd been doing days of testing at Kyalami and then he qualified just behind me [Hunt was on pole position, with Jody Scheckter second quickest in the Wolf, which the South African had used to give this new team a remarkable victory on its debut in Argentina]. Reutemann was suddenly much further back.

I managed to out-drag everyone on the very long run to the first corner [Crowthorne] but then I looked in my mirrors and there was the red bloody Ferrari. I knew this was going to get interesting. I reckoned if I could come through the final corner [Leeukop] as fast as possible and stay about thirty yards ahead of Niki for the first few laps, I would have a chance. Jody in second place would have given me a bit of a cushion – but not Niki. He took things really cool and steady; typical Rat! He sat behind me for five laps and then pulled out to have a look going into Crowthorne on the sixth. There wasn't quite enough room, so he dropped back. I did all I could to get through Leeukop as fast as possible. But he was right there and this time he started his run a few hundred yards earlier. There was nothing I could do …

It was the old Lauda as he gradually pulled away in the lead, preserving his tyres and looking after the car. Win number thirteen seemed to be guaranteed, barring misfortune. As it turned out, Lauda was about to be affected by someone else's truly desperate luck. He recalled:

There was pressure on me like you wouldn't believe in that race. There had been this mess at the first two races and I'd told the Old Man what I thought. So, I had to get moving and finally I was leading a race. And then I had two problems after about 30 [of the 73] laps. The car started to understeer – and I didn't know why. I remember feeling a bump at one stage, like I had run over something. For a couple of laps I gradually loosened my shoulder straps so that I could sit up a bit in the cockpit to see over to check the front wing. When I was satisfied it was okay, I tightened the belts and got going again. By reducing my pace to do this, Scheckter [having overtaken Hunt] came up behind me. I said to myself: 'After my experiences last year with the accident and whatever, and all this shit that's been going on, there's no fucking way this guy will pass me.' I remember thinking that very clearly.

With the problems I had – this strange understeer was still there – I knew I would have to drive tactically to make sure of staying in front. Coming onto the long straight, I would have to hold him up through the last corner, and then accelerate like hell because this was the only place where you can pass. I managed to drive away from him, thank God, because in the last six or seven laps I had this oil-pressure light coming on every time I braked and, again, I didn't know why it should be doing this. So then I had to brake less hard, not rev so hard and make the engine survive. Which was a clever move because the engine completely blew up just as I crossed the line to win the race. You wouldn't believe it. So, for sure, it was one of my best results ever, particularly after everything the previous year.

So I go to the podium and I remember the face of the Goodyear man [Bert Baldwin] when he came up to see me. He whispered in my ear and told me Tom Pryce had been killed. I had no idea. Absolutely none. It was a terrible shock.

Making up for a poor start in his Shadow, Pryce had just passed Jacques Laffite's Ligier for thirteenth place. At the start of the 23rd lap, the Welshman was overtaking Hans-Joachim Stuck as the pair approached a rise on the long pit straight. Just beyond the crest, Pryce's teammate Renzo Zorzi had pulled over and stopped. A young marshal on the opposite side of the track, seeing the Shadow catch fire, grabbed his fire extinguisher and ran – just as Stuck and Pryce crested the rise at more than 170 mph. It had been the spontaneous reaction of a well-meaning volunteer.

The marshal was killed instantly, as was Pryce when the 40lb extinguisher hit him full in the face, the impact being so violent that the extinguisher flew clean over the main grandstand and hit a car in the rear car park. With the driver's foot jammed on the throttle, the Shadow careered down the straight before veering right and rubbing along the wall. Its terrible journey ended by slamming into the concrete retaining wall beneath the author's feet on the outside of Crowthorne, several hundred metres from the original scene of devastation. Laffite, unaware of what had happened, had been trying to run round the outside of Pryce when the wayward Shadow struck the Ligier as they entered Crowthorne. Laffite escaped unhurt.

The impact with the fire extinguisher had ripped off part of the roll-hoop above Pryce's head and sent it spiralling onto the track. Lauda had unwittingly run over it, the mangled tube denting the underside of the Ferrari's front wing (producing the understeer) on its way to puncturing and becoming lodged in the left-hand water radiator. When the Ferrari rolled to a steaming halt seconds after taking the chequered flag, the twelve-cylinder engine had only four of its usual 12 litres of water left in the system. Lauda had been extremely lucky to get that far. 'The piece of roll bar must have been just over the crest,' said Lauda. 'I never saw it and only felt that strange bump. No surprise the thing was overheating and the oil-pressure light was on. At the end of the straight, I saw Laffite's car, which was a mess, but I could see he was all right. You are focused on the corner anyway and it was only afterwards I realised there was another car involved.'

That win may have been fortunate but it would be Lauda's last for quite some time. By using Ferrari's reliability to the full and consistently picking up championship points – coupled with race victories being spread among five other drivers – Lauda found himself at the top of the championship halfway through the season. He strengthened that position with wins in Germany and the Netherlands, the latter on 28 August being memorable for reasons other than a 21-point advantage over Scheckter with four races to go.

During the Dutch weekend, Lauda had signed with Brabham–Alfa Romeo for 1978. This may have caught observers unaware, but it was no surprise to the man himself. Lauda's relationship with Ferrari never recovered from, in his view, the insensitive treatment of his return post-Nürburgring twelve months before. The partnership had lost its dynamism; the time had come for a new challenge. Lauda had made his choice after speaking to a number of other teams, including Ligier. He had actually driven the French team's car during a test session at Zandvoort – in broad daylight, as it were. If a driver tried such a thing today, it would be across social media faster than it would take his employers to speak indignantly to their lawyers about the flouting of contracts. In 1977, it went virtually unnoticed.

Lauda asked for news of the Alfa Romeo signing to be kept under wraps until Enzo Ferrari had been informed. Having been keen to keep Lauda on board, and recalling that Niki had once said he would drive for Ferrari as long as Mr Ferrari lived, the Old Man was not best pleased at the thought of losing the driver he suddenly claimed he had 'treated like a son'. The parting of ways that day was less than cordial.

By the time Lauda reached Bologna airport, the news was out. As he requested permission to start his engines, Lauda was informed: 'You've got a delay of two hours. No more priorities; no more VIP treatment. You left Ferrari, you bastard.' Thinking quickly, Lauda told the air traffic controller not to be stupid; he would be driving for Alfa Romeo – which, of course, was Italian. Permission to take off was granted.

A more serious repercussion of his departure from Ferrari would occur at the United States Grand Prix on 2 October. Lauda arrived at Watkins Glen on race morning to find that his faithful mechanic, Ermanno Cuoghi, had been summarily dismissed after informing the team that he planned to follow his driver to Brabham. Lauda was even more incensed when he discovered that the abrupt sacking had left Cuoghi outside the paddock and without sufficient money. When he secured the championship later that day, Lauda made a point of bringing Cuoghi with him to the podium.

The one regret Lauda had was the end of a sometimes tempestuous but always productive working relationship with Mauro Forghieri, the designer Niki had referred to as a 'genius' in 1975. The feeling was mutual. Forghieri said:

> Niki was good; very good. He was concise, consistent – and honest; very honest – sometimes too much. In my opinion, he and Chris Amon were the best drivers I've ever dealt with. In Niki's case, you must also consider everything else that was going on. I'm not just talking about the technical things that we would need to discuss; I'm talking about the politik, dealing with Mr Ferrari, the press; Niki took care of everything, better than any driver I've ever seen. To win the championship in 1977 after everything that he experienced the year before is more than fantastic; it's a miracle!

Unfortunately, it was not the technical chief's place to intervene when Lauda's relationship with Enzo Ferrari went into even steeper decline a few days after the United States Grand Prix. Knowing that Ferrari had entered a third car for Gilles Villeneuve in the young star's home race in Canada (something Lauda had disagreed with knowing the championship might still be at stake), Lauda sent a telegram to Enzo Ferrari, thanking him for his efforts in helping him (Niki) to win another championship but regretting that he would be unable to take part in the final two races in Canada and Japan because he was not well. A powerful relationship, one Lauda had craved several years before, was well and truly shattered. He told Alan Henry at Watkins Glen:

One morning, I just found myself not feeling about Ferrari as I'd felt in the past. Like painters, we racing drivers have an artistic inclination and are individualists. Our task is to have a free head, come to the race and do more than normal people can manage. But it became like being married to a bad woman. If you're in that situation then you haven't got a clear head, you can't give of your best. I worked there for four years, some good, some bad. But I suddenly realised that I hadn't got the same feeling towards the team that I had in the past.

Okay, I'm not easy to work with and I expect other people around me to try to attain those sorts of standards. I worked hard this year with the team. I had always been prepared to give a hundred and ten per cent to Ferrari but, to do that, you've got to be in a very happy situation. For example, you might work all night for an employer who you like and get on with very well. If you do a normal job, without this special relationship, you simply take the attitude: 'Okay, it's five past five; time to go home.' You need so much to have a good relationship with the person you are driving for in this business.

As far as Enzo Ferrari was concerned, things began to change this year. Political problems, aggravation, Italian press. In the past I had done anything he wanted me to do. Suddenly my freedom had gone and I felt I didn't want to do more than normal. But to do that would mean not to win: I knew that I had to work hard to be successful. So I realised that if I didn't do what I did in the past, then we wouldn't be successful. I don't know a special point in time when it happened, but our relationship went all wrong.

I decided to go with Brabham because, after four years at Ferrari, I need a sympathetic climate. Second, I want a fresh challenge. To go to McLaren [as had been discussed], easy.

A winning team, everything organised, James is a nice guy. Sure it would be very nice to drive for them. But I look for more. I want to be in big problems and to come out from them. So, for me, Brabham is the right thing. Different engine with Italian people. I understand them, I speak the language. And there is something harder to come.

Harder, perhaps, than the 1977 World Champion was anticipating.

CHAPTER 12

Bernie and Brabham

At the end of 1977 Lauda said:

> One day, I went to England to negotiate with Bernie
> [Ecclestone, owner of Brabham]. We spent an afternoon talk-
> ing. Talking about how we get the money together, about
> my contract. Then he said: 'Come out to the back. I've got
> something to show you.' And there it was – the [Brabham]
> BT46, complete and ready to go. I was so excited; I knew
> that I just had to drive that car. If Bernie had said: 'Look,
> you give me £10 and you can drive that car.' I'd have said:
> 'Here's the £10.' I had to think: 'Easy, be sensible, draw back.'
> But it was terrific. That's when I realised that I wanted, so
> much, to drive it.

For Lauda, this was an uncharacteristically emotional response,
probably due to a complete change of scenery and the reputation and character of the Brabham's designer, Gordon Murray.
Brabham was a compact, typically British outfit dedicated to
racing. Tucked away on a nondescript trading estate in the
suburbs of south-west London, Brabham was far removed in

every sense from the Ferrari team and its attachment to a factory producing exotic sports cars. The only similarity was the presence of a dictatorial owner in love with motorsport and capable of controversial and sometimes irrational decisions. Enzo Ferrari and Bernie Ecclestone were streetwise and both had the good sense not to interfere with the design of their racing cars. Murray had used this freedom to produce F1 designs noted for a rare combination of ingenuity and sleek simplicity. That talent had not been lost on Lauda as he experienced its effectiveness in the hands of other drivers over the previous six seasons. Lauda said:

When thinking about going to Brabham, I've been thinking logically about Gordon Murray. All his cars have been fast from the word go. He's not just good, he's fantastic. Each car has been an excellent machine. Normally, a new car is difficult and you've got lots of work to do. I reckon the BT46 must be as good as it looks. So then you say, it might not be reliable. But what IS reliability? It's the easiest thing in the world. Just run the car. Get this thing working, look at it logically. Take, for example, if the brake pedal is getting soft. There's no point in just accepting it. It shouldn't be soft, so make [cooling] ducting that works. Then, when you come to a circuit like Zolder, which is hard on brakes, the pedal might get a little bit soft but, if it's all right at Zolder, you know it will be fantastic everywhere else.

So, yes, this Brabham BT46 is complicated – but that's exactly the point. The more complicated it is, the more I like it. The more digital stuff [dashboard instrumentation and monitoring the car's functions], jacks [built into the car to facilitate a fast wheel change], brakes, whatever; I love it. There's more for me to play around with; more to experiment with, more to make work.

Lauda's theory would be tested to the limit when, put bluntly, the BT46 failed to work. Instead of cooling through radiators mounted traditionally inside the bodywork, Murray had introduced so-called 'surface cooling'. Water and oil was cooled by passing through a number of thin radiators mounted on the outer skin of the chassis. The first test runs with the BT46 saw the water temperature skyrocket. And this was in the depth of winter at two British circuits. What chance would this car have in Buenos Aires and Rio de Janeiro at the height of the South American summer? It was to be one of Murray's few failures. But at least Brabham had discovered the shortcoming early on. No time was wasted turning to the previous year's car and instigating a development programme.

The first run with the revised car, the BT45C, would take place at Interlagos in Brazil, Brabham's test team being run by Mike 'Herbie' Blash. In the event of what was about to happen, it was fortunate Blash knew Lauda well. Blash said:

I'd first got to know Niki in the early '70s when he lived in that block of flats at Heston. I was a mechanic with Lotus and, because Mike Hailwood, Ronnie Peterson and other motor-racing people lived there, this became the place to be and I got to know Niki on the social side.

In later years – and particularly when you think of the image created by the movie *Rush* centred on the 1976 World Championship – James [Hunt] came across as the great womaniser and drinker. Well, Niki liked a drink as much, if not more, than James. I was with him at a Formula Two race in Salzburg in 1973. He wasn't driving but, because this was Austria, he had come along to watch. I went to a nightclub with Niki and he told me that he had just signed a Ferrari contract. This was obviously very big news. But my main memory of that night is Niki, sitting on the floor of the club, drinking neat Whisky out of a half-bottle. He was obviously very happy!

Since then, of course, he had built a fantastic reputation as a World Champion and we were absolutely delighted when he came to Brabham. I was looking forward to working with him at the first test session in Brazil.

So, he leaves the Interlagos pits in the Brabham – and doesn't come back. Thinking he's stopped out on the circuit somewhere, I jump in our hire car and drive round – there's no one but us testing that day. There's no sign of the car parked on the track, so I assume he's eventually made it back to the pits. I get there – but no sign of Niki or the car.

Charlie Whiting [a Brabham mechanic, later to become chief mechanic and, eventually, one of the most influential men in F1 as Race Director] gets in the car with me and we went round again. We've no idea where he is – until I notice some of the catch-fencing is flattened at the lower part of the circuit, down by a lagoon. He had gone all the way through the fencing, into the undergrowth and the mesh fencing had trapped him in the car. This was the original Interlagos track – five miles long – so he would have been like that for several minutes by the time we got to him. He had some bad scratches on the back of his hands but, otherwise, he was okay.

We discovered later that the problem had been caused when a hydraulic line to the rear brakes had not been fitted properly. Instead of going through a small gap designed for that purpose in the rear suspension, it had been squashed when the suspension was fitted. Basically, he suddenly had no brakes. Welcome to Brabham.

Of course Niki wanted to know, in his words, 'what the fuck had happened'. But he never complained. Other drivers would have shouted and screamed. You could say it was a reflection of what he had been through at and after the

Nürburgring in 1976. Anything else was insignificant by comparison. His attitude was: 'Okay, the brakes failed; I'm alive; I'm okay. These things happen.'

Lauda's pragmatism would surface in a subsequent test and continue to impress his team, if not the Goodyear technicians who had proudly brought their latest tyres from the United States for Niki to evaluate. Tony Jardine, a Brabham mechanic, was looking on. He said:

Goodyear had arrived with these brand new tyres and they were saying things like: 'Niki; you gotta try these new compounds; they're fantastic!' So, he'd be sitting in the car and say: 'Okay, let's try them.' He goes out, doesn't even complete a flying lap, comes back in and says nothing. The Goodyear people look puzzled for a second or two and then say: 'Niki. We've got these other tyres. Fantastic.' 'OK,' he says. 'Put them on.' Same thing: he does one lap, comes in and says quite simply: 'Take them off.'

'Okay, Niki; we got these qualifying tyres, super sticky, you'll really like 'em.' 'Okay, put them on.' Out he goes again. The Goodyear guys are standing at the pit wall, stop watches ready, waiting to see what his lap time will be – and he comes straight back to the pits again, rolls to a halt and switches off the engine. In the silence, all you can hear is the muffled voice from inside the crash helmet: 'Those were joke tyres! Take them off.' The poor American guys were completely crestfallen. They'd never had such direct comments from any driver before.

'That was typical Niki,' said Blash. 'He was very straightforward technically: "Yep, this works. No, that doesn't." But he wouldn't really go into why something worked or didn't work.

For him, that was a job for Gordon and the engineers to work out what was going on.'

Lauda's arrival at Brabham brought a new dimension for John Watson, who had moved to Brabham in 1977 following the Penske team's withdrawal from F1. He recalled:

It was Hockenheim [for the German Grand Prix] in 1977 when Bernie had asked what I thought about Niki coming to Brabham in 1978. Bearing in mind that I'd never had a teammate of that quality – a World Champion and, at that stage in 1977, going on to be a double champion – I said to Bernie that I had no problems; I was happy to have anybody as a teammate. In any case, I liked Niki. I told Bernie that we had a friendship, not close, but a friendship, and all that I would ask was for an undertaking that we have equal treatment. Bernie said that was the way it would be; no problem.

But I was being naive insofar as not recognising the skills that had evolved over the years during Niki's time at Ferrari and how he had learned to manipulate and organise things favourably for himself and not necessarily his teammate. I had never come across this before. I believed that – forget all about the technical stuff with qualifying tyres, car set-up and so on – racing was basically about two athletes competing as athletes do in, say, a 100-metre race; just the two of you, and that's it.

Niki had a leverage which I didn't have. He was now a two-time World Champion – which was significant in itself – plus the fact that his personal sponsor was Parmalat and he brought the dairy company to Brabham as title sponsor. So, one way or another, he was in a very strong position. On top of all that, he and Bernie really liked each other – right until the day Niki died. So there were a number of things stacking up, and Niki's stack was considerably taller than mine.

As the 1978 season got under way, a couple of podium finishes for Lauda and Watson, plus pole position for Lauda with a heavily revised BT46 in South Africa, failed to disguise the fact that Brabham were working hard to recover following the failure of the surface cooling.

An incident during the Brazilian Grand Prix would sum up the run of bad luck that seems to attach itself to any team finding itself on the back foot. Having qualified on the fifth row of the grid, Lauda was in a mid-field fight with Stuck when a wheel balance weight flew off the German's Shadow. The lead slug smashed Lauda's windscreen, sliced through the air intake behind the cockpit and embedded itself in the leading edge of the Brabham's rear wing. Travelling with the speed and force of a bullet, the lead weight missed Lauda's head by less than an inch. Blash said:

He took that sort of thing in his stride, just like everything else in his life. Nothing seemed to bother him too much. We were due to go testing at Paul Ricard. I flew with Niki to Salzburg to spend the evening with him – and the first thing we did was have a large beer and a schnapps. We flew off the next morning and it was foggy when we got to the south of France. We were trying to find the Paul Ricard track and the little airport beside it, but we couldn't see much. So we went along the Mediterranean coast until we found Bandol [a small town] and then we followed this twisting road as it climbed all the way up to where we knew the track was, high on a plateau. And he was doing all this – no problem at all – in a small jet! He was an excellent pilot.

He was also a deft manipulator, as Watson had noted earlier and was now feeling the effect of:

I forget what it was exactly – a reliability issue or something not happening as I felt it should – but I went to Bernie and said: 'Look, Bernie: you told me you were going to give us equal treatment and I feel this is not happening. I want to know what you're going to do about it.' Bernie doesn't like to be put in those positions. He turned round immediately and said to Ann Jones [Ecclestone's PA]: 'Get Watson's contract; get Lauda's contract; tear them up; make Watson number 1; make Lauda number 2.' Then he said: 'John, I'm telling you, what's on a piece of paper is not what's important. It's the way that person goes about their business that's important.' That summed it up.

Prior to each Grand Prix, Bernie would instruct the team to go to a circuit in the UK and run all three cars. It was my duty to drive each one for five or ten laps because Bernie had a thing about spending a bloody fortune, only to have these cars do one lap and break down. On one occasion, I noticed Niki's car was doing something slightly better than my car. When I asked Gordon, he was a bit sniffy about it, saying Niki had a stiffer rear roll bar but, as I was happy with my car, what was my problem? I said I was happy until I had driven Niki's; I asked if they could do the same to mine. So, the differences were primarily in that kind of minor adjustment.

It was all part of learning how Niki went about his business; it was something I had never seen before when inside a team. Niki was exceptionally good in building a team to support him. He was always working to secure his best options. He had the clout to do it and he won over the team, which, if you understand what's going on, is fine. I didn't understand it initially but, eventually, the penny dropped. Niki was thinking of just one thing: winning the championship again.

By the time he had flown to Sweden for the eighth Grand Prix of the 1978 season, Lauda was fifth in the championship table with half the number of points scored by the leader, Mario Andretti. The American was beginning to dominate thanks to the recent arrival of the Lotus 79, a car that would set new standards thanks to the use of so-called 'ground effect', which utilised air passing through the sidepods to effectively suck the car onto the track, particularly when cornering.

Gordon Murray had his own ideas about maximising aerodynamics. Radical wouldn't make a start when describing his thinking.

CHAPTER 13

Up, Up and Away

'I tell ya, no matter the politics and legal bull that surrounds this car, it's gonna have to be stopped for safety reasons.' Mario Andretti was not mincing his words after the first practice for the 1978 Swedish Grand Prix. The Lotus driver's colourful concern had as much to do with the alleged danger created by this car as it did with the Brabham's sudden threat to the American's lead in the championship.

Andretti was referring to the Brabham BT46B – henceforth known as the 'fan car'. Murray's sense of innovation was demonstrated in all its shrewdness when he mounted a conventional radiator horizontally over the engine and ostensibly cooled it by a gearbox-driven fan. But the trick was to use flexible skirts to seal the rear so that the fan also helped suck the car to the ground and generate hitherto unimagined levels of downforce.

When the Brabham was rolled out of the team's transporter in Sweden, it created a massive amount of interest – followed by outrage when the rear of the car sat down on its skirts each time the throttle was blipped and then rose slightly when the revs died away. Rivals immediately claimed the car was illegal because the primary function of the fan was to provide aerodynamic assistance — which was not allowed. Murray claimed the fan's primary function was to cool the engine, citing the simple but effective premise that, if the fan was disconnected, the engine would overheat. While arguments continued, the car was allowed to run during practice. Blash said:

We had run the car during testing and we knew imme-diately that it was quick. But we didn't want to show our hand straightaway during practice in Sweden. Other teams — particularly Lotus and [team boss] Colin Chapman — were watching us like hawks. Each time we ran, we had the cars heavy with fuel to avoid accidentally producing a quick lap time but, of course, we didn't want anyone to know that. So, we were playing games. The car would be on the track and Bernie, making sure Chapman was within earshot, would be shouting: 'Get that car in! It's low on fuel! What idiot let it go out like that?'

Andretti claimed pole, with Watson alongside the Lotus and Lauda third fastest. Watson would eventually be forced to retire when dirt got into the throttle slides of the Alfa Romeo engine, but Lauda was content to shadow Andretti before choosing his moment, snatching the lead and going on to take his first win of the season. Lauda said:

It was the easiest win I ever had. You could do anything with that car. I was pressing Mario really hard when one of the Tyrrells dropped oil all over the racing line and the track became very slippery. Mario's Lotus was sliding all over the place and my Brabham was just sitting there, like it was on rails. Then Andretti made a small mistake coming through a corner, I pulled over to the inside and just nailed him coming out — no problem at all.

You had to alter your technique to drive it properly. I remember when we were testing at Brands Hatch on the club circuit, when you came through Clearways [a long, dipping right-hander at the end of the lap] you didn't back off to kill the understeer, as you would on a normal car. You just booted it even harder – the thing just sat down on the track, you were through the corner and away. Incredible car!

Rivals, naturally, did not share Lauda's enthusiasm for the Brabham, claiming that the rear-mounted fan was firing dirt and debris directly at anyone following. Since this win had occurred at a time when Ecclestone was beginning to unite the teams into a collective bargaining force that would earn them – and Bernie – healthy sums from television and other commercial rights, Ecclestone craftily played the long game and agreed to withdraw the BT46B even though it was never declared illegal. Murray was incensed. But he wasn't the boss. Work resumed on developing the BT46.

Lauda would win one more Grand Prix in 1978. But it was a race he would rather forget. A multiple collision shortly after the start of the Italian Grand Prix saw Ronnie Peterson removed to hospital with leg injuries that were not thought to be life-threatening. Lauda finished third on the road but was elevated to first when the two cars ahead were deemed to have jumped the start and penalised. A win is a win but all of that became academic the following morning when news from the hospital revealed that Lauda's friend and former 'master' had died of an embolism.

Retirement from the final two races summed up Lauda's 1978 season better than two wins under controversial circumstances. Aware that he needed to exploit ground effect to the full, Murray persuaded Alfa Romeo to switch from the flat-twelve engine to a V12 shape that would be better suited to utilising the flow of air around the back of the car. Under the guidance of Carlo Chiti, the legendary designer of Alfa Romeo racing cars and engines, the Italian firm's willingness to help was impressive. Unfortunately, the remarkable speed in producing a new engine in just three months was not matched by making it reliable. While Murray's latest creation, the BT48, looked the part, it would also prove as excessively ambitious as the V12. Giorgio Piola, reporting for *La Gazzetta dello Sport*, would see this at first hand:

> Lauda was testing this Alfa engine for the first time at Paul Ricard. He was there, waiting for the car, and it came on a trailer – not in a big truck – because they had carried out a shakedown at Balocco [Alfa Romeo's test track] before coming. But they forgot to put water in the system, and the engine was broken. When they got to Paul Ricard and went to start the engine, it was dead. Niki went mad! Chiti looked at me and said: 'Piola, you are the only journalist here – don't write this!'

The Brabham's lack of competitiveness was tough on Nelson Piquet, a Formula Three champion plucked from the ranks of promising drivers by Ecclestone to replace Watson, who felt the opportunities would be more favourable at McLaren. Piquet was similar to Lauda in his early days insofar as the Brazilian's mind was like a sponge, absorbing everything, with the added ploy of spending as much time as he could with the mechanics, both at work and socially. It was a clever plan but, in Lauda's opinion on one occasion, a move too far. Piquet said:

> During the British Grand Prix weekend at Silverstone, the car was 18 kilos overweight. Before qualifying, I got the mechanics to take out first gear, because I didn't need it for

a flying lap. I got them to take out the fire extinguisher, too, which put my car just on the minimum weight. Niki saw the car on the scales, and went to complain to Bernie; he wanted to know why his car was 15 kilos heavier than mine. After that, my mechanic was taken off the job and I was not allowed to visit the Brabham factory any more, because Niki realised I was spending my days there doing these things.

Rather than sour the relationship, the incident cemented the friendship as Lauda realised they were two of a kind. Piquet said:

What I learned with Niki was how to communicate with the team. Before I drove for Brabham, I never worked with any engineer. I had my own car and I made all my decisions about the set-up; I just told the mechanic what to do. Niki could describe what the car was doing, whether it was rolling or understeering or oversteering. I tried to feel the same things to tell the engineers. That was a good thing I learned.

But, for me, the most important thing when I came to Brabham was that Niki never left me by myself. He would take me with him to the restaurant at night, and I don't think today there is any relationship between teammates like that. Usually when drivers are new in the team, no one wants anything to do with them. But Niki was so helpful on this point. He also gave me horizons in other directions. We started to talk about flying; he helped me to understand about aeroplanes; he convinced me to buy a plane; he told me what to do. All these things I got from Niki were very good for me. He was a fantastic guy.

Piquet also noted Lauda's simple and direct method of communication. Blash said:

That's what we all liked about Niki. Everything was black and white. There were no grey areas. No bullshit. If you bullshitted him, he would lose all interest – so don't even think about it. But there were times when you had to be firm.

I was running one of our tyre test sessions at Anderstorp [in Sweden] in 1979. One way of keeping a check on whether or not a changing track surface might be affecting lap times was to use what were known as a set of control tyres. You'd run them at the start of the test and then, every two hours, put them back on again to see if anything had changed.

It was getting late in the day and Niki had finished his run with a set of tyres we were testing and he said he had to leave. I told him we needed to run the control tyre before we could stop. He didn't want to do it. When I insisted, he was pissed off. He said: 'Listen, I can tell you exactly what the time will be [on the control tyre]; I'm going to do a 1 minute 27.23 seconds' – or whatever the lap time was; I can't remember exactly. He did his laps, came in – and I wouldn't show him the lap times. He looked at me, knowing exactly what I could see. The lap time was as he said it would be; absolutely spot on. It just showed the level of the man as a driver.

Bernie Ecclestone was in no doubt about his driver's ability. There was the added bonus of Ecclestone and Lauda speaking the same direct language, neither being afraid to call a spade, a spade. Ecclestone said:

He was very special. As a team owner, he was no problem whatsoever. During qualifying in Austria, we had been given five sets of qualifying tyres for the team. Niki and Nelson had each used two sets of qualifying tyres, and Nelson was quicker than Niki on this occasion. Niki came in and said: 'I think I can find a bit more time, so put on that last set of qualifiers.' I said to him: 'Nelson doesn't think he'll be quicker; he IS quicker. So he gets the tyres to be quicker still.' When Niki said he was supposed to be number 1, I said to him: 'Niki, you're number 1 in my heart. But you're number 2 today as a driver.' And that was it. We didn't have an argument; there was no big discussion about it afterwards. Nothing. That's just how it was with Niki. Very straightforward. A guy who was very comfortable with himself.

Lauda had a mere 4 championship points on the board going into the penultimate race of 1979 in Canada. Apart from an unexpected win in a non-championship race at Imola in Italy and a mere two finishes in the top six, his season had been a catalogue of retirements; a disappointment for Gordon Murray as much as his driver. Murray said:

I really liked working with Niki. He got on very well with Nelson and they both worked well with the mechanics. The arrival of Nelson, a potentially quick young guy, didn't change anything as far as Niki was concerned; he had a strong enough character. He enjoyed working on the BT48 but I have to admit not scoring any points took the edge off it. It wasn't very good for somebody with his reputation but, saying that, he just took it as being one of those seasons. He didn't have many moods and he had very good control over himself.

Having had more than enough of the Alfa Romeo, Ecclestone decided to switch to the Ford–Cosworth V8 engine, used by the majority of teams. Murray would have a new car, the BT49, ready in time for the race in Montreal. Things were about to change – in every direction.

The Brabham mechanics had been working flat out to build and prepare two BT49s, ready for Friday morning practice around the Circuit Ile Notre-Dame. The man-made island in the middle of the Saint Lawrence had been prepared for Expo 67 and then used for the 1976 Olympic Games. The rowing lake ran alongside much of the track.

As might be expected of a car that had not run before, Lauda was in and out of the pits during the morning and made no impression on the list of lap times. Shortly after the afternoon session had started, a memo, V-9 (representing the ninth official notice on Vendredi [Friday]), was issued. It was brief and to the point. Handwritten and signed by Roger Peart, the clerk of the course, the document referred to Brabham number 5 and said: 'Please be advised that this car will be driven by Ricardo Zunino, and not Niki Lauda.' By which time, the double World Champion had left the racetrack – and motor racing.

The motor-racing world was stunned; the media caught totally unawares. In the midst of hurriedly writing appreciations of a spectacular career, journalists also had to try to fathom why the double World Champion had suddenly chosen to walk away. It's one thing to quit; quite another to do it in the middle of a race weekend. Even allowing for Lauda's abrupt pragmatism, this was unprecedented. Lauda said:

The main thing for a lot of human beings is that maybe the money involved makes you do a lot of things that maybe you wouldn't do if the money wasn't there. Was I racing for the money? You know, $2 million to have or not to have makes quite a difference – particularly if you're thinking of going into the aeroplane business. I had no problems for 1980; everything looked good. We'd got rid of the twelve-cylinder Alfa and I knew Gordon would design a competitive car. But maybe I had started wondering if I was now going racing just for the money.

That morning, when I looked out of my hotel window, it looked very grey and I didn't feel good about everything for some reason. I didn't feel excited. I thought that by the time practice starts and I get in the car, the feeling will come. When I got in the new car for the first time, I immediately felt a kind of tickle in my back that came from the vibration you got from the Cosworth engine – which I hated. (No coincidence, perhaps, that the last time he had experienced the British-built V8 had been in the awful March 721X in 1972.)

I started to practise, did a few laps – and I felt nothing. I thought: 'What are you doing here?' I returned to the pits and had a think to myself: 'Come on; keep going; you are paid to drive here. Do another five laps.' I went out again. This time the feeling was worse. It hit me hard. I felt I had to do something else. I got out of the car and went to Bernie and said we need to talk. He thought I wanted a set of qualifying tyres or something. He said I could have the tyres but when I said: 'No, I need to speak to you', I think he could see from my face that this was different. He said we should talk in the motorhome.

The positioning of the Montreal facilities was unusual in so far as the teams' caravans and motorhomes were located at the far end of the Olympic rowing lake, a five-minute walk from the pits. Blash said:

Niki had got out of the car and said to me: 'We've got to see Bernie.' So we had that long walk down to the paddock. That's when he told me what he was going to do. I must admit I was a bit surprised at the time but, looking back later, I could see that he had been losing interest. The one thing I didn't do was question his decision. There was no point. He'd clearly thought about it, made up his mind, and nothing anyone said was going to change it.

Lauda arrived in the team's motorhome and, as ever, came straight to the point. If Ecclestone was surprised, he hid it well. He said:

> When he said he wanted to stop, I wasn't particularly surprised because, with Niki, you had to be ready for these things. When it came to doing deals with Niki, he was not so much a tough negotiator but he was tough as a guy who would simply say 'No' – which is not always the best way to negotiate. He was the first driver to get a $2 million contract, which I gave him because I thought he was worth it. He was good not just as a driver, but as a person, as a mate. I didn't want to lose him. But when he said he wanted to stop, I knew that was likely to be final. Once he'd decided, I said: 'Get in your car and drive away. Leave your helmet and overalls here. Just leave them; I'll deal with it. Go! Go! And don't just go back and stay in the hotel; go to the airport.' Which is what he did.

'Bernie was the fairest guy I ever met,' said Lauda. 'He said he understood, but told me not to rush a decision I might regret, to go away and have a think. His attitude was great but, after a few minutes, I went back and said: "Bernie, I'm sorry; that's it." He said: "Okay, go now – but do me a favour. Leave your helmet and overalls here because I need to find another driver."'

Ecclestone said: 'I got hold of [Ricardo] Zunino. He was a young [Argentine] guy who'd been looking for a drive for a long time. I said – pointing to Niki's overalls – try these. "What d'you mean? These are Niki's. What's he going to say?" I said: "Don't you worry about Niki. Just let me see if they fit!" They did.'

Lauda's instant departure had an immediate effect on Murray, who clearly needed to learn more about his new car. But once the initial shock had subsided, the Brabham designer was scarcely surprised. He said:

It was obviously a disappointment initially. I was surprised – and, then again, I wasn't. I was surprised that it happened then and there, but I wasn't surprised by the fact that Niki had retired before the end of the season: he was that sort of character. If he decided something, then he wouldn't 'um' and 'ah'. If he woke up in the morning and decided something, then that would be it. It did surprise me that it was that particular morning because we did talk the night before about how the car should go. I spoke to him that morning but he wasn't saying very much. I think it was a sign that he'd made up his mind before he drove the car. He was very quiet; very different that morning.

At the start of the season in Argentina, Blash had met Walter 'Wally' Brun, a senior captain with British Caledonian Airways, and introduced him to Lauda. Blash said:

We met by the pool – as you do. Wally liked racing and he lived not far from our factory. British Caledonian were flying DC10s at the time and he arranged for Niki and I to go to the McDonnell Douglas factory at Long Beach a few weeks later, when we were in California for the United States Grand Prix West. They had a simulator and we met Pete Conrad, the astronaut who was vice president of McDonnell Douglas. On the way back to the racetrack that day, Niki said he was going to buy a DC-10 one day.

As he walked out in Montreal six months later, he said: 'I'm off to buy that plane.'

Anyone watching from the pit lane knew there would not be a backward glance. Lauda had applied the same ice-cold logic to this decision as he had when using life insurance as collateral for the necessary funding to launch his international motor-racing career seven years before. In his mind, this would have been another simple choice, similar to the decision to return to the cockpit in 1976 even though he resembled a dead man walking. The initial shock felt by fans and F1 insiders when learning of such a sudden retirement was gradually replaced by a sense of regret. The sport had not only lost a fine racing driver but also a distinct personality with an ability to cut to the chase and the quick. It was tempting to wonder if the aviation industry truly knew what was about to hit them.

CHAPTER 14

Flying High

'You give me a single-engine plane, and I'll take it up for a circuit. Nice, but no challenge. You give me a Jumbo with four engines, 5,000 things that might go wrong; fantastic; a challenge. Let's get on and try to fly it.' Niki Lauda was talking about the pleasure derived from driving a complex racing car and comparing it with flying, a skill that had intrigued him from the moment he had been given a lift in a single-engine Cessna in 1974. By the following year, he had taken up flying lessons, gaining his pilot's licence in late 1976 – not even the physical setback of the Nürburgring crash interfering unduly with his plans to get airborne. The healthy pay cheques from Ferrari made possible the purchase of a twin-engine Cessna Golden Eagle and rapidly expanded his aviation horizons in every sense.

Once the Golden Eagle 'held no more secrets for me', Lauda thought about upgrading to a jet. Typically, he had made that financially possible by acting as a promoter for an aircraft charter business and receiving favourable terms on a Cessna Citation. At the same time, he used a pilot from the charter company to accompany him in the cockpit, as required in a business jet. Having been attracted by the technical challenge, Lauda

discovered that flying could also be put to practical use, particularly as the Citation would carry six passengers.

'I used the Citation to go to races,' said Lauda. 'I even flew
it to California for the Grand Prix at Long Beach. Flying time
was 23 hours 17 minutes, which included seven stops. We
went Salzburg–Glasgow–Reykjavík–Narsarsuaq (Greenland)–
Sept-Iles (Canada)–Cleveland–Kansas City–Albuquerque–Long
Beach. What would have happened had there been a breakdown
in Greenland? We didn't have one. Anyway, I enjoyed the slight
madness of a journey like this.'

The Austrian F1 journalist, Helmut Zwickl, himself a skilled
and experienced pilot, had accompanied Lauda on this and other
flights. He said:

You can see in the way he flies that he is in the world champion
class. He so quickly understands the complicated instruments,
and his gift of quick comprehension and his ability to concentrate are quite out of the ordinary. That is to say, even as a
simple private plane pilot he has reached the level (though not
the experience) of an airline pilot. His reflexes are so rapid that
even in the most unexpected simulated emergency, he always
intuitively does the right thing.

That was an incredible trip to Long Beach. Niki had a
professional pilot with him. We encountered severe turbu-
lence when coming into land in Greenland and Niki said to
the pilot: 'You have more experience than I have; you do the
landing procedures. If I make a mistake, we'll miss the Long
Beach Grand Prix!'

While in California, Lauda had visited the Northrop Corporation, a leading aircraft manufacturer. This led to an invitation
to fly in their two-seat F5 supersonic fighter plane during a
demonstration at the Paris Air Show at Le Bourget. Lauda said:

It was very interesting. It was frightening, only because the pilots do aerobatic things with you and they never tell you in advance. So, whatever they do, you're always surprised. You can't follow up: you're always behind instead of ahead. This guy, the chief test pilot, when he passed Mach 1, he just looked at the speed meter and, at that moment, he made a roll. I said: 'Shit! What's going on?' If they tell you in advance, it would be much easier. But they don't. For me, it was a very strange feeling because I wasn't doing anything. I'm not really interested in aerobatics: it's a bit of a show. I only want to fly normally. This white-haired chief pilot was very relaxed as you might expect. Even so, I was surprised by the almost casual way he would ask the control tower for permission for a supersonic flight like he was asking to take off in a [Fokker] F27 [passenger aircraft] for Brussels or Amsterdam.

In fact, an interest in starting his own airline was accelerated by the possibility to acquire flying rights for certain commuter routes in Europe. It was no coincidence that this should occur as Lauda walked away from motor racing. By now he had passed the exams necessary to earn a professional pilot's licence and he was poised to form Lauda Air, operating out of Vienna International Airport at Schwechat.

Being entitled to use aircraft with a maximum of forty-four seats, Lauda bought an F27, which seemed an ideal size for the purpose of charter flights south to the Mediterranean. Another advantage – or so he thought – with the F27 would be the avoidance of a clash with Austrian Airlines. This would be a naive assumption; one that underestimated the national airline's ruthless determination to rule everything in the air and crush opposition – any opposition – before it had a chance to leave the ground.

None of this was a surprise to Otmar Lenz, a former Austrian Airlines captain and soon to become CEO at Lauda Air. Lenz said:

One of our mutual friends suggested to Niki that maybe I could help him run his airline. I was happy to do this because I had to stop flying for medical reasons. Almost immediately we were running into difficulties because of Austrian Airlines. This company was completely politically orientated and they had much better networking whereas Niki was never interested in politics. He did not have the same kind of network. He could only use his publicity to achieve anything because, of course, people knew who he was and would listen to him. But that was not much help when you were trying to do things like find finance for an aircraft. The Austrian banks would initially say they'd like to do it – and then the Austrian Airlines guys would step in and convince the Austrian banks not to do it at all.

So, I would go to Barclays Bank and make a presentation. When they said this is a good thing and they would like to invest, I then said they should ask for co-financing from whatever Austrian bank they were associated with. When that bank then realised that such an important financing company in the UK was involved, the bank's board could be persuaded to come on board with Lauda Air. This is what you had to do to avoid Austrian Airlines using their political network to try and stop things.

Niki thought that the F27 would be okay because it was smaller than anything Austrian Airlines used. He had no wish to compete with them because Austrian Airlines had a monopoly and this way, as he said: 'I have an easier life.' He thought he could operate side-by-side and perhaps co-operate sometime in the future. None of this was correct because they even fought with him over the F27.

Lauda discovered that the maintenance-heavy turboprop was slow and noisy and did not appeal to passengers who preferred aircraft such as the Douglas DC9 jet. 'Niki eventually understood that it made no sense to use small aircraft and try to avoid competition with Austrian Airlines because they would try to kill you anyway,' said Lenz. 'It would be better to actually compete by getting a wide-bodied aircraft for long-haul and, at this time, the DC10 was a good aircraft to have.'

Which brings us to Lauda's departure from the racetrack in Montreal on Friday, 28 September 1979, a flight that afternoon to California, followed by a visit to McDonnell Douglas and the payment of a $300,000 deposit on a DC10. Lauda said: 'I was fed up with these people at Austrian Airlines making life difficult no matter what I did. I'd tried to keep out of their way but in the end, it was very simple: I'll go upmarket and operate a DC10. The US dollar at the time was strong for us and the tourist market good. The possibilities were good and this was probably on my mind a lot when I was driving round in circles for the last time in a F1 car in Montreal.'

The timing may have seemed right for Lauda. In fact, it could not have been worse; the DC10's reputation was about to nose-dive in every sense of the expression.

In May of that year, an American Airlines DC10 had crashed on take-off from Chicago, killing 258 passengers, 13 crew and two people on the ground. The cause was found to have been improper maintenance leading to damage to the pylon structure holding the left-hand engine and allowing it to break free. Several months later, two more DC10s had crashed, one due to a failed attempt to land in poor visibility at Mexico City, and the other when an Antarctic sightseeing flight hit a mountain. These tragedies may have been caused by human and environmental factors unrelated to the aircraft but it was enough, coupled with Chicago and other incidents, to ensure the sales of the DC10 would go into decline. This was bad news for Lauda who, if he could not complete the purchase for whatever reason, had hoped to cash in on the fact that demand at the time of his order outstripped production. Max Mosley witnessed how his former driver found a solution:

What you did in those days, was you ordered one [DC10] and you put a deposit down. At a certain point, you would pay more, and then more after that. What used to happen was airlines that were expanding and wanted a DC10 found that the waiting list was something like three years. So, the thing to do was buy a position on the waiting list. Niki put his deposit down with the intention, if he couldn't afford the aircraft, of making money – and then these accidents happened, fairly soon one after another, and the bottom dropped out of the DC10 market. Niki had this DC10 coming down the line with the first big interim payment due, he'd got no money and there was no chance of selling it.

I happened to be with Bernie [Ecclestone] when Niki came in to get some advice. Bernie told him how to handle it. He said McDonnell Douglas wouldn't want a big scandal with a World Champion racing driver. He said Pete Conrad, the former astronaut and the airline's vice president, would understand that. Bernie told him exactly how to play his cards. Niki went off and got out of the deal. It's like so many of those financial deals where you can't lose – until you do.

With a surge in fuel prices and continuing intransigence on the part of Austrian Airlines and the government, Lauda Air rowed back its operations, leasing a pair of F27s to Egypt Air and operating executive jets out of Vienna. Otmar Lenz, having previously known Niki Lauda as a motor-racing champion, was discovering his attributes as a businessman. Lenz said:

He was very professional; very focused on what he wanted to do. We worked out what we could really do together and the nice thing was that we could have a discussion, establish our goal and then we would go for it. It was straightforward with him. He was very analytical and that was one of his big assets. It was nice to run the company with him. With some companies, it takes twenty-four hours to reach a decision; you need meetings and phone calls to check and cross-check and so on. With Niki, you called him and he immediately picked up the phone. It wouldn't be through secretaries or whatever. He'd say 'Yes', 'No', 'Do it', or whatever. He knew what he wanted.

Lauda may have known in which direction he needed to go with his airline but there would be an unexpected diversion lurking in the shadows of Formula One. Having not felt inclined to watch any of the Grands Prix in 1980, Lauda's mild curiosity got the better of him in August 1981 when he accepted an offer to join the ORF (Austrian Television) commentary team at their home Grand Prix at the Österreichring.

Lauda was immediately struck by the appeal of not just the raw elements of the sport that had been his life – and almost killed him – but the way the cars had changed. With turbo-charged engines on the increase and continual performance advances through aerodynamics, the inquisitive side of the former champion wondered if he could handle one of these machines; would he be quick enough to not just be competitive but also to win races?

By chance, Willi Dungl was holding a training camp at Bad Tatzmannsdorf, 170 kms east of the Österreichring. Lauda flew across and asked the opinion of his fitness guru. Dungl, as usual, didn't say much. He beckoned Lauda to get on a bike and join in a ride up hill and down dale. At the finish, Lauda didn't need to be told he was unfit any more than he wished to have his trainer quietly but pointedly draw attention to the fact that the women present had left him standing. Lauda asked Willi to prepare short- and medium-term fitness programmes – just in case he should feel inclined to drive a Formula One car again.

That inner urge became more public when Lauda turned up a month later at the Italian Grand Prix. It was one thing to appear at his home race; quite another to bother to travel to the hotbed of speculation for the coming season that is forever part and parcel of Monza in September.

The irony for most British journalists was that Lauda's second appearance at an F1 race was suddenly lending credibility to a flyer taken some months before by the social gossip columnist Nigel Dempster in the *Daily Mail*. On 21 April, under the heading 'Lauda can't bear to be a quitter, so he's roaring back', Dempster wrote:

Just two years after he quit motor racing, former world champion Niki Lauda is on the threshold of a surprise comeback. Lauda, 32, has been in Britain this week discussing plans for his reappearance driving the Marlboro MP4, which is being prepared by McLaren International at their workshop in Surrey. Champion in 1975 and 1977, Lauda quit the sport in favour of running his own private airline (he has a DC10 on order). But while this enterprise is successful, he has been telling friends that he doesn't get the same excitement from it. Although financial considerations have not motivated his decision to return to the Grand Prix circus, Lauda, father of two and resident of Monte Carlo, could reasonably expect a retainer of around £0.5 million a year.

The estimate of Lauda's financial expectation may have been as short of the mark as this entire speculative piece had been in April but, five months later, it had been given legs overnight.

Media suggestions that Lauda might be making a comeback were accompanied by possible motives. News of the DC10 being cancelled fed rumours of Lauda being in financial trouble and needing the income from racing. One story followed another.

It was true that the charter business had not been as successful as hoped and the operation had been brought to a close. But claims of insolvency became more personal when it was reported that Lauda had been ordered to pay more than £130,000 in back taxes. Then word came out that he had been called up by the Austrian army and rejected as medically unfit – which, apparently, begged the question of his fitness to fly. When questioned by the *Sunday Telegraph*, a British newspaper, Lauda nailed each claim in turn:

> First, the tax. In 1974, my lawyers went to the authorities who agreed that my income should be paid into a trust fund in Hong Kong, from which I would draw a monthly allowance. I pay tax on that and there was absolutely no problem until 1978, when they suddenly decided to recheck everything. They went through all my expenses and said I should travel by boat rather than aeroplane. 'Listen,' I said, 'if I ever go back to racing and I go by boat, the race will be over before I get there.' Then they asked things like 'Where were you on August 17, 1975?' They fought me like hell and, in the end, I had to pay. I checked it out properly and they now agree that I can fly wherever I want.
>
> The tax people also checked with the army. Although there is national service for people under 35, I think they had forgotten me. Then I had a letter to go for a medical. It took just two minutes. They said I was not fit enough to join because of my burns. I said: 'Thank God' and left. Next day it was in all the papers, and the civil aviation authority made me have three separate medicals before I could continue with

my flying licence. I am Austrian and I like living here but I don't see why the government makes it so difficult for me. I don't care how people interpret it [rumours of a comeback]. The only motivation is enjoyment.

Would he enjoy driving one of the latest F1 cars? That question continued to intrigue Lauda almost two years after he had walked away with no feeling whatsoever for this intoxicating sport.

CHAPTER 15

Comeback 2

'Ron Dennis broke my balls for a year and a half after I had retired. He called me on a regular basis every two or three months asking if I wanted to come back. I always said no. Because if you retire, you retire. But then he caught me at the right time in my life,' Lauda said.

Niki Lauda should have known what to expect. Dennis was in an expansive and acquiring mood. He had established a fine reputation in the late '70s for meticulous preparation through his company, Project Four Racing. His partner, John Barnard, was equally regarded for his scrupulous attention to detail as a first-class designer. Meanwhile, the McLaren team that Lauda had fought against in 1976 and 1977 was a shadow of its former self, the decline having been noted by the title sponsor, Marlboro, and the ambitious owner of Project Four Racing.

Marlboro could see Dennis and Project Four Racing as a means of extricating McLaren from the performance cul-de-sac in which the former champions had become stuck for two seasons. In 1980, the situation had become so untenable that Teddy Mayer, the McLaren boss, was given no choice if his team wished to retain considerable financial support from

the Philip Morris tobacco brand. Mayer was made to realise
he could either merge with Project Four Racing (Marlboro
having agreed with Dennis's latest offer to buy 50 per cent of
McLaren) or preside over the depressing demise of a once-
great name.

At the end of 1980, it was announced that Dennis and Mayer
would be joint managing directors of a new company to be
known as McLaren International. Mayer would take care of
administration and accounting, Dennis would be responsible
for sponsorship; and Barnard would have complete command
of the technical side.

Barnard's first McLaren, the MP4/1, took F1 design to a
completely different level when he produced a car made primarily from carbon fibre rather than aluminium, which had
been the tradition for fifteen years and tended to fold around
the driver in the event of an accident. Not only was the
carbon-fibre chassis stronger, it was also lighter; a win–win
in every sense when John Watson took the MP4/1 to its first
victory in the 1981 British Grand Prix – and then proceeded to
unintentionally prove the integrity of the chassis several weeks
later during the Italian Grand Prix at Monza. Watson put a
wheel on a kerb at the exit of a 95-mph corner, spun across
the track and hit a crash barrier that effectively tore the car in
two. Apart from a sore neck, the Ulsterman stepped unscathed
from the cockpit. Lauda watched with interest. The McLaren
represented the sort of technical innovation that intrigued
him. Lauda said:

When I was at the Austrian GP, there was a big start line crash
and I didn't feel awful. I felt normal; didn't feel good; didn't
feel bad. This was different for me because, for a year and a
half, I had no feeling for motor racing. Whenever I heard
something or saw something on television about Formula

One, I thought: Don't mention all that crap. But this was interesting. The cars; they're different and things change.

Then I went to Monza on my own because I wanted to check my feelings. I saw Watson's crash where the engine came off the car because he hit so hard – and even with an accident as severe as that, I thought – 'Pah! No problem! The risk element is reduced. I don't care any more; there's no more fear.' So the feelings I had before for racing just came back. I spoke to [John] Hogan [of Philip Morris] and he didn't seem surprised that I might be interested in driving one of these cars.

Then Ron rang me again and said: 'Come to a test at Donington.' It was typical of him that he should pick exactly the right moment. I thought this would be a good opportunity to see if I really want to come back. I told Marlene that we were going to London – but not to a racetrack, because she would have hated it. I said: 'You go to Harrods: I have to drive somewhere.'

I went up to Donington and McLaren were waiting with one of their cars ready for me to drive. I did quite a few laps. After two years, it was nice to be back in a racing car. I enjoyed it and actually felt quite emotional about it. By the first corner, I had forgotten the emotion. I was already a racing driver again, giving all my attention to controlling the car.

The first thing I noticed was that I couldn't drive more than three laps. I was out of breath and didn't have the strength. I came into the pits and asked for something to be looked at. I was a bit shocked at my lack of condition but not really worried about it because I knew that Willi Dungl would have me fit within a couple of months. I was out of shape because I hadn't trained, but my times compared well with Watson's and it was enough to tell me that, with suitable preparation, fitness and so on, I could do it.

'He took the test very seriously,' said Dennis. 'He had got Willi Dungl to get him ready for it as best they could in the short space of time. He did a lot of laps, about 50, I think. Then he said he'd think about it and let me know. I was expecting him to take at least a couple of weeks to make his decision but, as we were going down the M1 from Donington in the pouring rain, Niki was driving and he suddenly said: "Yup, I'll do it."'

Lauda did not say he would drive for McLaren; merely that he had made up his mind that he could do it. He wanted time to think this through. He recalled:

I came back to the hotel in the evening. The phone rings – I'll never forget – and it's Frank Williams. 'Hello, Niki. How are you? Are you enjoying yourself in England? How did the test go? If you're going to make a comeback, come and see me first.' I don't know how he found out; he said it was his business to know everything that was going on – which was typical Frank, of course. I would have liked to have driven for Williams; at the time, it was a very good team. But the first problem was, while all this was going on with Frank on the phone, Marlene was standing next to me. 'What the hell are you doing?' She wasn't happy. I said I could do what I wanted and things calmed down after that.

Frank Williams had put two and two together and made four. There had been talk of Lauda testing a car – but it was generally thought to be with his former team, Brabham. Dennis had deliberately chosen Donington Park in the Midlands because of its comparative seclusion and absence from the list of usual F1 test venues. Nonetheless, *Motoring News* had got wind of the test, their F1 correspondent Alan Henry following up with a telephone call to his old friend, Lauda. On Thursday 8 October, the weekly paper carried an exclusive at the head of its news page, starting with a direct quote from Lauda:

I made my decision the day I drove that McLaren at Donington. But I decided to keep quiet and give myself a couple of days to think about it, to make sure. But if you think I'm coming back for money, then you must be mad. You can't give a total commitment to something as dangerous as Formula One if you're not totally in control of yourself. Worrying about money isn't the way to go motor racing.

The reason I drove the McLaren was to see how I would handle the mental side of F1 again. Honestly, there is still the choice between Frank Williams and McLaren. I think that I've been really stupid not to try for a test drive before now. If I had tested earlier I would have found the answer to my personal question — do I want to race? — much earlier.

So I took the opportunity to drive the McLaren and I felt all the old adrenaline pumping through me. These cars are cornering more quickly but they have much more solid suspension now and are total rubbish. It's not driving: it's just being bashed around. But I needed to find out for myself whether I could drive these cars; whether I was still feeling competitive. And I was. It was a terrific feeling.

You've got to remember, that I must discount my previous experience to a large degree. I'm effectively starting from zero once again. It's a totally new challenge. So I have the choice between an established team such as Williams, which has a very good car with proven capability, or going to McLaren. In many ways, it would be a good thing to go with McLaren. They are growing and they have great potential. I don't think that they've yet fully realised the potential of the organisation, but that's not a criticism of John Watson. Remember, John

Barnard is just completing his first year in F1 and it takes quite a time to make a team work successfully and smoothly. At the moment, I don't know which way I'll go.

Pino Allievi of *La Gazzetta dello Sport* had heard about the test in the McLaren, but knew no more than anyone else about Lauda's plans. Allievi said:

I had always got on well with Niki. On the Thursday before the Grand Prix in Canada in 1978, when he was driving for Brabham, he asked what I was doing that evening. When I said I didn't know, he asked: 'Why don't we go to the cinema?' So we went to the movies that night – I don't remember which one – and this is the only time I've ever done that with a Grand Prix driver!

So, in November 1981, he called me and said: 'Why don't you come to Vienna tomorrow afternoon?' 'Yes, okay, but to do what?' 'It's a surprise.' 'Okay. But do I have to bring pyjamas and something?' 'Yeah,' he said, 'just a couple of things.' I flew to Vienna and he was waiting for me when I arrived at about seven in the evening. We went to a restaurant and then to a nightclub; it was a fantastic night. We went back to the hotel – which he paid for – and I said to him: 'Niki, what are we fucking doing here?' He said: 'Tomorrow morning, I show you. Do you have the passport?' 'Yes, I have everything.' 'Okay, be ready at five o'clock in the morning.'

When he came for me, it was snowing. We went in a Mercedes 500 to the airport. When I asked where we were going, he said England. We got to London and somebody picked us up. We went to McLaren, in Woking. Niki didn't introduce me to anyone; no one knew that I was a journalist; he said I was a friend of his. I waited for him in reception and when he came back, he said he had signed. 'Signed what?' 'A contract with McLaren. Now I have to go testing.' Incredible! We had a big scoop in the newspaper: 'Lauda comes back!'

When the news was officially announced, a quietly delighted Dennis stressed that McLaren's decision had been based on Lauda's continuing potential. Dennis said:

It's not correct to say I'm a fan of his. I admire his driving abilities. I think the modern Grand Prix driver is more than just a talented individual who can climb into a car and drive around the circuit. I think he needs to be a much more computer-orientated person who needs to be calculating and intelligent. With due respect to the current drivers, a considerable quantity of them do not have the brainpower to make a fundamental decision. That decision is to drive the car into the position it can attain on that day. If the car can come second, come second, don't crash trying to come first. If it can come fifth, don't finish tenth and stroke around. I think that's where Niki's strength lies.

Lauda took the opportunity to further expand on his reasoning. He said:

People say that comebacks never work out. Well, that's another reason why I want to come back – to prove them wrong. How can I say things will go? Maybe they'll be good, maybe bad. Maybe I'll finish up in hospital. Who knows? But if I didn't feel I could come back and be competitive, I wouldn't think about it. For the past few weeks, I've been training like hell, getting myself fit. After all, I'm not a racing driver at present; I'm a pensioner coming back!

Lauda may have been in his thirty-fourth year but he used all of that experience and guile when renewing personal sponsorship with Parmalat (the Italian dairy and food company that he been associated with since 1976) and arranging his deal with McLaren and Marlboro's John Hogan. John Hogan said:

> Niki came along to me at Monza and said: 'I've been think-ing. I should maybe come back.' So, we had a bit of a chat. I used to use James [Hunt] a lot as a sounding board, so I immediately went to him and asked if he thought a comeback by The Rat was possible. James said something along the lines of: 'If you play sport, or anything, to a high level, it never goes away. You can always hit the same ball in the way you always did. It's only a question of if you want to do it. If that's the case with Niki, there will be no problem; he will be fine.'

Hogan continued:

> It's important to remember that the environment at the time was such that anyone making a comeback must be mad. Of course, that was perfect territory for Niki; all the more reason to do it. Then Ron became involved and, typically, he was very good at pulling everything together; getting a car, get-ting this, getting that.
>
> Then we had to discuss money, of course. A Philip Morris accountant asked how much we should pay him. Niki was in the room at the time and, before I could answer, he said: 'You pay me one dollar for driving the car, and the rest for promotion.'
>
> It was a hell of a lot of money. But he knew, as did we, that the Lauda name was worth a lot in the world outside motor racing. The people in Philip Morris who had been around the block a few times absolutely loved him. James hadn't

The author captured a fresh-faced Lauda preparing for his first major
international event at Mallory Park in March 1971. Neither of them could have
imagined where this would lead during the next four decades.

Vienna, 28 SEptember 1971

Dear Sirs,

In consideration of your permitting my son, Andreas Nikolaus
Lauda, to delay payment of the sum of S 2,500;000 Austrian
Schillings due on the 29 September 1971, under his contract
with you datet the 23 September 1971, until 31 October, I
undertake to pay the suit sum to you on the latter date,
should he for any reason fail to do so.

Yours faithfully

E. Lauda

The letter, purporting
to be from Lauda's
father, ensuring his
place with the March
Formula One team.

Lauda cut his single-
seater competition
teeth with a Kaimann
Formula V in 1969.

The McNamara Mk3B
Formula Three car with
which Lauda tended to
make more impact with
the scenery than on the
results sheets in 1970.

Driving his distinctive yellow March, Lauda made a solid impression on the Formula 2 scene throughout 1971.

The opening paragraphs of Lauda's contract with March for his first full season of Formula One in 1972.

Left: Max Mosley with Lauda at Monza in 1972 as the fledgling Grand Prix careers of March Engineering and the young Austrian driver became intertwined.

Right: Manhandling the unloved March 721X at Jarama in Spain during a struggle to impress in 1972.

Top: Driving the BRM to its limit during the 1973 Monaco Grand Prix brought Lauda to the attention of Ferrari and ended the struggle for proper recognition.

A leg-up from Louis Stanley and BRM in 1973 helped Lauda recover from a disastrous debut season the previous year.

Below: Always game for a laugh, Lauda has fun with the cockpit top of his Ferrari at Nivelles in 1974 before finishing second in the Belgian Grand Prix.

Lauda (yellow shirt) joins fellow F1 drivers and personnel for a charity cricket match on the day after the 1974 British Grand Prix.

Pressing on with the Ferrari 312 B3 on his way to second place in the 1974 French Grand Prix at Dijon. Having won his first Grand Prix a couple of months before, Lauda was in the reckoning for a championship he would ultimately lose through inexperience.

Pause for thought. Lauda put any doubts about safety behind him as he became the first man to lap the Nürburgring Nordschleife in less than seven minutes in 1975, the year he became World Champion for the first time.

Enzo Ferrari (white coat) makes one of his occasional visits to Fiorano in 1974 as Lauda tests the 312 B3.

Lauda points out a feature of the Ferrari 312T2 to chief engineer Mauro Forghieri during an early-season test at Fiorano in 1976.

Above: Daniele Audetto (left) found life tricky as team manager in 1976, particularly in the aftermath of Lauda's accident at the Nürburgring.

Left: Lauda formed a fine working relationship with Luca di Montezemolo from the outset in 1974.

Lauda powers through Casino Square on his way to dominating the 1975 Monaco Grand Prix and giving Ferrari their first win in twenty years on the classic street circuit.

Rivals and mates. James Hunt and Lauda shared the same sense of humour, evident since competing against each other in the junior formulae.

Lauda, pictured with Clay Regazzoni in the pit lane at Monza in 1975, formed an easy working relationship with the colourful Swiss.

Prior to the 1976 German Grand Prix, Lauda took journalist Helmut Zwickl and photographer Alois Rottenstein for a lap of the Nürburgring to point out some of the hazards of the Nordschleife.

Above: Officials and drivers tend to the burning Ferrari after Lauda has been extricated from the cockpit and removed to hospital. Brett Lunger's Surtees sits to the left, where it came to rest after ramming the Ferrari amidships.

Right: Lauda was given the Last Rites once he had reached the Intensive Care Unit in Mannheim Hospital.

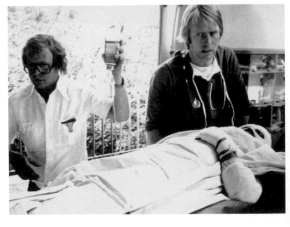

Lauda's livid head wounds were painfully evident during his return to the cockpit at Monza in 1976.

Marlene played a key role in Niki's racing career, particularly in the aftermath of the Nürburgring crash.

Lauda's appearance in the controversial and rain-soaked 1976 Japanese Grand Prix was brief.

As reigning World
Champion, Lauda
carried the number
1 on his Brabham
BT46 during 1978
but would have little
success.

Carrying the colours
of Parmalat on his
cap, Lauda waits
for a helicopter at
Monza in 1978.

Nelson Piquet
(centre) listens on
as Lauda gives his
thoughts to Gordon
Murray, designer of
the Brabham.

Lauda impressed everyone when he won the United States Grand Prix at Long Beach, three races into his return in 1982.

John Watson and Niki Lauda were reunited at McLaren in 1982 and continued the friendly working relationship which had begun at Brabham four years before.

Lauda and Prost fought hard and fair as McLaren team-mates throughout 1984, Niki beating Alain to the championship by half a point.

Lauda enjoyed his role as television pundit (interviewing Nigel Mansell) and struck a good working relationship during twenty years working with RTL's presenter Florian König.

Daniel Brühl won Lauda's full approval when playing Niki in the film *Rush*.

A passion for flying led to the formation of Lauda Air with the Fokker F27 forming the backbone of Niki's early fleet.

Lauda surveys the shocking scene of devastation after the Lauda Air 767 had crashed in mountainous jungle in Thailand in May 1991. It would prompt a relentless search for the cause and a battle – which he eventually won – with Boeing.

An attention to detail was perfect for flying, Lauda being fully qualified to pilot all of his aircraft, including the Boeing 777.

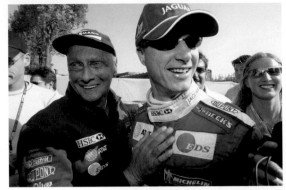

Lauda struck a good working relationship with the like-minded Eddie Irvine, particularly when the Jaguar driver finished third at Monza in 2002.

Lauda applied his experience and pragmatism to assisting the Mercedes F1 team to several world championships. Here, he joins Nico Rosberg and Lewis Hamilton in celebrating the first in 2014.

Lauda played a significant part in persuading Lewis Hamilton to move from McLaren to Mercedes, the Briton appreciating the former champion's deep understanding of a racing driver's world.

Lauda cemented a warm relationship with Toto Wolff, boss of the Mercedes AMG Petronas Formula One team.

Lauda enjoyed the love and respect of Lukas (left) and Mathias, the two sons from his first marriage, and quietly supported both in their various careers associated with motor sport.

Lauda displays a pig's ear and his sense of fun at the scene of the crash in which he received burns to his head and right ear. He is joined by (left to right) Arturo Merzario (who helped pull Lauda from the burning wreck), Karl-Heinz Zimmermann and Bernie Ecclestone on the 25th anniversary of the near-fatal accident at the Nürburgring.

St Stephen's Cathedral, Vienna. 29 May 2019.

always been flavour of the month because he was always trying to shag someone's daughter. But the mothers and the matrons and the senior executives just loved Niki. He was very European; very well mannered; very old school due entirely to his upbringing. You could see it in the reaction to the way he would kiss the back of a lady's hand in the proper manner. Little did they know he was a bit of a rascal with a wicked sense of humour.

Given the reputation attached to any high-achieving sportsman, particularly during this era, Lauda was quite subdued and far from outrageous; certainly, nothing like the rapacious James Hunt. He was well mannered and polite in female company and had a deep respect for Marlene. Lukas had been born in 1979 and, a few months before Niki began contemplating his return to the cockpit, Marlene had given birth to Mathias in January 1981.

Typically, though, family responsibilities did not impinge on Lauda's desire to go racing again. There may have been some truth in stories of financial constraint associated with running his airline but the overwhelming motivation was a successful sportsperson's abiding need to compete and measure their own ability. Better than anyone, Niki Lauda knew the risks involved. He would pull his crash helmet over a head and mind devoid of fear or worry about doing this for the wrong reason. The focus would be on one thing only: winning and being the best – yet again.

CHAPTER 16

Strike Back

'I feel more open; that there's more freedom. Before, I was protecting myself so hard against all the shit that comes with all this; building walls up and up. Now, I'm in a period when the walls are down. I'm open, relaxed, easier to get on with if you like and, in a way, easier to get on with myself.' Lauda was speaking in the pit lane in Detroit on 4 June 1982. He had needed all of that inner calm to cope with a wide variety of incidents that had come his way since the announcement of his return.

During testing at Paul Ricard, a rear suspension failure at more than 175 mph sent the McLaren off the road and through layers of wire-mesh catch-fencing installed specifically to slow down a wayward car. Having ducked his head in order to make his profile as small as possible, Lauda was very relieved to feel no pain or injury when the McLaren eventually came to a dusty halt. He remembered Willi Dungl's advice to sit still for a moment or two, breathe deeply before undoing his seat harness, then climb out slowly, walk a few yards away from the car, sit down and breathe deeply again.

When a rescue vehicle finally arrived, Lauda's fitness guru

was on board, pleased to see his man in one piece and a safe distance from the wreck. Dungl took Lauda's pulse and was impressed by a reading of a mere 90 bpm after what had clearly been a major crash. Apart from anything else, had Lauda been injured, there was little time for recovery before the first Grand Prix of 1982 in South Africa on 23 January. Lauda got there all right, but no sooner had he arrived at Kyalami than he appeared to be suggesting there should be no race at all.

As a returnee – and despite his status as a double World Champion – Lauda had his fair share of paperwork to sign in order to compete. One such form was a Super Licence, recently introduced by the Fédération Internationale du Sport Automobile (FISA). The sport's governing body required novices to have taken part in (and preferably won) a certain number of races in Formula Three and Formula Two. Lauda agreed with the theory of preventing drivers with more money than talent buying their way into a Grand Prix team that was perhaps desperate for funds.

However, he did not approve of a new clause that, in effect, tied a driver to his team and prevented a switch to a rival without the present employer's approval, regardless of whether the agreed term of their contract had expired. As Lauda put it succinctly: 'If we sign this, we could be shafted by our respective team bosses.'

More alarming still was the realisation that most of Lauda's colleagues were on the point of signing without being aware that F1 was about to enter the world of transfer fees, similar to soccer. Lauda's first call was to Didier Pironi, the Ferrari driver who was also president of the Grand Prix Drivers' Association (GPDA): 'I said to Pironi: "What the hell is all this rubbish about?" He said that I shouldn't worry; the whole matter was under control. So I told him that he might carry on like that in France, but I was an Austrian and, where I come from, the whole thing made no sense at all. It was rubbish. If I leave McLaren, I might not be able to get another drive according to the terms of this licence form. Fortunately, Pironi got the message, but we knew we had work to do.'

With more than 100 Grands Prix to his name, Lauda was experienced enough to realise the drivers needed to be united in the physical sense because, once under the control of their individual team managers at the racetrack, divide and conquer would be child's play. As the 31 drivers arrived at the Kyalami circuit gates on the Thursday morning for the first day's practice, Lauda was waiting – with a bus. Abandoning their wives and girlfriends, all the drivers (with the exception of Jochen Mass, who was late) boarded the coach and set off for the Sunnyside Park Hotel in Johannesburg. The plan was to stay there all day – and all night – if necessary.

Pironi, meanwhile, entered into discussion at the racetrack with Jean-Marie Balestre, President of FISA. Balestre was unmoved. As deadlock continued into the evening, the drivers settled into a function room and prepared to spend the night on the floor. Lauda ensured there was no contact with the drivers' respective teams, despite some managers attempting unsuccessfully to force entry. With no drivers present at the racetrack, there had been nothing for the paying spectators to watch. It was a strong hand, which Lauda used to assuage the doubts creeping in among five novice drivers.

The following morning, as the result of a phone call from Pironi, Lauda led the drivers back to the racetrack, where new terms were verbally agreed. The drivers took part in practice and the race. Balestre may have had the final word as he fined the drivers (after the race had started), but this was seen as a pompous token gesture. The hard truth was that the drivers had won – and Niki Lauda was back.

Following the drama off track, Lauda played himself in

gently by finishing fourth at Kyalami. He could have done even better in Brazil had his nemesis, Carlos Reutemann, not used his Williams to thump the back of Lauda's McLaren and cause a rear suspension failure. As it happened, this would be the Argentinian's last Grand Prix. Seven days later, he announced his immediate retirement. Lauda's career, meanwhile, was about to go in a more positive direction on the bumpy streets of Long Beach.

At the end of the first day's practice, a seven-lap run of controlled and sustained precision gave Lauda the fastest time. The downside from his point of view was a request by the organisers for him to attend a post-practice press conference; an unfamiliar exercise in F1 but common in North America where the racing media expected immediate access to the leading player. Even worse, the interview room was in a convention centre, an excellent facility but one that was a fair stretch from the pits.

Lauda walked in briskly, stepped onto the podium, adjusted the microphone and said: 'Tyres good. Engine good. Car good. Goodbye.' Then he nodded and walked off. His obligation to appear may have been fulfilled but loquacious members of the local media were stunned. Their European counterparts could only smile and quietly shake their heads. Welcome back Niki Lauda.

Two days later, he returned to the same place, this time as winner of the Toyota Grand Prix of the United States (Long Beach). Lauda didn't care about the lengthy official title of the race; only that he had won it with a typically clever combination of speed and experience.

Running third behind the pole position Alfa Romeo of Andrea de Cesaris and René Arnoux's Renault, Lauda had been about to attack the Frenchman when he spotted the Alfa Romeo of Bruno Giacomelli dodging around in his mirrors as they charged along the back straight. Rather than block the

Italian, Lauda moved to one side and left the door open. The overexcited Giacomelli accepted the invitation, steamed past the McLaren, promptly misjudged his braking for the oncoming hairpin and rammed the back of Arnoux. Lauda was second.

Over the space of the next nine laps, he whittled down de Cesaris's five-second lead and seized his moment when the Alfa Romeo got caught behind a backmarker. Niki Lauda was leading a Grand Prix for the first time since the British at Brands Hatch four years before and he would remain unchallenged for the remaining 60 laps.

This was a moment to savour. When he appeared with that nonchalant, flat-footed walk, red Parmalat hat and waspish grin, the media centre burst into spontaneous applause. Not waiting to be introduced by the host commentator, Lauda ambled up to the battery of microphones and, in between gnawing an apple, barked: 'Any questions?' He fielded a number with his familiar precise answers. When asked which of his 18 Grands Prix wins he savoured the most, he replied that the last one is always the best. At which point, he nodded crisply, called a halt and sauntered off.

It was good to be back but Lauda was to receive a shocking reminder of his profession's perils a month later at Zolder in Belgium.

In line with almost everyone in F1, Lauda had grown to like Gilles Villeneuve, the sublimely gifted French-Canadian who had brought his free spirit and spectacular driving to Ferrari. In a misunderstanding with Jochen Mass during the final moments of qualifying, Villeneuve had clipped the slow-moving March and somersaulted off the road. Villeneuve died in hospital that night.

Lauda laid the blame at Mass's door in such a direct manner that there was talk of him being disciplined by FISA, the governing body clearly uncomfortable with the former World

Champion's direct words. An official inquiry would later attribute the cause solely to Villeneuve's error and state: 'No blame is attached to Jochen Mass.' Such an unequivocal statement angered Lauda even more. Some months later, Lauda told Alan Henry:

> I was touched by Villeneuve's accident like never before; that's a fact. I think he was the best driver of his day, taking every factor into account. And I think that the accident that killed him was the most stupid motor-racing accident that I've heard about. I don't want to go into any more details because I've done that once. But the whole thing was absolute shit. It should never have happened. No, it's not a question of reminding me how dangerous this business can be; not at all. It's just a question of how the best guy in the business comes to get killed in a stupid accident. These are the facts that worry me and get me very upset.
>
> Look, we come here [Detroit] and nobody talks about him [Villeneuve]. I think that is fucking sad. Life is moving on so quick, especially with sixteen Grand Prix races; one a fortnight; another winner and everybody writes about him. Next race, he finishes nowhere and nobody is interested. So, the best thing from your point of view as a driver is not to worry about it at all. The only thing is to know what you want; see that your line is a strong one and a good one – and then stay on that one line and don't move off it.

He also subsequently commented that 'Villeneuve was perhaps the only driver around who would have chosen the risky option of overtaking a slower car going flat out off the ideal line'. Lauda stayed on his chosen line in July when he won the British Grand Prix at Brands Hatch. It was a circuit he enjoyed and this made up for controversial incidents at the same track in 1974 and 1976.

On his slowing-down lap, Lauda made a point of signalling to each marshals' post in turn as a way of saying thanks for the invaluable services of these enthusiastic and often overlooked volunteers. It was a considerate gesture that was well received; an indication of how his thinking had been revised during the two-year absence from the cockpit. Lauda said:

I never thought that coming back might be the worst thing I could do. You can sit at home and say you want to come back but then you have to make a major decision about whether you are able to do this mentally. Physically it is no problem because you just run and train; that's the easiest thing you can do. You look at the watch and run for ten minutes, then twenty minutes or two hours, or whatever, and then you're fit. But mentally, you can't train yourself because this is something that changes every day. The rain comes down, you feel miserable. The sun shines, you feel happy. Mentally, it's been a much bigger fight for me than physically. Things change every day and you have to adapt yourself differently to the job.

Lauda had turned 33 the previous February, putting him among the oldest on the grid. In Lauda's view:

It's been much more difficult for me than some of these younger guys. When you're eighteen and you race for ten years, you are single-minded and your brain only works for motor racing because you haven't done anything different. Being away from motor racing, spending two years flying aeroplanes or doing other things, you suddenly get a completely different view about everything; you get a wider view.

So, you come back into motor racing and you're up against the other fuckers who are single-minded. They don't know anything else and it's easier for them in a way. On the other hand, I think it's a big advantage not to be so single-minded because you get a bigger view. I think if you can get your aggression back – the killer instinct, if you like – then this, with a wider view, I think makes you a better driver. I don't know what the others think: I can only judge myself on my own capabilities.

If anyone was familiar with Lauda's capabilities, it was his teammate in 1982. Niki's signature on a McLaren contract had renewed his partnership with John Watson after a year racing together in 1978. Watson was comfortably established, having moved to McLaren in 1979, gone through the growing pains of the revised organisation and scored a memorable home victory at Silverstone two years later. Watson had known what to expect when told of the Austrian's imminent arrival, even though he felt this might be a different Lauda from the one who had ruled the roost at Brabham. Watson said:

I think any driver who stops for whatever reason and then comes back will be different. The benefit of continuity is very important. When Niki tested the car at Donington Park, he wasn't race fit by any means. But you knew he would go off with Willi and get stuck into heavy training – which is exactly what he did. When he had the first race in South Africa, he was back to the normal Lauda – with the drivers' strike thrown in.

There was a big love affair with the comeback, helped by the fantastic story that came with winning the third race at Long Beach. To be honest, I began to feel like a third party in a two-party relationship. It was a bit like: 'Excuse me . . . d'you think I've just farted or is there a bad smell in here?' But, on a personal level between Niki and I, everything was perfectly fine. We were having a lot of fun as before and getting up to whatever tricks were being played. But, as the season went on, it suddenly got very interesting. Niki's win at Brands Hatch meant we had two wins each – and I was still ahead in the championship.

Prior to the British Grand Prix, Watson had won in Belgium but neither McLaren had finished in Monaco due to mechanical problems; in any case, they had not figured large in the race story due to the McLaren being ill at ease on the street circuit. On that basis, little was expected when the scene shifted to the even bumpier surfaces of downtown Detroit. Not only would the result defy all predictions, for the first time in his life Niki Lauda was to be totally eclipsed by his teammate.

CHAPTER 17

Not by the Book

'I don't think Niki could quite understand how, if I started behind him in a Grand Prix, here I was overtaking him and pulling away. That just did not compute in his analytical mind.' John Watson had been on good form from the moment the Formula One circus arrived in Detroit for the first time. Anxious to polish the tarnished image of a once great metropolis, the city authorities had pushed forward the idea of a Grand Prix along the riverfront and through the downtown streets. Unfortunately, they failed to convey much of the detail to local businesses.

There was outrage on the first day when office workers found their regular commute blocked. The entire scene descended into complete disarray when a proposed F1 acclimatisation session was abandoned because the teams demanded changes to the tyre barriers and escape roads. Having secretaries snag their tights against the rough edge of concrete walls was one thing; to suffer such indignity and inconvenience for no apparent reason as the track remained silent, quite another. Friday's edition of the *Detroit Free Press* made uncomfortable reading at the F1 breakfast tables. And when the F1 cars finally got going, the American motorsport media, more accustomed to Indianapolis-style ovals and speeds approaching 200 mph, poked fun at these funny F1 cars averaging a 'mere' 82 mph.

Lauda and Watson felt they would be lucky to reach even that speed. The McLaren simply could neither put down its power nor deal with the succession of angular corners. Starting tenth and seventeenth respectively, neither held out much hope of a decent result. That looked to be the way of it as the race started and the red and white cars made little progress. Then, predictably, others collided, blocked the narrow track and caused the race to be stopped. During the ensuing 60-minute wait, Watson decided to try fitting a tyre with a harder compound. It would transform the McLaren from a ponderous machine to a nimble, precise racing car that was particularly sure-footed under braking.

Watson was to make good use of it as he took the restart from thirteenth on the grid, six places behind Lauda. As the race got going and some of the leading group either ran into trouble or each other, Lauda found himself fourth, behind Keke Rosberg's leading Williams, the Ferrari of Didier Pironi and Eddie Cheever's Ligier. Watson, meanwhile, was on the move. As editor of the annual *Autocourse*, this was my take on the fast-moving story:

Once Watson caught the Pironi-Cheever-Lauda battle for second, it was assumed he would meekly join the queue and play safe. Not a bit of it. Watson had built up a rhythm which he was anxious to keep going and he knew if he became involved with the battle ahead, his pace would be reduced to their level. So, he simply overtook them. All three. In one lap. It was the most impressive piece of precise, confident driving seen for some time as he out-braked each in turn, almost before they knew he was there.

By the end of lap 33, Watson was in second place and making enormous inroads into Rosberg's lead. When he made up as much as 6 seconds in one lap, it was clear the Williams with its Goodyear tyres was no match for the McLaren/Michelin combination. By lap 37, Watson was in the lead.

When Watson took the chequered flag 25 laps later, Lauda was walking back to the garage, his car parked against the wall after a botched attempt to take second place from Rosberg. Watson said:

In situations like that, I never had any problem passing Niki, because he was always very clean. I was, I think, better on the brakes; I could brake later and I could handle that situation. Part of that was because, once we had set up our cars, I always felt my car was a better race car. His car would work extremely efficiently whereas I didn't have that narrowish window and I could hustle my car. I felt I was a better over-taker.

In Detroit, part of Niki's rationale was: I'm in a line of cars, I can't pass, so I'll just stick with it. Then, this idiot comes past and immediately goes on to take Cheever and Pironi with no trouble at all. So, once he's seen what can be done, Niki gets going, passes Cheever and Pironi and goes after Rosberg. I had caught Keke at the end of the pit straight and passed him without difficulty; Rosberg was always firm but fair. So then Niki comes up, by which time I'm way down the road, and he makes a mess of it. Keke has to take his line, cuts across the front of the McLaren and Niki spins into retirement.

I know that Ron was pissed off with Niki because, in reality, he had been ahead of me and he should have won that race and it would have been a McLaren one-two. But Niki had predetermined you cannot pass. It was an aspect of his personality; once Niki had decided something, that was it.

Lauda's success at Brands Hatch six weeks later would give the McLaren drivers two wins each as a bizarre season – there would be eleven different winners – counted down to the final round in Las Vegas.

Victory in the Swiss Grand Prix (which, strange as it may seem, was in France) had helped Rosberg to the top of the championship. He stayed there despite failing to finish in the points in Italy. After the race at Monza, Pironi (sidelined by injuries) was three points behind the Williams driver and eight ahead of Prost. Watson was third, three points in front of Lauda but, if an appeal court overruled his disqualification on a technicality from third place (four points) in Belgium, Niki would be champion if he won the race in Nevada and the others did not score big points. Watson, meanwhile, had an outside chance that required Rosberg in particular not to score. Watson said:

It was a very interesting situation. There were a number of us that could win the championship. Keke was best placed to do that and Niki and I both had a chance. But my mathematical chance was more favourable than Niki's. I understand that, on the Saturday night, Ron spoke to Niki and said: 'Here are the facts. John is better placed than you to win the championship. If he's behind you, will you let him go?' In other words, he was being asked not to block me if the occasion arose.

Niki didn't know what to make of it. In all his career, he'd never been asked to do something like this. Niki hadn't fully appreciated the reality that Ron didn't care a damn about either of us personally. All he was concerned about was McLaren. That had been Ron's ethos all the way through his time at McLaren; it was the team and not the individuals that mattered. Suddenly, Niki was being asked to do something which was anathema to him.

As it happened, on the day, I was ahead of him anyway. I finished second, but fifth place was enough to give Keke the title. Niki retired [with engine trouble] but I think he just went through the motions. As soon as the race was finished, he was gone; he just vanished. I think his race was over on Saturday night.

Rosberg carried personal sponsorship from Marlboro. Keen to cash in on their support for the 1982 World Champion and their association with McLaren, Philip Morris arranged a promotional tour to eleven cities in six days. The perfect way to do it would be with Lauda flying Rosberg, Watson and Patrick McNally (Marlboro's sponsorship executive) in Lauda's Falcon 10 private jet. Peter Windsor, sports editor of the British publication *Autocar*, joined them on the legs to Rome, Paris, Brussels, Stockholm and London.

In between the whirl of executive cars and press conferences with increasingly familiar questions, Lauda did the flying, accompanied in the right-hand seat by a 28-year-old co-pilot. Shortly after taking off from Paris en route to Stockholm, the automatic deployment of oxygen masks at 12,000 feet indicated a problem with the cabin pressure.

With a clear view of the cockpit, Windsor noted:

Everyone looks frontwards but Lauda is hard at work, pressing buttons, turning knobs, radioing back to Paris. Ears begin to pop. Lauda works his bottom jaw but rushes nothing. Rosberg and Watson begin playing with masks. 'Pressure valve has got stuck,' Lauda says a few minutes later. 'We're going back to Paris.'

It is cold and grey by the time they land. Rosberg, McNally and Watson head straight for the Falcon lounge and cups of coffee. Lauda, in the cold, is talking to mechanics and inspecting the Falcon's air pressure system. Finally he strides over to the lounge and addresses the group: 'These things happen. A plane is only a machine. It may take one hour to fix; it may take all night; they don't know. I suggest we hire another plane and fly to Brussels.'

With everyone having agreed on the latter, Lauda became a passenger on the charter flight, choosing to squeeze between Watson and Rosberg to allow himself a clear view of the flight deck. Nothing escaped his attention, as Windsor noted:

'The left–hand engine temperature gauge is still at zero,' said Lauda. 'Let's see how long it takes them to notice it.' As they taxied along the runway, Lauda pointed to the strobe lights at the end of the wings. 'Very unprofessional,' he said. 'No way you should use the strobes while you're taxiing. It's unnecessary and you can get reflections.' When the pilot opened the throttles, Lauda added: 'Look, he's not dead centre on the runway. See that? He's left of centre. If something went wrong now, if he had a blowout or something, he would have less room to play with.'

'That was typical Niki,' Watson recalled. 'He flew by the book. These pilots were like taxi drivers; just get in the plane and take off. Niki was very thorough with his flying and these guys clearly irritated him. They were not doing things by the book.'

As Lauda's fellow passengers were scarcely comforted by his dry observations as the aircraft became airborne, Niki resorted to ribbing McNally about how much he was being paid. 'When I signed in 1982, I said that you could pay me 99 per cent for my PR work and 1 per cent for my driving. When I renew I want 100 per cent for both . . . '

McNally could never be sure whether or not Lauda was joking. But the one certainty was that he was becoming increasingly serious about an important detail that would have a major bearing on his future competitiveness in the McLaren.

When Niki walked away from F1 at the end of 1979, Renault had won a race with a turbocharged engine; the first victory for a type of power plant that had been allowed – but ignored – since 1966. Initial derision over Renault's exploration of this alternative had given way to a reluctant acceptance by the British-based teams that turbocharged engines were the future now that they had reliability to match their superior performance. BMW (suppliers to Brabham) and Ferrari had joined Renault, with Alfa Romeo and Honda due to come on stream with turbo engines in 1983.

Lauda was not blind to the future, particularly when the Ford-Cosworth V8 in the back of the McLaren was breathless compared to the power of the turbos. The message had not been lost on Dennis and Barnard (now in complete control at McLaren after buying out Teddy Mayer and another former director). With typical acuity – and not wishing to be a customer to an engine manufacturer such as BMW – Dennis had done a clever deal with Porsche to design a V6 turbo. McLaren had entered a partnership with Techniques d'Avant Garde (TAG), a Saudi-connected corporation already familiar with F1 through a previous involvement with the Williams team. The TAG-Porsche engine would be built and designed to Barnard's exacting requirements. In the meantime, Lauda and Watson would have to persevere with the McLaren-Ford in 1983. Despite Lauda's reservations, the McLaren MP4/1C would have its moments – and sometimes embarrassing misfortunes.

Part of the problem was not of McLaren's making. A late rule change going into 1983 had banned ground effect at a stroke; all F1 cars should now have flat bottoms and none of the trick aerodynamic tunnels in the sidepods. Barnard was horrified; not only had his clever design to accommodate the narrow profile of the forthcoming TAG Turbo been made redundant, the existing Ford-Cosworth car with its V8 engine would lose two-thirds of its downforce. McLaren and other teams persisting with the Cosworth would be at the mercy of the turbos and their prodigious horsepower. In addition, it would take time for Michelin to adapt their tyres to suit the McLaren. It led to a couple of bizarre performances.

At Long Beach, problems setting up the cars for the city's streets resulted in Watson and Lauda qualifying in twenty-second and twenty-third places. Come race day, however, the Michelin tyres proved more durable than their rivals and this, coupled with collisions up ahead, allowed the McLarens to slice through the field, Watson leading a totally unexpected one-two finish for the red and white cars. Lauda said:

> The problem was that we couldn't work out any harmony at all between our car and our tyres. We made the mistake of not running enough wing [downforce] in places and we just could not get the car to work on slow circuits. Okay, so we had a good result at Long Beach but we were really lucky. Nobody really knew why we were so bad in practice or why we won the race. It was just one of those strange things which can happen in motor racing, but it certainly wasn't planned.

That was proved by neither McLaren qualifying for the most prestigious race on the calendar, the Monaco Grand Prix. By the time they reached the vast open expanses of Silverstone a couple of months later, Lauda had endured enough as the turbos blew away the normally aspirated McLarens during practice. When completion of the TAG Turbo car continued to be some way off, Lauda decided to take matters into his own hands. Typically, it would be pragmatic. And definitely not by the book.

CHAPTER 18

More Power, Please

Lauda said:

I was pissed off with this stupid Cosworth car because everyone was passing me! People said we were doing well because we were the fastest of the non-turbo teams [McLaren, Williams, Lotus, Tyrrell, Arrows], but who cares? Nobody cares because it's one race; there isn't one Ford-Cosworth race and one turbo race. It has been a complete waste of time in my opinion. A joke. We had to get going with the turbo engine. John Barnard was a very detailed man who would never release anything if he was not convinced. I told him: 'Listen, you must start early with racing the turbo car because this season is over for us already.' Ron said they couldn't do anything; he agreed with John and wanted to wait until the start of 1984.

Lauda had also been making his views known to John Hogan on the basis that McLaren's title sponsor was not going to receive value for money unless Dennis and Barnard accelerated the programme with the new car and its turbocharged engine.

Hogan said:

> Niki started really leaning on the situation; he used every
> trick in the book. My boss, Aleardo Buzzi, the president of
> Philip Morris, was at the British Grand Prix. Niki was sit-
> ting in the car, way back on the eighth row of the grid, and
> I watched this happen. Buzzi liked to walk the grid and, as
> he reached Niki's car, Niki beckoned him over. I don't know
> exactly what he said, but I could guess because Niki knew
> Buzzi was a very competitive person who felt he had to win at
> everything. Next thing I know, Lauda is in Lausanne [Philip
> Morris headquarters] the following morning.

'I flew to Lausanne to see Buzzi,' said Lauda. 'I told him I knew
there was a clause in the Marlboro contract with McLaren that
whenever the next development was ready, they had to use it.
I said to Buzzi: "Tell your friends in England that they have to
get the turbo car going."'
Buzzi called Hogan immediately. Hogan said:

> I got a typhoon in my ear, asking why can't we get onto
> Ron and make him put pressure on Barnard to finish this
> bloody thing. 'We expect to win and we're not going to
> do it if we stand still with the Cosworth car,' was the gist
> of what Buzzi said – courtesy of Mr Lauda, of course. Ron
> was called to Lausanne. When he heard what Buzzi had to
> say, Ron's immediate response was to claim it wasn't possi-
> ble. The new car would be ready for 1984, but not before.
> Buzzi's response was to say something along the lines of:
> 'Okay, let me put it like this, Ron. If the turbo car doesn't
> appear, I'm not paying you. Even better, you can pay us our
> money back.' Ron picked up the phone to Barnard more or
> less straight away.

John was mega pissed when he heard this. He said he didn't give a damn; the engine had got to be right and the sponsors would just have to suck it up. But Ron knew this had reached the stage where Marlboro might pull the plug. Tomorrow.

If he was unhappy about this latest edict, Barnard was not unnecessarily surprised by its cause. He had got to know Lauda well and appreciated some of his finer points. Barnard said:

He is very decisive. Because of that you can get feedback from him very quickly. There have been occasions when you need to analyse the feedback for yourself and decide whether it's right or wrong. He's quite prepared to accept that he is wrong. He's very positive. He will decide in his own mind that he likes the cars set up in that way and so you can proceed in a certain direction. If you find that the direction is not as quick as you should be, he is the first to stop and listen and try another direction. Because of his positiveness and decisiveness, he gets you going down a path and you can proceed.

From a racing point of view, he's obviously a very good, thinking driver. This situation we have now with turbos and normally aspirated [engines] catches him out a little bit at the moment because his normal racing approach is to let things settle down in the first 15 laps or whatever and then start picking up the pace and making his attack if he is behind, or, if he's in front, keeping it under control. But with the turbos, the only chance you get to be in touch with them is right in the beginning of the race before they have a chance to open up this gap. So you've really got to go out and give it one from the start.

Barnard was speaking during an interview on 4 May 1983. A couple of months later, he was getting the full force of Lauda's 'decisiveness' as Niki pursued his belief that the McLaren TAG Turbo needed to be on the track sooner rather than later.

'I was pressurised into doing an interim car [MP4/1E] and I wasn't happy about it,' said Barnard. 'The turbo was still only a dyno development engine at that stage, but Niki was pushing. As things turned out, it was probably useful.' The makeshift car (effectively a 1982 chassis with the Porsche engine in the back) was made ready for a test at Silverstone.

'I was at the last corner, waiting for Niki to come around,' said Hogan. 'He appeared at what seemed like a million miles an hour and he was aiming straight for me. At the last minute he turned away and, as he went past, he gave me two fingers. He said later that the turbo engine just kept pushing; that it was like taking off in his Learjet. He was happy – well, happier than before.'

Barnard was not so pleased. His irritation was now being directed at Porsche when the Silverstone run showed the new engine to be consuming oil at a prodigious rate. He said:

Porsche's response was to use a bigger oil tank. I said: 'This is not a 24-hour sports car; it doesn't have an empty passenger seat to take something the size of a dustbin! Your piston rings are probably too loose – that's a favourite way of making horsepower – so you need to sort it out.' Which they did. We had the clout to tell them to go away and make their engine work because we were paying for it. That was an important part of the deal and it worked in our favour. If Porsche had been left to their own devices, we'd never have got the job done.

All of which convinced Lauda that his determination to get the car up and running had been correct. The McLaren with its TAG-Porsche engine turned up at the Dutch Grand Prix – but only after a great deal of effort that involved mechanics adding the finishing touches on the cross-Channel ferry and in the paddock at Zandvoort. It had been hoped to have two turbo cars ready but the second chassis would remain unfinished in the paddock, purely as a source of spare parts. The latest car would be entrusted to Lauda. He may have qualified four rows from the back of the 26-car grid and four places behind Watson in the Cosworth car, but lessons were being learned, almost by the lap. Lauda said:

Ron had been pissed off with me, and Barnard didn't speak to me. They even got Watson to drive the car at the Porsche test track or somewhere before bringing it to that test at Silverstone. But I didn't care because it worked and were finding out things all the time with this TAG Turbo car.

For example, when it was sitting in the pit lane [at Zandvoort], I compared it with the other turbo cars and I noticed we had the same rear wing used with the Cosworth car. I asked them how they thought this was going to work and they told me just to drive. I drove – and what happened? The rear wing was too small. You needed a bigger one to deal with all the power from the turbo engine; that's what everyone else with a turbo was doing.

Hogan looked on with mild amusement as Lauda got down to work in his inimitable style:

Niki was smart. He wasn't going to sit back and think everything would be okay now that we had a turbo. We were having dinner and Niki said: 'I told Barnard the effing thing is not right – but we're going in the correct direction.' He was talking about things like too much turbo-lag and so on but it was clear from what he said that, despite his expected complaints and search for perfection, the potential was there.

It was typical Lauda, the computer; processing everything and coming up with conclusions that were entirely logical.

Lauda, in fact, disliked the computer analogy. With a hint of irritation when questioned on the subject he said:

Look, I'm a human being like anybody else, right? All this computer nonsense was tagged onto me, I think, when I was driving the Ferrari and winning a lot of races. They all said, well this success can't be down to a normal guy – so he must be a computer. Right? He must be something else. But I'm a human being and I make mistakes like any other human being. All I want to do is not make the same mistake twice. The problem that catches so many people out in this business is that they make a silly mistake – and then they make that same mistake again, and again, and again. I always try to remember each little mistake and never ever make it again. So, logically, if I do that I will come to the time when I make no more mistakes. Okay, perfection may not be possible – but I'm working on it!

The search for perfection with the TAG Turbo was just beginning. Lauda worked his way up to twelfth place in the Dutch Grand Prix before brake trouble intervened. Watson, meanwhile, drove a storming race to finish third in what would be the last outing for a Ford-Cosworth-powered McLaren. A second turbo car was made ready for the Italian Grand Prix, the learning process continuing as both cars retired from this and the European Grand Prix at Brands Hatch with various technical problems. Lauda told Alan Henry:

We are facing a series of quite understandable problems with the new project. It's the sort of things which are going to crop up when you start working with a huge engine manufacturer such as Porsche sitting in Germany and McLaren International sitting in England. This sort of partnership throws up a lot of little problems, which perhaps come from suddenly doubling the number of people around the car and involved in the project.

So, we have to make all these different people, of different nationalities, go in the same direction. This is the main thing we have to do. I don't think we've achieved it yet. From the moment we first started testing the TAG engine, I realised it's a question of educating both sides, Porsche and McLaren, to give each other a fair chance and, at the same time, work together in total harmony so that the end result is a complete success.

To work with the turbo project, means the car we have now is basically a compromise. Suddenly, with the new engine, there are so many new aspects you need to consider. So I do have difficulty, sometimes, to find the right words to explain things to John and our engineers about what the hell is going on. We've never been in this sort of situation before, so it's very difficult to interpret what the driver is trying to say. But I believe a good designer is the one who can translate the comments of the driver into a technical reality and change the car so that he can go quicker.

With a turbo, there are so many potentially misleading factors entering the whole equation that need the closest co-operation imaginable between driver and designer, because otherwise it will not work. I think, personally, between John and I there is a lot more potential to come, a way of developing a better understanding. And I think it's about time we got it out of the drawer and got on with things, because the new project offers too many pitfalls if we don't. If there's any misunderstanding, or lack of trust, between the two of us, then the new car will not function the way it should.

There appeared to be every sign of good communication going into the final race of the season in South Africa, Lauda actually admitting McLaren might achieve a decent result at Kyalami, provided the car held together. McLaren qualified in their now customary middle of the grid positions (Lauda ahead of Watson) but race day took a downturn just before the start.

A third car, acting as a spare, had been made ready, which was just as well because Watson had need of it when his engine developed a misfire on the way to the grid. Jumping into the back-up car and rejoining the parade lap, Watson made the mistake of weaving through the field to assume his grid position rather than, as required under such circumstances, starting from the back. He would be disqualified after 19 laps.

Lauda, meanwhile, was making impressive progress, working his way into second place and closing down Riccardo Patrese's lead in the turbo Brabham–BMW. With just six laps to go, the McLaren rolled to a halt with an electrical failure. The engine itself was sound. Lauda said when reviewing the year with Henry:

This is good. We've begun to develop that car as I'd hoped. Okay, it's been a shit season from my point of view; I didn't come back to Formula One to finish eighth, or whatever it is [tenth, in fact], in the championship. Basically, as long as you keep your feet on the ground, it's all part of the game. These things happen.

In these circumstances, you really get to know the true qualities of your partners in the team. The most important thing is that in times of difficulty you should find yourself moving closer together if you trust each other. You shouldn't start polemic arguments: I've never done that. We've had a bad time but we proved that we could start to overcome it. Now we had a lot of lost time to make up compared with other teams who've had turbos before us. So, I believe that over the winter, preparing for next season, it's going to be a question of quality, moving in the right direction and progressing quickly enough. We have to try many things during the off-season if we want to be competitive next year.

Ron Dennis was already thinking of 1984, but from a different perspective; one that would not have amused Lauda had he known about it. The South African race had settled the 1983 Championship in favour of Nelson Piquet and Brabham. Alain Prost was not only the loser but also the fall guy for Renault's failure. The motor manufacturer had missed out once again on winning a title that ought to have been theirs after investing so much effort in turbo technology in the first place. Renault had flown a posse of media to South Africa to record what should have been the crowning of France's first World Champion. Instead, they were writing Prost's career obituary. As Alain walked from the Kyalami paddock, he knew his three-year relationship with Renault was likely to be at an end. With typical perception, Dennis was alert to Prost's vulnerability and availability at this particular moment. Dennis said:

We were in a queue waiting for a helicopter and Alain was standing in line with us. We'd been aware that Renault were so convinced they were going to win the championship they had brought a very large quantity of champagne. I jokingly told Alain not to worry because there is always a positive in every negative. When he asked what the positive was, I told him I had managed to buy the champagne at half price. He did see the funny side.

I then said quite simply: 'Why don't you just come back to McLaren?' [Prost made his F1 debut with the team in 1980.] Alain was very critical of Renault in the media, because they were very critical of him. They got into a war of words and that escalated to the point where they just parted company. But Renault didn't play it very well because they ended up with the contractual obligations still intact. The amazing thing in the negotiation – and, of course, I can say this now – is that Renault paid Alain's retainer in 1984. It was quite an interesting negotiation as you can imagine. But that's how it unfolded.

This was bad news for Watson, who had been holding out in the expectation of a contract renewal based on the premise that McLaren would be hard-pressed to find anyone with suitable qualifications, one of which was having a good working relationship with Lauda. Prost's sudden arrival in the marketplace, at a bargain basement price, changed all that overnight. Within days, Prost and Dennis were in Hogan's office in Lausanne, thrashing out a contract. Niki Lauda was about to have a new teammate; a very different proposition from the departing John Watson.

CHAPTER 19

Playing the Long Game

Lauda viewed the change in personnel at McLaren as unsettling:

Prost coming to the team really annoyed me. I wanted Watson to stay; I got on well with him. I had been aware Prost was quick from the moment he first turned up in F1. I can't remember exactly when that was; it doesn't matter. All I knew was that he was up and coming and he could be trouble; a perfect French frog! Meanwhile, Wattie had been screwing around with his contract with Ron. I tried to convince John to do something because, as I said to him, you never know what's going to happen. Sure enough, Prost lost the championship to Piquet and so, suddenly, the best up-and-coming guy was available, Watson was out and I had a new teammate who was going to be bloody quick.

I had done all this hard work, helping Ron build the team and doing all the development work on the TAG Turbo – don't forget, I had to push Dennis and Barnard to run the thing in the last four races of 1983; they didn't want to race it until the start of '84. So, we do all that and now this quick little French guy is coming in to take advantage of everything. I was pissed off – but that's the way drivers are. Sure, I would work with Mr Prost. Of course. He seemed to be a sensible guy.

Niki Lauda may not have known a great deal about his new teammate's background, but the opposite was true when it came to Alain Prost's knowledge of the double World Champion. Prost said:

When I was young I had two idols in Formula One: Jackie Stewart and Niki Lauda. I can't say for sure why I chose them. It had a lot to do with perception because all you had in those days was the TV commentary and what you read in the newspapers. Jackie and Niki seemed to be a little bit different; cleverer than the rest.

Then, after Niki had the accident at the Nürburgring [in 1976], I remember very well waiting to see his comeback at the Italian Grand Prix. I really wanted to watch him closely and, when he did what he did, it was God-like in a way.

I can't remember exactly the first time I met him but it was obviously after his comeback in 1982 and I was racing with Renault. To be honest, I was not sure about this comeback. I was not convinced at all. I'd never experienced something like that before, so I could not tell how difficult it would be. I thought two years away would be a little bit too much. But then he proved the other extreme by winning races again, which was quite incredible and typical Niki.

It was also characteristic of Lauda that he should establish a few ground rules before the season got under way. Rather than show concern – and possible weakness – directly to the team, Lauda decided to have his card marked by John Hogan. Hogan said:

As soon as Niki realised what was happening with Prost coming to the team, he phoned me in Lausanne. He said he wanted to come and have lunch. This was on a Sunday morning. I said, 'Okay. But you have to come here.' He flew in to Geneva airport; I wouldn't even pick him up. I told him how to get to the restaurant – which he did. It was what you might call a family restaurant and he had Sunday lunch with myself, my wife and, I think, my oldest daughter.

I said: 'What the hell are you doing here?' Typical Niki, he said: 'Listen, this Prost in this team – I don't trust the little guy.' When I asked why, he said: 'I tell you, he's bloody quick. Are you going to screw me?' When I said I wasn't, he asked about Ron and I said he ought to know how Ron and John [Barnard] worked. Both cars would be exactly the same because John always had this philosophy that you can't make one unique part; you've got to make a set. Niki thought about that for a minute, nodded, went back to Geneva and flew home. Ron had to do a bit of tricky negotiating with him for his retainer – but it was straightforward in the end.

Although it was never written as such – and Lauda would insist 'This is not my team; I'm just a driver' – he was the de facto number 1, a situation that Prost was happy to accept. Niki did, however, have a clause in his contract that said he had priority in testing. He used it to full effect, Alain having to spend most of the time at Paul Ricard cooling his heels while Niki pounded round and round with an MP4/1E.

Both drivers, however, would get time in the cockpit of the all-new MP4/2 when it arrived at the French circuit not long before the start of the season. Within a few laps, Lauda and Prost both knew Barnard's latest beautifully crafted creation was a potential winner. And so it proved – in the manner that Lauda had feared when Prost won the opening race in Brazil.

It had not been for the want of trying on Lauda's part. He may have qualified sixth, two places behind Prost, but Niki was soon on the move, taking advantage of a poor start by his teammate and quickly working his way into third place. On lap ten, he dived down the inside of Derek Warwick's Renault with an uncharacteristically aggressive move that saw the right-rear wheel of the McLaren thump Warwick's left-front.

Looking back on his career in later years, Warwick would harbour a quiet grievance over the incident – since this race had otherwise represented his best chance to win a Grand Prix – because of what happened next. When Michele Alboreto's Ferrari retired with brake trouble, Lauda found himself in the lead. But not for long; an electrical problem was about to bring retirement. Warwick took the lead, only for the suspension to fail, probably as a result of the earlier contact with Lauda's McLaren. Lauda recalled:

In the beginning, I had said: 'There's no problem; I can fight anybody.' That was my very simple approach to it. In Brazil, Prost out-qualified me – right away. By five-tenths. I thought: 'Okay; but there's always the race.' I took the lead and had everything under control until my car failed. I drove back to the hotel, saw the last laps as I arrived and saw that Prost had won with 'my' car that I had developed all through the winter. This was the worst thing for me. I said to myself: 'Next race, he will not out-qualify me. I will try harder; take more chances; more risks.'

That theory was blown apart immediately when Prost out-qualified Lauda by an even bigger margin in South Africa. But, this time, it was Prost who ran into trouble, leaving Lauda to open his winning account in 1984. The victory in Brazil may have been rather fortunate for McLaren but luck had played no part in this one, particularly as Prost, forced to start from the pit lane after a last-minute switch to the spare car (set up for Lauda), had carved through the field to finish second and keep Lauda on his toes.

In Belgium, however, both drivers were off the pace in qualifying and then retired from the race. Any hope this may have given McLaren's competitors proved to be a false dawn. Prost won at Imola (Lauda retiring from fourth place with engine trouble) to put the Frenchman at the top of the championship table, 15 points ahead of Lauda in fifth place. It was as big as the gap would get during the subsequent twelve races, even though Prost arrived for his home Grand Prix quietly confident he could extend his lead. He was holding second place at Dijon when a front wheel worked loose, two lengthy pit stops to cure the problem dropping Prost out of the points – just as Lauda moved through to make it two wins apiece, with Alain just 6 points ahead.

From here on in, the 1984 championship would be about these two. Lauda, as ever, was not deluding himself, particularly at Monaco where Prost was on pole with Lauda eighth on the grid. Studying the lap times and noting how Prost was more than a second faster, Lauda turned to Barnard and asked simply: 'How does he do it?' There could be no hiding it; for the first time in his career, Lauda had a teammate who was undeniably quicker.

Compounding his unease the next day, Lauda spun off while lying second during a wet race. There had been a problem with locking rear brakes, but Niki would have none of it. 'McLaren no problem. All Lauda!' he snapped when asked about the cause of his McLaren parked heavily against the crash barrier at Casino Square.

The fact that the race was subsequently stopped prematurely would prove pivotal. Had Jacky Ickx, the clerk of the course, not waved the red flag when he did, Prost's position at the front would have been seized by Ayrton Senna's Toleman-Hart and, not long after, by the Tyrrell-Cosworth of Stefan Bellof. Prost was declared the winner but, because three-quarters distance had not been reached, half points would be awarded (4.5 to the winner instead of nine). This would be crucial when the championship figures were totalled at the end of the season. Lauda said:

I began to hate the turbo car because of Prost. With these engines, you had more boost [power] for one lap in qualifying. So we had 1200 horsepower and these sticky qualifying tyres. Then, in the race, you had 600 horsepower. I hated this; to get the power up then change the engine and bring it back; completely stupid. I was not motivated in the end by having this huge difference in power but, in the meantime, I had to do something about Prost.

It had been very clear after four races that Prost was *the* fastest guy for these days with this turbo bullshit. I had to accept that he was quicker. Yeah, sure I was pissed off that Watson wasn't on the team. But this question of 'with or without Prost' wasn't worth discussing because it was with Prost this year and it was a fact of life that I had him in the team with me. In one sense, this was very positive because he's a very competitive driver indeed and he forced me to the limit. On the other hand, we would obviously have to wait until the last few races to see who was going to finish ahead of whom – and no one really knew how that was going to work out.

There were no team orders. We could do exactly what we wanted. We both enjoyed the freedom to race each other as if we were competing for different teams. We weren't stupid and there was no danger of either driving the other off the road. Basically there was a very good level of communication between the two of us. I told him everything I knew about my car's behaviour and he did the same. We liked our cars adjusted in the same way, neutral with just a touch of understeer. That was useful when we had only a single car available for testing. I knew that I would be happy with my car set to his adjustments and vice versa. In the old days with John, we both had different tastes: he liked his cars to oversteer, which wasn't to my taste at all.

So with Prost being bloody quick, I changed my strategy. I said: 'Fine. I still want to win the championship with my car.' I concentrated on not getting upset by his qualifying speed but to work on the race, the car, the tyres; all of these things. This was the right switch at the right time because I won at Dijon and Brands Hatch – and also Austria – where Prost crashed because he was making mistakes, thank God.

If it was a mistake, it was an understandable one. Starting from the outside of the front row at the Österreichring, Prost had set off in pursuit of Nelson Piquet's pole position Brabham-BMW. These two were in a league of their own, Piquet getting some respite after several laps when Prost's fourth gear began to play up. Alain had to hold the lever in place, not an easy prospect on a track known for its high-speed corners.

On lap 29, just after half distance, there was an incident that, ultimately, would have a bearing on the outcome of the championship. Elio de Angelis, holding fourth place behind Lauda, had a sudden engine failure, the Lotus-Renault spewing oil through the final corner, the downhill and very quick Rindt Kurve. The marshals were slow to react, Piquet arriving on the scene with Prost tucked beneath the Brabham's rear wing. Even with two hands on the wheel, Piquet barely managed to stay on the road. Prost, unsighted and one-handed, had no chance.

This put Lauda into second place – and he was closing the gap on Piquet as the Brabham driver struggled with this rear tyres. With 11 laps remaining, Lauda took the lead and seemed to be heading for an easy win. It would be anything but.

A couple of laps later, there was enormous bang as Lauda snatched fourth gear while accelerating hard out of the Bosch Kurve at the top of the circuit. Niki shoved his arm in the air to warn other drivers as he lost power and began to coast to a halt, his race ostensibly over. But Lauda being Lauda, he figured it would be a long walk back to the paddock and prepared to crawl towards the pit lane using third gear. He tried fourth again, got no response – but found fifth. Maybe this was not as bad as he had imagined.

Lauda continued past the pits, where his signalling board told him Piquet was 17 seconds behind. By managing as best he could without fourth, Lauda reckoned he was losing between four and five seconds a lap. To his surprise and huge relief, the gap to Piquet remained the same. The Brazilian was nursing his tyres and had assumed Lauda was adopting his usual tactic of backing off and playing safe in the closing laps. It was only when Niki told him of his troubles as they went to the podium that Nelson realised how an easy victory had been lost. When the McLaren mechanics stripped the transmission, a dog ring tooth was found to have smashed its way into the side of the gearbox. Had it found its way out, Lauda would have lost his gearbox oil, along with a fortuitous win.

Lauda led Prost by 5.5 points. The gap was reduced by three points when Prost led a one-two finish for McLaren in Holland, and opened up again after Prost's engine suffered a rare failure and Lauda took another win at Monza. It was difficult to predict who would score the most at the penultimate race, the European Grand Prix at the New Nürburgring, a tame facility set in the shadow of the ferocious Nordschleife that had almost claimed Lauda's life eight years before.

If Lauda won this race, he would become champion, regardless of Prost's finishing position. But nerves were clearly taking hold. During the warm-up on race morning, Prost put a wheel on a kerb made wet by overnight rain and lost control. That would have been harmless enough had the spinning McLaren not hit a safety car parked just beyond the protection of a crash barrier. The irony of the moment was pushed aside by concern over the state of the McLaren, the left-rear corner of which had come off much worse than the damaged Volkswagen Passat. Prost's anguish was heightened by Lauda speeding by to set the fastest time in the 30-minute session.

With the spare car allocated to Lauda (the drivers took it in turns at each race to have the benefit of the back-up car), Prost's mechanics set to and changed the damaged parts, as well as the engine, which was found to be leaking water. Not the start needed to such a significant day in Prost's career. In the event, he led from start to finish – and it was Lauda's turn to make a misjudgement as he spun during a mix-up with a backmarker and finished fourth. Now, it would be all to play for in the final race in Portugal.

Having been in this position before with Renault, Prost appreciated the different atmosphere at McLaren and the friendly relationship he had with a teammate who had once been his hero. He said:

I had been really pleased to go back to McLaren, and very happy to be with Niki. I was happy to be a number 2 because, at the end of the day, it was not a big difference. He had priority on the development and things like this, so I had to adapt myself to that, but it was no problem; I accepted it. I had been confident coming to McLaren and a lot of that was to do with working with Niki. I had been looking forward to it.

I had a vision created several years before. I knew he was clever, he was intelligent. I would learn a lot and I did not expect any problems in 1984 – and that was how it turned out. It was like being in a dream team. It was a family; a pure racing team. I had to stop sometimes and think about when I had been racing go-karts and I had been following this guy, Niki Lauda. And then he becomes your teammate, and then your friend.

When I say a friend, that means somebody with whom you can share a lot of things. We were talking about everything: about life, women, children, all kind of things. We really, really had fun. People found it hard to believe we could have fun in this way because his nickname was 'The Computer' and mine was 'The Professor', which gave a very serious impression. And yet he was the teammate with whom I had the most fun.

On the track, of course, he was different; exactly as you would expect. I think he was only faster than me once during qualifying. But in the races, he used his brain. I knew that's how it would be in that last race in Portugal. I would be quicker, but . . .

CHAPTER 20

Three Times a Champion

The Portuguese haven't played host to a Formula One Grand Prix for more than 20 years, so they can be counted as beginners. They have had beginner's luck. This afternoon's race is not only the last of the season, it will also decide the World Championship. Usually the matter is settled earlier on. This time the main contenders are racing right down to the wire, and the wire is made in Portugal.

Grand Prix races are held on Sunday, with the Friday and Saturday for qualifying. This time, however, some of the familiarisation has been tagged on the front, because nobody has previously seen the Estoril circuit, which the Portuguese were still refurbishing on Wednesday evening. On Thursday morning, not all the large pieces of earthmoving equipment had left the perimeter and there was wet paint everywhere.

But the police were ready. The Portuguese gendarmerie are a high-profile body of men and here was a chance to strike paramilitary attitudes in a macho atmosphere. The lower ranks, of whom there were hundreds, had truncheons hanging from their belts. Their senior officers toted swagger sticks. One had sun glasses, shaped battle dress fitting tightly over a corset, spurred riding boots and a riding crop. The horse to go with all this was nowhere in sight. There were a lot of dog handlers and their dogs, all of which had been to snarl school.

Clive James, with his inimitable sardonic prose, described the scene in a piece for the *Observer* on Sunday 21 October 1984. Along with sports writers from around the world, James had been sent to Estoril, an attractive town on the Portuguese Riviera but straining at the seams to handle the sudden influx of motor-racing people. Not all of them would be enamoured with what Estoril had to offer. 'The hotel stinks. The rooms are terrible,' said Lauda. 'Prost moved out after the first day, but I can't be bothered. Willi [Dungl] is here, performing wonders in the kitchen, and the switchboard pulls the plug in the evening and promises I won't be disturbed again. All in all, I can put up with it. The hotel is right next door to the circuit.'

Despite the hype associated with the championship, this was another race that Lauda would deal with as it happened – just as he had more than 150 times before. Lauda said:

I don't dwell on things that have gone before. I really believe if you are going to make any sense of this life, you've got to look ahead all the time.

For example, you win the British Grand Prix. Good. But what does that really mean? I promise you, it doesn't mean a thing to me in the long run. Sure, I'm happy to win because I'm tired the following morning when I wake up. But I've never moved on to the next race, using my most recent memory as some sort of mental cushion. This weekend there is another race to be won and what happened at the previous race doesn't matter.

One of the problems with this business is that too many people spend too much time reflecting on things which have happened in the past. Okay, so I don't know what happened in racing twenty years ago. I can carry on about all these races I won during with my time with Ferrari, but they don't mean anything, do they? Not to me they don't. The pleasure derived from winning is in the actual business of winning, so when it's over, it really is over. Okay, so the memories are good but what matters is getting on with the programme and dealing with what you've got here and now.

At Estoril, Lauda needed comparative peace and quiet. The high profile created by past exploits meant his bid for a third championship after all he had been through was high on the news agenda. And if Lauda was not available, then anyone associated with him was fair game. Even the reticent and monosyllabic Dungl would be invited to share his thoughts. Geoffrey Levy focused on the 'Grand Prix guru who rules Lauda's body and soul' for a piece in the *Daily Express*. Referring to a previous race, Levy wrote: 'When Lauda roared into the pit and stepped out of the car, the solemn little man was waiting with a bowl of muesli, wheat germ, strawberries, honey and a cup of wild flower tea. "Eat," he said. And Lauda ate. "I'm here in case he needs me," said Dungl. "After eight years Niki is like a part of me. If this guy feels pain, I feel the same pain. Niki and me, it's like brothers, or father and son."'

Dungl must have felt some mental pain during the two days of practice as his man ran into enough technical difficulties to qualify eleventh on the grid – ten places behind Prost. Lauda had spent most of his time at the racetrack in discussion with Steve Nichols, an American whose laid-back approach accompanied solid engineering skills and an understanding of his driver. 'I had started with the team in October 1980,' said

Nichols. 'I had been Niki's race engineer in 1983 and again in 1984. It had been an interesting season. Niki had been trying his hardest; I've never seen anyone with such iron will and determination: he tried everything he could. So, we get to Estoril and he has a horrible qualifying thanks to a spin and an engine that was down on power.'

Lauda took those thoughts with him back to the hotel on Saturday. There, he followed his normal procedure, as outlined some time before in an interview with a British television channel. 'I usually go to bed at nine – something like that,' said Lauda. 'I normally sleep well, no problem. Wake up quite early as normal, at about six, just hang on in bed, start thinking about your race and what you are going to do in the first corner and the next corner and the first lap and so on. But as experience has proved, whatever you think in bed is always different to what happens on the racetrack, so the best thing is to stop and say let's wait-and-see.'

Lauda had plenty to keep his thoughts occupied during the warm-up on race morning when a new engine, installed on Saturday night, developed a water leak. Unlike today, when one engine must last for a third of the season, never mind a third of a race weekend, there was no alternative but for Lauda's tireless mechanics to wheel another V6 from the back of the Porsche truck and set to work.

Lauda returned to the sanctuary of the McLaren motorhome. 'It can seem like a prison,' said Niki. 'I have to sit there for hours and wait. Anywhere else, if you have to wait for four hours, you just go for a walk and look at the planes, or the cars, or whatever. But you can't do that at the racetrack because, as soon as I leave the motorhome, I have to sign autographs and speak to people, which I don't want to do because I need to concentrate and wait for the race to start.'

The waiting in Estoril did little to ease the pressure that had been building since Thursday. 'It was such a tense weekend,' said Nichols. 'Everyone was really on edge and it stretched really tight. Niki sort of freaked and was shouting at everybody in general and me in particular about the preparation. He probably didn't realise that all of us were pretty tense.'

Problems during the race morning warm-up were not new at McLaren, the hopeful omen being that, in almost every case, the cars would run faultlessly when it really mattered during 190 miles of racing in the afternoon. Lauda said:

I knew that I had to finish second behind Prost to win the title. But funnily enough, before the race, even though I was way down the grid, I knew that if I didn't make a mistake, like running into somebody and breaking my wing, then I could make it. Once you are in the car, you're not aware of anything which happens around you; you are waiting and concentrating on the start. This is a very difficult procedure because you have to contain revs and make sure there's not too much wheelspin. So you just concentrate very much on that and tell yourself that you have to do a very good start today.

You're nervous, there's no doubt about it. But I think everybody is nervous because nobody knows what's going to happen. Everyone wants to beat the other guy into the first corner – which is the worst time because something could happen over which you've no control. But, once the green light comes on, there are no more emotions. There is nothing. You're dealing with whatever is happening around you.

When the lights flicked from red to green and the twenty-seven cars squirmed away from the starting grid, Prost was elbowed down to third place. Lauda was twelfth, with a lot of work to do if he was to reach second place, the minimum needed if Alain won and Niki was to take the championship. Prost, intent on doing all he could, gradually moved forward, taking the lead on lap nine. Lauda was ninth, mired in a midfield battle – but thinking this through, working out what he needed to do without compromising the reliability of his car.

'Slowly but surely, he was using the revs, the boost and the power to manage his race while looking after his tyres,' said Nichols. 'Prost, in typical style, was out there winning the race, doing everything he had to do. Meanwhile, Lauda was working hard and eventually made it to third. But that would not be enough.'

Lauda was half a minute behind Nigel Mansell's Lotus. With 30 laps to go and a host of backmarkers to work through on such a narrow circuit, it seemed Lauda might not make it despite breaking the lap record time and again. Then Mansell spun off when brake trouble forced the Englishman to end his race in the gravel. Lauda was second; the championship would be his and there was nothing Prost could do about it. 'Winning the championship was just fantastic,' said Nichols. 'Everyone was overjoyed – except for Alain, his race engineer Alan Jenkins and his mechanics. I could really feel for them. But Niki had won the championship simply because of his determination.'

Barnard said: 'It was the one time I saw Niki just chuck everything at it and go for it big time. He came up the field like I've never seen. You could tell it was "This is my one chance." He was passing people here and there. He just came storming through.'

Keke Rosberg had witnessed Lauda's resolve at first hand. 'Niki has driven harder this year than I have ever seen before,' said the 1982 World Champion. 'He's had Prost so big in his eyes. I've been with him in a few corners, and I've been given a very clear picture: either I move or something is going to happen. Absolutely clean – but also absolutely uncompromising.'

It was a mellow 1984 World Champion who arrived at the podium, where a magnanimous Prost asked Niki to join him on the top step. In the end, half a point, the narrowest margin there's ever likely to be in the World Championship, separated them. Recognising Prost's obvious and understandable disappointment (Prost had led 352 of the season's laps; Lauda had been in front for 152. Alain had won seven races; Niki had claimed five) Lauda reassured his teammate that his turn would come the following year. Lauda said:

It had been a very hard year; my hardest time in competition. With Watson it would have been easier! We developed the car to the point where we were hard to beat. There was very good engineering and back-up but, as I said before, if we had not started on the turbo car when we did, we would have not been competitive in the first four races.

So, I won by half a point – half a point! Prost had showed me how quick the next generation can go. The relationship with Alain had been very good. He was absolutely straightforward; there was no bullshit. I cannot say anything negative about him. We had a very good working relationship; we pulled together; I accepted his performance. He liked me, I think; we never had a personal issue. He was quicker and I was running out of age, basically. He once said to me when he got his first driving licence for the road, I was already World Champion. So, Prost was the future for McLaren. No question. That's what I told him on the podium in Estoril.

Alain Prost said:

I really appreciated his sincerity. At the end of the day, he had used the brain. I had been fighting more against Piquet [in 1983] and I could not believe from the beginning that Niki could beat me, because he was not the quickest one. Okay, maybe reliability problems made the difference; whatever. But he became World Champion and that moment on the podium meant a lot.

I was very happy for him because I was also happy for the team. It had been the sort of season you would want to have when you are a racing driver. I always wanted to fight for the championship until the last race if possible, because that's when you have massive fun. But when also you have the kind of ambience we had, that added to the pleasure. I was happy for him because he was my idol when I was young and there was something very nice in being able to share something exceptional like this.

The positive working relationship between the two drivers had made life easy for Ron Dennis, particularly when compared with the open hostility to come when Ayrton Senna joined Prost at McLaren a few years later. Dennis said:

I was very fortunate in that the competitive tension between them wasn't a destructive partnership – it was very constructive. I think that Niki and Alain were at very different points in their respective careers, and that meant that there wasn't the need for them to constantly be outdoing the other.

They were both extremely professional, extremely mature. Collaborational. That made my job easier because I knew that they understood and respected each other. They knew that they were each there to get the job done; they knew that the car was a very good one. We didn't know at the start of the season that it would deliver in the way that it did, of course, but we were quietly confident that we'd approached that season and that car with the very clear intention of building something without compromise – which I think we did.

Alain and Niki derived their speed in different ways – you could see that Alain was incredibly fast, extremely ambitious; Niki was perhaps more prudent, wiser through experience, and more patient – again, a product of age and experience. The thing about Niki was that he brought a mental and physical discipline to the job of being a driver that few other drivers had in those days. He taught me, indirectly by observation, how to get an edge by always being focused.

In 1984, this difference in character meant their races were invariably quite diverse – in fact, now, I can't remember a race in 1984 when they raced each other together. It was more common for one to win while the other failed to finish, as I recall. That also added to the absence of animosity – although they both knew they were fighting the other for the championship, it was more of a mathematical battle than a purely physical one. It was an unusual situation for the team. It's still one of my greatest satisfactions, that 1984 season.

The racing may have finished but the weekend in Estoril was by no means over. Having the luxury of knowing that one of his drivers was going to win the championship, Jo Ramirez, as team co-ordinator, had organised a post-race celebration. He said:

That last race was incredible. The party started from the moment the chequered flag dropped. The Marlboro motorhome was a complete wreck – champagne, water, wine, cream; you name it, it was spread all over the place. From there we moved to a restaurant in Cascais for a late dinner, finishing up at the Penny Lane [club]. I had booked everybody to get back to England on the Tuesday, which was just as well because the party didn't finish until nine o'clock on Monday morning and we were not in a condition to go anywhere. Unbelievable.

Niki had had a difficult time with McLaren because Prost was so much quicker than him. He always tried to beat Prost outside the car; inside the car, he knew he could never beat him. I always felt in that particular year, because of the way the championship counted, it wasn't quite fair because Niki won five races and Alain won seven; Alain should have been the champion. But that's the way it goes.

Of all the drivers I've worked with, I had a very good relationship with just about all of them. But with Niki, he was a very enigmatic kind of personality. All of his closest friends were Austrian and he used to come with his friends; it was not easy to get close to him.

Having run his preview on race morning, the following edition of the *Observer* carried a follow-up by Clive James on the actual race. Describing the scene on the starting grid, James wrote: 'The French media, as always, focused on Prost to the exclusion of the world. For him it was a dubious privilege, because those chaps would have woken up Napoleon for an interview on the night before Waterloo. Much further back, Lauda said the necessary, but not a word more. Mr Minimax long ago found the secret of hiding without running. You can get near him, and you can't get to him.'

With similar apt syntax, James concluded: 'At 60 laps with ten to go, it was Prost, Lauda and the rest. Lauda was 40 seconds behind Prost but it could have been 400 as long as his car held together. Both of them turned down the boost to save fuel and avoid stress. The Grand Prix year spiralled gently to an end. Prost won the race and Lauda won the championship. The new boy won the battle and the old hand won the war.'

One question remained: how long would the battle-scarred 'old hand' wish to continue at such a furious pace?

CHAPTER 21

Hard Talk

The atmosphere at McLaren had been good, but halfway through 1984 I was feeling a bit uneasy about the way things were going. I knew Ron was unhappy about how much he'd had to pay me – it was a lot of money, I know. But that's the way it worked. Ron was as difficult as he always is, in a positive way and a negative way. But, I must say, I could handle him because I knew exactly what he was – and is.

I had a nice argument with him about renewing my contract for '85 because my original contract was coming to an end. I asked him for $4 million – and Ron had gone mad. He said he was going to get Rosberg and Piquet to drive instead of me. So, I went to Piquet and said: 'Nelson; you know the number is four million?' He said, 'Really? That much? Good to know.' I went to Rosberg and said: 'The number is four million.' He said: 'No way! You're lying.' I said: 'Keke; ask for four million, make it simple. But don't stop my salary.'

Then Ron argued with me forward and backwards and we had a real bad relationship. I thought I have to do something now because I'm trying to win the championship and to race under these conditions is not good. So I invited Ron and his girlfriend Lisa to Ibiza; picked them up with my plane and flew them down and we went out on a boat to an island to have something to eat. Lisa was lying in the sun, so I went out with Ron and said: 'Let's talk now – like men – and we solve all these problems.' It was a two-hour talk; he says I'm an arsehole; I say he's an arsehole; forward and backwards. Peace? Okay fine, now we are friends again, please let's discuss my contract.

That's when Ron said to me: 'Now I have to change my hat. I'm your boss. I'll pay you half of what you're getting now.' I didn't say another word, took them back in the boat and said goodbye. He said: 'What d'you mean goodbye?' I said: 'I've changed my hat, I'm fed up. See how you get home . . . ' That's when I started to think about maybe driving for someone else.

Lauda, in fact, had already been in discussion with Renault. The negotiation picked up speed in the light of the brief 'friendship' with Dennis at Ibiza having come to an abrupt halt. After much, as Lauda would say, 'forward and backwards' with Renault, an agreement was reached in principle. Pino Allievi, F1 correspondent for *La Gazzetta dello Sport*, was about to see evidence of the dialogue when he least expected it:

Myself and a colleague had arrived on the Thursday of the Dutch Grand Prix in 1984. It was unusual because the press and drivers were using the same car park and we saw Niki. There was speculation at the time that maybe he would stop racing in 1985 and we asked him if he thought that might be possible. He said: 'I have a fantastic offer.' From who? 'Oh, you can't imagine; you can't imagine.' And he opens his briefcase and shows us the contract that Renault has offered to him. We read it. It was true. Incredible! We could write about it, he said, on the condition that we did not mention the amount of money that they offered to him.

Not long after, Lauda would receive a call saying the proposed deal was off. The Renault board had become nervous about paying a large retainer in the light of an ongoing dispute with the car manufacturer's workforce and the trade unions' collective outrage over the figures being rumoured in the media.

That lobbed the ball back into Dennis's court – and he remained resolute; it was to be half Lauda's existing pay packet or nothing. After an intervention by Philip Morris (prompted by Lauda, of course), a compromise was offered. It was not the $4 million Lauda had wanted but, taking into consideration how well he had been paid, plus the fact that he wished to get on with trying to win the championship, agreement was reached for 1985 – albeit reluctantly on Lauda's part. He said:

Listen, if you cut my salary to less than half what I've been earning, then obviously I am going to be very fed up. I think it's unfair. The reason I got paid so well was that people expected me to do the job – and I think I've done the job. I think it would be reasonable to cut back by about one third, which would give the team some extra money to develop the engine and chassis further. This is a team effort and everybody has to work together, but I believe that things should be kept in proportion. Anyway, this is the situation and I'm not quitting because of it.

Having become World Champion for the third time in October 1984, Lauda had a full six months to think about the first race of the following season. 'After you've totally exhausted yourself going through a hard season, it's difficult to accept that to do it again, you have to work even harder,' said Niki. 'It's difficult to put yourself in that mental position again at the start of the year. It's something that you don't want to do automatically because you're exhausted and you think: "Shit! I've really got to push even more."'

Lauda had the added complication of going into the new season knowing that McLaren's tyre supplier, Michelin, had pulled out of F1 and the substitute tyres from Goodyear did not, in his view, provide as much reassuring grip. But that would become a minor issue in the light of an appalling run of luck; Prost would finish first on the road in three of the first four races (disqualified from one on a technicality) while Lauda would score points just once with a lowly fourth place. It got so bad as the season progressed that, going into his home Grand Prix in the middle of August, Lauda was twelfth on the points table while Prost was in the running for his first title. Speculation about Lauda's future began to focus on possible retirement – and those suppositions were not confined to the media. John Barnard said:

I remember Niki saying to me, 'This fucking little Frenchman is always half a second quicker than me, I've got to figure out what to do.' Niki had the nous to suss out his competition and play games with them mentally but, at the end of the day, Prost was just quicker. And it used to piss Niki off no end, because he couldn't figure out how to find that [lap] time.

The '84 car was nailed down at the back, which meant you were nearly always trying to dial out that entry understeer, which Alain could kind of drive around. Niki had to dial it out a bit more to be comfortable. I think Niki would go in a little deeper and a little harder, so he needed a bit more grip from the car's front end.

In 1985 it had become clear early on that Niki had started

to lose his edge, his will to win. He climbed into the new car and immediately saw it didn't have the grip of the previous year's. He was going to have to work a lot harder and it was clear to me that he had started to have doubts.

Lauda, who had turned 36, did not exactly refute his technical director's point in July 1985 when discussing his season thus far with Alan Henry. He said:

This year I think I made an improvement because there have been races where I've only been three-tenths away from Alain. I mean, this isn't good. I don't want to say I'm happy about it. In fact, I'm not happy. But it's better than being 2 seconds away, which I was at some circuits last year.

Everything happens so quickly with a turbo. You have to get used to it – but there's no time to get used to it. I mean, it's just straight onto the track, one chance at a fast lap, and that's it. You don't have time to work into a rhythm and you're suddenly presented with 300 bhp more. You have no choice. It's all happening. It's just a big kick up the arse and you've got to get on with it and I can't handle that as well as the others; it's as simple as this.

But I'm working on it. In that respect, there are circuits that help me; the faster circuits with wide-open bends where you get into a rhythm, where the power application is more spread out over the whole lap. But at somewhere like Montréal – stop, start, stop – I hate this. I find myself suffering more. There is no question there has to be a point where you say: 'Right, I've done everything, I'm just repeating myself.' But I don't know where that point comes with me.

Lauda went on to draw a comparison with his sudden decision to quit at the end of 1979:

When I retired then I had a rest from it all and then came back. But I don't think you can take my career before 1979 into consideration when you are thinking like this. It was a different era and then I started all over again in 1982.

It's difficult repeating the same thing over and over again. It's normal that motivation can vary from circumstance to circumstance and I'm trying to put myself in a situation where I am fully motivated for this year, to try and beat Prost again. But sometimes I don't know whether this is enough for me. I really need to be in deep trouble. I need a major problem to solve and kick myself in a big way. I am in the best team and have the best car. I'm happy in this situation and with these people. But maybe at the end of the season, they won't be happy with me. So then I'll have to make a decision.

Putting in the effort to win a World Championship is like walking up a mountain. The air is thin and you have trouble breathing when you get up high. But when you come down again, you're satisfied with your achievement. Going for another championship is like being told you've got to go back up that mountain – but climb higher. Knowing what you already know, maybe you take it a little too easy to start with, knowing that you've got to conserve the oxygen for when you get higher. The risk is that when you're taking it a bit easy, somebody else goes past and beats you to the top. It's a normal reaction, I guess, and I'm trying to fight it.

That fight, weakened in its intensity by five more mechanical failures in successive races, reached a conclusion in the week leading up to the German Grand Prix on 4 August. Lauda told Dennis he intended to retire at the end of the season. Dennis accepted the decision. He asked that Lauda keep it under wraps until such time as Dennis had secured the services of another driver, the logic being that, once the news got out, rival teams running the leading drivers would immediately tie down any contracts that were outstanding. A week later, Dennis informed Lauda that McLaren had signed Keke Rosberg for 1986.

The timing was convenient. The next race was in Austria; an ideal place for Lauda to make public his retirement. He asked Marlboro's press attaché, Agnes Carlier, to arrange a press call for nine o'clock on Saturday morning on the understanding that this would be a Niki Lauda press conference and nothing to do directly with either McLaren or the team's sponsors. Ron Dennis had other ideas.

When the two appeared together in front of a packed room, the feeling in the audience was that this could go either way; Lauda was either staying for another season or, more likely, he would be stopping sometime soon. Lauda picked up the microphone and got straight to the point:

> As I've used eleven years out of my life to follow the fascination of driving Formula One cars, which I really loved and still do, I think it's about time to take the decision to do something else. As Lauda Air is taking hundreds of people daily to their holiday places, we're going to expand and buy new aeroplanes. And I want to devote all my time to operate the airline, which is based in Vienna.

With Dennis by his side, Lauda thought it appropriate to add: 'More important than that announcement is that I especially thank Ron Dennis. For four years I've driven for him and we've had our ups and downs, but we won the World Championship. For me, it was fantastic last year. Certainly I must thank John Barnard and all the sponsors who have been involved through my eleven years.'

When asked if he would consider making another comeback, Lauda said: 'Nothing is ever definite. The difference is that last time I made a sudden, emotional, decision. This time, I have thought it through much more. I can't say what will be in my head in three or four years' time, however. Last year my motivation was to win the championship, but this year I have not been able to find a new motivation. I'm having a bad year – which is nobody's fault – but, really, I can't find a good reason to go on next year. So ... I stop.'

At which point, a po-faced Dennis took the microphone:

There is one thing that Niki has consistently left out in his statements. And that is that our success last year is principally the result of John Barnard's fantastic car. Both the drivers had a tremendous season last year. When Niki refers to me, he should be referring to both myself and John, because we share the responsibility of running the team and the company. Very rarely are so many journalists together as now. So many of you tend to overlook the role the designer plays. He's certainly as important as the drivers, and certainly more important than any other member of the management.

As regards to Niki's retirement – or stopping for a year, to be more accurate – our position will always be the same. We presently operate McLaren International to win Grands Prix, and will certainly have two drivers next year who will be capable of winning Grands Prix. Who will replace Niki is not decided yet, but you'll obviously be very high up on the list as regards knowing who, when.

The audience stood in stunned silence. The failure to thank or pay tribute to the driver to his right was, even by Dennis's sometimes gauche standards, a new low in a lack of grace. Nigel Roebuck, reporting for *Autosport*, summed it up in his usual succinct manner: 'Greatness,' wrote Roebuck, 'is not confined to the drawing board or the balance sheet, as most of those present appreciated.'

Naturally, there were a considerable number of Austrian journalists present, among them Gerhard Kuntschik of *Salzburger Nachrichten*. 'Niki was very angry after this; really angry,' said Kuntschik. 'All he wanted to do was tell us about his decision to retire and Ron Dennis comes out with all this stuff about John Barnard. We had the impression that Ron was upset because he hadn't been able to make the announcement; that Niki was the one who was in charge. Niki could hardly speak afterwards and what he did say about Dennis, we couldn't print his exact words!'

On race day, it looked like Lauda might get his own back in the best possible way. With the Österreichring favouring aerodynamics – a strong suit on Barnard's car – Prost had taken pole for the first time in 1985, with Lauda third, his personal best as reigning World Champion.

It looked like 1984 all over again as these two pulled away from the rest, Prost upsetting the symmetry by making a stop for fresh tyres at half distance. The potential for a rare and tasty battle began to emerge as Prost slashed the lap record and made inroads on the leading McLaren. At this rate of going, and in the absence of team orders, calculations indicated they would be at each other in the closing stages.

Then, with 13 laps to go, Lauda pulled to one side with yet another failure on his turbo. Flicking off his belts, Niki was out of the car and away before many of the spectators had realised what had happened. On learning of the home hero's retirement, most of the crowd went home too.

Typically, though, Lauda was to have one last shout.

CHAPTER 22

Win or Bust

Lauda said:

1985 was Prost's year, no question. I was happy for him. So, we get to Zandvoort and a funny thing happened. I was nowhere on the grid and, because I had already decided to retire, all I wanted to do was finish the season off. Herbert Völker, a journalist who I had worked with, leans into the cockpit and says: 'You're going to win today.' I said to him: 'Are you completely mad? I hope my engine blows up after one lap and I can go home. I'm not interested.' When he looked at me, I could see in his eyes that he was wondering why a guy he thought he knew pretty well could say such a stupid thing. But that was my feeling; I was just the second driver; Prost was leading the championship. I really didn't care.

Lauda's retirement – and the behaviour of Ron Dennis at the announcement – was clearly at the forefront of Niki's mind seven days later as he prepared for the start of the Dutch Grand Prix. Conversation between the two had been minimal; restricted to professional necessities as Dennis asked Lauda to cede his right to the spare car at Zandvoort, a request that was readily accepted given Prost's challenge for the championship. Lauda said:

> I didn't make any fuss about it. It was correct that Prost should have the car. But as we talked, Ron couldn't help himself. He started talking again about how he and John worked like crazy but when a McLaren wins all you guys write about is Lauda and Prost. He said I was lying in the sun in Ibiza while all this work is going on and then I fly in and get all the credit and have the photographers all around – and stupid things like this. I wasn't interested in talking to him any more.

Lauda had other things on his mind after a wet practice on Saturday had ruined the chance of making up for lost ground when various technical problems intervened on Friday. He would be sharing the fifth row of the grid with the Brabham-BMW of Marc Surer, an experienced Swiss driver who was coming to the end of what would be his last full season of F1. Surer said:

> For me Niki was always such a cool, logical thinker. When we would have drivers' meetings and something was being discussed, going round and round without getting anywhere, he would say: 'Okay. What's the problem? What can we do? We can do this . . . ' and tack-tack-tack, he would go through each point and make it seem straightforward. 'Simple!' he would say. It was unbelievable. We would come out of the meeting and it would be Niki who would sell it to the press, explaining what had been said and what we were going to do. It made everything seem logical – and not many drivers could do that. For him, it was never emotional. 'This is what we have to do – so let's do it.'

As a driver, he didn't give you advice as such, but he would say something like: 'When this happened to me, I did this and this,' and let you decide. When we were racing, there was one thing I didn't like with him. Okay, he usually had a faster car and lapped me most of the time! But when he came to lap you and you leave him room, he would hesitate. This is the worst thing that can happen. You've left room and he doesn't come through because he's not sure if you're going to let him. He comes halfway and then you get in trouble because you are on the outside and you can't turn in to the corner, and you both lose time. You're being lapped, but you're having your own battles and you don't want to lose time. Prost, for example, was – boom! – he was there. There was no question about his move and you could follow him out of the corner with neither of you losing too much time. When I was fighting Niki with the Brabham – as opposed to being lapped – he was okay. He would close the door early – or not. So, he was absolutely fair.

Despite starting on the same row, Surer would be lapped by Lauda in this race, but only after the Brabham had been hobbled by a chronic exhaust problem just as he was set to equal a career-best fourth place. On this occasion, Lauda most certainly did not hesitate on his way through; Prost was ensuring he did not have that much time. And Völker's prediction of a win for his friend was having a surprising effect. Völker said:

I was very rarely at motor races then because my interest had moved to general motoring and other things. I had to finish this last book with Niki – it was our fifth book altogether – so I decided to visit just one more Grand Prix to get the feeling again. While we were on the grid, it occurred to me that it would be nice if he could win the race; I don't know why I said it, but it seemed a good idea at the time. I made a joke about it, but this became more and more serious with the way the race evolved.

Lauda had been lucky at the start. Piquet had stalled his pole-position Brabham while Thierry Boutsen, ahead of Lauda on the grid, made a very slow getaway in his Arrows-BMW. 'I swerve around him,' says Lauda, 'and find Mansell also moving slowly, and then I nearly hit Nelson. After all that, I'm fifth at the end of the first lap – just behind Prost. I say to myself: 'Shit! I was thinking how stupid Völker was – and now I'm thinking I'll give it a go and try and win this race!'

Lauda was up to third when Prost took the lead as Rosberg's Williams retired with engine trouble. The race had just reached one-third distance when Lauda made an early pit stop and dropped to eighth, the McLaren having been at a standstill for 10 seconds (a quick stop in 1985). The gamble appeared to have failed as Lauda had immediate handling problems. Lauda said:

After the tyre stop, I had oversteer like you wouldn't believe and I was sure something had happened during my pit stop. I later discovered Ron had decided to put on a hard tyre – but only on the left-rear; it was his decision, not mine – or anyone else's. I was really struggling with the car but I knew Alain had yet to stop and they [Dennis] had done something either to make sure he won or because they thought I didn't care about winning. I remember thinking at that moment: 'No way is Prost going to win this fucking race!'

Lauda was to be inadvertently assisted when Prost came in just before half distance. The stop would take 18 seconds because of a jammed wheel nut, Prost rejoining in third with Lauda now in the lead. It took Prost 12 laps to catch and pass Senna's Lotus. Lauda was seven seconds in front. And determined to stay there.

By lap 54, with 16 remaining, the gap was 3.8 seconds. These two were racing absolutely flat out, as could be gauged by Prost slashing the lap record and yet only shaving a tenth of a second or two off Lauda's lead. The gap came down to 2.5 seconds – and then Lauda extended it slightly. A backmarker gave Prost the chance to close up, the Frenchman putting two wheels on the grass as he tried to seize the lead. Lauda would have none of it.

On they went, into the closing stages with nothing to choose between them. During the final 2.6-mile lap, Prost was darting left and right but Lauda was not going to be unsettled. They crossed the line 0.232 seconds apart. Prost said:

It was an incredible race. Niki kept shutting the door but I didn't really have a problem with that because I knew he had nothing to lose even though I was fighting for the championship. It was interesting because, in those races, we were limited by how much [turbo] boost we could use in the race. I had not used any in that race. When the race was over, you could look in the cockpit at the gauge, and see how much boost had been used. Niki used a lot; I could sense that by the way his car was going when we were running close together.

When that race was over, he came over to my car and had a look. When he saw I had not used any boost, he said 'Thank you' and said some very kind words. Coming from him, that was nice. He knew it was difficult for me because a win at Zandvoort would have helped me, obviously, trying to win the championship.

It would take another three races before Prost finally managed to become World Champion at Brands Hatch. Lauda may not have been present to witness the moment thanks to injuring his wrist at the previous race in Belgium, but he better than anyone appreciated what Prost had been through. Prost said:

Niki had always been very nice; very helpful. I learned a lot about him. His philosophy, his mentality; these things were very different. He was different also because of his accident [in 1976]. His health problems meant he was not doing a lot of sport whereas I was doing a lot. I remember saying to myself before some tough races: 'Okay, this race is going to be difficult for him; he's going to be tired.' But he was never tired! And he was just eating some carrots and things like this and I'm wondering how he does it! Of course, Willi Dungl played a big part in Niki's life. And Willi was a big help for me too; a big, big help because, thanks to Niki, we shared everything.

I remember in Long Beach, not long after I had come to McLaren from Renault, I was eating some steak and French fries one hour before the race – because that was what I was used to when racing with Renault. My weight at the time was about 62 or 63 kgs. As soon as I started to work with Willi and eat differently, I dropped to 58 kgs – and I'm still 58 today. I learned a lot about that and different exercises and so on. Niki pushed me to go in this direction. He didn't need to do that. Other drivers would have said: 'Willi is my trainer. You must get your own.' For me, that was a sign of how Niki was confident about everything he did and said.

This applied to things like – I don't remember which race it was – but I was destroyed afterwards because for the second race in a row I had been leading and lost. Afterwards, he asked where I was going. I said I was humiliated and I was going home. Niki and Willi both said: 'No, you're not going home. Come with us.'

So we went out to a nightclub. He gave me a Whisky Cola. And then two and three. After one I was drunk completely. Niki said to me I had to understand that what has happened at the racetrack, has happened. It's over. You can't change things. So drink a little bit, sleep well and promise me, tomorrow morning, you think about what comes next; never think back. Those were maybe just words that are easy to say but, coming from Niki – and Willi, too – this changed my mind about how I did things. When I cannot change things, even in my life, I no longer regret anything. I have to thank Niki for that.

Niki was strong for sure. When he wanted to tell you something, he could do it in a good way; I never remember him being rude or doing something in a way that was too tough. I never had a problem with him. There was never a problem in the team when we were together, even though we were both fighting for the championship. Niki may have been very tough when talking with Ron about contracts and things like that, but the ambience in the team was always really good.

Dave Ryan, the crew chief at McLaren, concurred after being in a position to quietly observe Prost and Lauda at close quarters:

It was a really positive period. Alain was just a fantastic guy; a mega driver. He was one of those guys who would spend time with the mechanics. I can remember him on the podium at one race saying: 'A monkey could have driven the car today'; unlike some drivers who get up there and say: 'I got the most out of this car', suggesting that no one could have done it better. Alain was one of those guys who would always give credit to the team; genuine credit, I feel. He was just a very good guy to have around.

Niki was different, but not in a bad way, I had to teach him to come into the garage before he left the circuit and say 'Good night' to the guys. The best it got was: 'Okay, I go. Thank you. Goodbye.' He felt he was the driver and he didn't appreciate the benefits of having a relationship with the garage. But he was very good to have as a driver in your team. When he won his third race in his comeback in 1982, you could see it building up because he was so methodical.

It was so tight between Niki and Alain in '84. Before the final race at Estoril, they bought five gold watches between them and decided that whoever won the championship would have the watches and give them to selected people on the team. I wasn't there because I'd had to fly back to New Zealand after my father had died. So I didn't get a watch. Niki said he had one for me but every time I saw him he would look at his wrist and ask: 'Got the time?' I never did get the watch!

Even with that intense rivalry, the mechanics' perception was that there was no back-room dealing; no underhand methods. It was an open fight between the drivers. There was a rivalry between the two sides of the garage, but it never got nasty. It was as level a playing field as you could have hoped for. Everything worked very well and I just remember a lot of very good times.

Those good times came tantalisingly close to having a fairy-tale ending at the final race of 1985. Australia was hosting a Grand Prix for the first time in Adelaide; a typical street circuit and the last of 171 Grands Prix for Lauda. The prospects looked grim when Niki qualified sixteenth, six rows behind Alain. Lauda was soon on the move and, by lap 15, he had worked his way into sixth place. On a day when more than half of the twenty-five starters would succumb to mechanical trouble (Prost, for instance, with a broken engine) or mistakes on the unforgiving track, Lauda found himself in the lead at two-thirds distance. But not for long.

The dream result would go the way of his brakes as a failure when he needed them most at the end of the 180 mph straight sent the McLaren nose first into the wall. Lauda stepped out, his international motor-racing career ending much as it had begun with a wayward F3 car fifteen years before. He headed for the airport, ready to face new challenges as Lauda Air was effectively reborn.

CHAPTER 23

Winging It

The turf war with Austrian Airlines had continued unabated. Keeping a low profile and overheads, Lauda had carried on leasing his Fokker F27s to Egypt Air while operating two or three executive jets out of Vienna. Then, for no apparent reason in August 1982, the Austrian Transport Ministry had threatened to revoke Lauda Air's licence. The news had been leaked by someone within the Transport Ministry.

Lauda called the ministry immediately, only to discover that the leading officials were on holiday and the letter of withdrawal was ready to be mailed. Not one to stand on ceremony, Niki flew to Majorca where the Austrian Chancellor, Bruno Kreisky, was on holiday. An audience with the socialist leader earned a stay of execution while the matter was investigated. A few weeks later, Lauda was called to the Transport Ministry, where it was claimed no such letter existed and Lauda didn't know what he was talking about. No more was heard on the matter, but it was typical of the unnecessary time-wasting obstacles being thrown in the path of Lauda Air.

Two years later, Lauda became involved with two other individuals to establish Lauda Touristik AG, which would become the country's second-largest tour group. Two BAC 1-11s were chartered from the Romanian airline TAROM, the operation later expanding with the lease of a pair of Boeing 737s; one in December 1985, the other in March 1988. The gloves were off. Lauda was taking on all comers, and relishing the fight. Lauda Air CEO Otmar Lenz said:

When Niki stopped racing, he was concentrated totally on the airline. He could switch from one thing to the other with ease. I remember this impressed me when he invited me along to one of the Grands Prix at the Österreichring. During practice, he came into the pits, had a look at the computer while the mechanics did some changes on the car. As soon as he saw me, he was immediately talking to me and showing me how this worked, how that worked and then asking me about other things. Everyone was running around him in the garage. When they finished a couple of minutes later, he put his helmet back on, got in the car, closed the visor and set the fastest time at that moment. This was one of his secrets; he could change from one second to the next; concentrate on one thing and, when that was over, immediately give a hundred and ten per cent to the next thing.

The impression always was that he was very keen if he believed in whatever it was that you were doing. He was very rational; very calm. We had the same ideas about making travelling, not as it is today, where you pay for water and have a very hard seat, but to provide a very good service. That's when he started talking to Attila Doğudan about bringing a new standard of catering on board. All these ideas we were very keen to do; we had a lot of fun building up the airline. But, of course, all the way we were fighting with Austrian Airlines because they had all the rights and were making life difficult.

So, we had to think about different destinations. I knew a little bit about Australia and I suggested we should do that because we knew Austrian Airlines couldn't; they only had an Airbus A310, which was inappropriate for Australian flights. By this time, we had a Boeing 767 and we knew we should get the schedule licence because Austrian Airlines couldn't fly there. But even then, there were all sorts of tricks to stop us.

One 'trick' in particular would prompt a startling retort, as Niki explained during an interview in 2011:

We were making our inaugural flight from Vienna to Sydney in 1989; this was a big deal for us. On the day before the flight, I had a phone call from an official in Canberra saying my aeroplane books did not turn up in time. These were technical papers for the 767, so they said they couldn't give permission to fly over Australian airspace. I knew this was bullshit. Somebody was making some moves, trying to stop us. I said to this guy: 'What do you want me to do? I have 223 people, all ready to go.' He said: 'I don't care.' So I said: 'Neither do I. I'm coming so, if you want to stop the flight, you'll have to shoot me down!'

This is confirmed by Lenz:

Yes, he did say that! We were sitting in the office together and I actually took the call. They said we had no landing rights because they had not received the books for the Boeing 767. We knew that was wrong because Qantas [the Australian national airline] had been using this type of aircraft for three or four years, so the Civil Aviation Bureau in Canberra knew the 767 very well. Then, when they admitted to receiving our papers from Boeing, the guy said he hadn't had time to study them. That's when Niki had enough and said he didn't care; he was going to fly the aircraft to Sydney and they'd have to shoot him down!

Lauda continued:

I flew the plane to Bangkok. We got start-up clearance from there because, thank God, they didn't know about what had happened with the Australians. I flew down to Australia and there was the mayor of Sydney, a music band and everyone there to inaugurate the new flight. I told them it was easier to win three World Championships than to fly to bloody Australia!

Because of the regulations for an inaugural flight like this, it cannot be a commercial flight, so you give the passengers a voucher for Bangkok to Sydney and they go free. Qantas are obviously not happy about Lauda Air coming into their territory but we're there, on the ground, with the mayor, who was glad to see us. The Australians were happy too because the influence of Qantas was heavy – like Austrian Airlines in Austria – and the Australians wanted more choice. So, the television cameras are there and I say: 'It's not a commercial flight. Whoever wants to go back to Bangkok free of charge, then come to the airport.' Suddenly, lots of people turned up. It was the best bit of PR I ever had!

Potentially the most damaging piece of PR was about to knock Lauda for six. Nothing would prepare him for an ordeal far worse than anything he had experienced during such an extraordinarily eventful life as a Grand Prix driver.

CHAPTER 24

Flight 004

At 16.02 on Sunday 26 May 1991, Lauda Air flight 004 took off from Bangkok, bound for Vienna. This was the final leg of a journey that had originated that day in Hong Kong. The Boeing 767-300 ER, named 'Mozart', was under the command of Captain Thomas J. Welch, 48; an American with 11,750 flying hours who had been with Lauda Air since 1990. Josef Thurner, the 41-year-old co-pilot from Austria, had accumulated 6,500 hours. Everything was routine as the aircraft, with 213 passengers and 10 crew, gained height and headed north-west from Don Mueang airport.

Niki Lauda was at home in Vienna. At 21.50 local time, he received a telephone call from a TV news channel, asking about a reported crash involving one of his aircraft on a flight from Bangkok. Lauda said he was unaware of this, but would check. He immediately called his company headquarters and asked them to get in touch with Flight 004. No contact could be made. The aircraft had disappeared from air traffic radar at 16.17 hours local time. Fearing the worst, Lauda called together his management team, among them the CEO, Otmar Lenz. Lenz said:

I had already received a call from our dispatch. Then Niki called and said something had happened to one of our aircraft and we had to meet at the airport. As soon as we realised that something had happened near Bangkok, Niki immediately said: 'Listen, you have to stay here, deal with everything including media and television. I have to go immediately to Bangkok. This is something I have deal with; it's important that I know what's going on and try and find out what happened.'

It was also important for the Thailand and Chinese people; a courtesy to them that the owner is immediately at the scene. He also had to do it because it's very typical of an aircraft manufacturer that, when they sell you an aircraft, they are your best friend – and we always had very good co-operation with Boeing – but when something like this happens, you can't get information. They stop everything because they're careful what they say. So Niki knew straightaway that he had to be there.

In all his experience running an airline, Lauda had never been confronted with a terrible situation such as this. When he arrived in Bangkok, Lauda was flown by helicopter to a mountainous region in the Dan Chang District, approximately 94 nautical miles north-west of Bangkok. Lauda said:

We landed, took a car and drove into the jungle. Suddenly, I saw some white stuff on the ground and wondered what this was. Then I realised they were napkins with Lauda Air on them. It's a big shock when you suddenly see this in the middle of a jungle. The closer we got, the bigger the pieces of the aeroplane. It was spread over five kilometres. I've never in my life seen a disaster like this. I'd never seen dead people without heads, without arms, with the local people stealing rings and watches from the remains of these people. There was luggage all over the place; I saw handbags of cabin attendants who I knew. It was the worst experience you can possibly imagine; it was a scene which I will never, ever forget.

I was flying these planes myself as a pilot and I had to find out why this aeroplane had come down. I had a Boeing representative with me, who I brought from Vienna. I had asked him if he had ever seen a crash. When he said he had, I said: 'Come with me. You can tell me what to expect.' But nothing he said prepared me for this.

We looked around; one engine here, the other engine over there, the frame of the aircraft in several other places. When I asked him if there was anything he could tell from what we could see, he said: 'No. It's all a mess.'

I noticed on one engine, the thrust reverse was deployed. On the other engine, which was two kilometres away, the thrust reverse was not deployed. [Thrust reversal – or reverse thrust – is the temporary diversion of an aircraft engine's thrust so that it acts against the forward travel of the aircraft, providing deceleration on landing.] When I asked why this was like this, the Boeing man said when a plane crashes into the ground from that height, this is what happens. That's the way it is.

We went back to Austria. In these days I was crying with tears, many times. But never with other people, only when I was alone. But something automatic kept me going, because I was always asking myself: 'Why, why, why?' I was very proactive. If there was no news, I wanted to know why not. I was being called by relatives of the victims, about fifty calls each day, always asking me the same question: 'Mr Lauda . . . Why?' I immediately realised that the most important thing for all these people in all this sadness, losing their loved ones, was to give them a reason.

The problem was the flight data recorder was completely destroyed; the aluminium tape in there had been so badly burnt, we could get nothing from it. We didn't expect this because it should cope with up to 900 degrees. But that tells you how long it had been in a big fire. We found the cockpit voice recorder. This showed that the flight had been normal. Then, suddenly, there was a huge noise in the cockpit. The pilots only spoke to themselves, not with each other. I knew something must have happened so fast that these two guys didn't even have time to communicate with each other.

Five minutes and 45 seconds after take-off, the crew had begun to discuss a yellow flashing warning light relating to a possible fault in the thrust reverse system. ('They did exactly what they had to do – following the instructions from the checklist,' said Lauda. An investigation would later state that 'No corrective actions were necessary and none were identified as taken by the crew.') The Boeing 767 had reached 24,700 feet and 598 mph when, 15 minutes and 1 second into the flight, the co-pilot was heard to say: 'Reverser's deployed', followed by a sound similar to the airframe shuddering. The cockpit voice recording ceased 29 seconds later with multiple bangs thought to be the break-up of the aircraft after it had turned over and plummeted earthward. Lauda said:

Despite believing it must be something to do with the thrust reverser, for eight months it was Lauda Air's fault that these people got killed. This was the worst thing for me. I had to give a press conference to explain what I knew. For me, the first emotional effect was I was running the company and I was captain on these aeroplanes. So basically I knew everything about it. I said if this was my fault then I would stop Lauda Air. I would stop running an airline because I was not capable of doing it; I was not able to let an aeroplane fly safely from A to B.

This was a tough statement at the time, but it would allow me to concentrate completely on finding the cause. I didn't care whose fault it was; it could have been mine; it could have been somebody else's; I just wanted to know. I was pushing and pushing and pushing to get the truth. It was really annoying because all our aeroplanes were still flying worldwide. What happens if the next one crashes? So, there was a huge fight between me and Boeing to get this thing resolved, because my only interest was to find the cause and fix the aeroplanes, so that travelling is safe. This was a huge mess.

In Otmar Lenz's view:

Niki was very angry. As an airline, you stay alone and they [the aircraft manufacturer] don't help you; they're not willing to give you information. It was a really tough time. I never saw him so concentrated on anything. He was very pushy because he needed to know – we all did – if it was a failure of the pilot or of the maintenance, or whatever. If that had been the situation, I think probably Niki would have quit aviation; he would have said, I cannot live with this. For eight months Lauda Air had to keep flying while not knowing the answer. It was a terrible time for everyone. We eventually thought we knew – but Boeing would not say anything.

The turning point came when Lauda attended a mass burial for 23 unidentified victims in Bangkok. Niki said:

I went to there to pay my respects. All the friends and loved ones of these poor people were there, looking at me, and no one could tell them why this had happened. There was one little kid and he threw some marbles into the grave. There was a huge noise when they fell so far down and hit the top of the coffins. I asked the grandmother about this and she said these were the marbles that the parents had bought this child on their last holiday together. They were both dead.

This was a very difficult moment. I decided immediately to fly straight to Seattle [Boeing's headquarters] and have this dealt with properly. I flew via Hong Kong and there was a pilot I knew from Boeing coming in the other direction. I met him at the airport and asked him what was going on at Boeing. He said they knew something was wrong with the thrust reverser and I should try to get in the simulator because they had been in there and tried to save it (with reverse thrust deployed) and no one could handle it. He knew they had done this.

It had taken a long time to get all the computers from the engines and everything worked out. It turned out this was a failure of the design of the thrust reverse system. Basically, an O-ring in a direction control valve failed; it fell out of the valve, which pushed the thrust reverse out – which it should never do when you're in the air – and the thrust reverse deployed. This was on the left engine. Therefore, the left wing stalled at 28,000 feet and the aeroplane turned over. It was clear what had happened but Boeing did not want to say anything. Everyone thought that an aeroplane could continue to fly under those circumstances – but it had become clear to me that it couldn't. And now I heard about this from the pilot.

When I got to Seattle, at first they did not want to let me fly the simulator. I said: 'Listen, this was my fucking aeroplane, my name, my damage . . . so let me do it.' They eventually agreed. I tried several times to recover the aircraft, but it was impossible. It was absolutely clear why the plane had crashed. As soon as the thrust reverser comes out, the aeroplane turns over. You can do whatever you want, but you cannot control it.

I asked Boeing to issue a statement. They said they couldn't because it would have to be checked by lawyers and it would take another couple of months. I said: 'Do we know the cause?' Yes, they said, we know the cause but we have to make sure there is no risk in getting sued – and this and that. We have to find the right wording. I said: 'I cannot wait another three months. Why do I have to carry all this responsibility on my back for eight months that this plane crashed? We know what happened.

'Okay,' I told them. 'This is what we'll do. Tomorrow, I will hold a press conference and say we are going to take a 767, load it up like it was with my two pilots, deploy the thrust reverser in the air and everything will be okay. I'll be on board and you can show me that it works. Simple. I will ask you to do that for the sake of all the victims. The relatives of these people need an answer as to why they all got killed. That's the most important thing.' I went back to my hotel – and they were waiting for me when I got there. They issued the statement.

Finally it was all over. This was the first time in eight months that it had been made clear that the manufacturer was at fault and not the operator of the aeroplane. But the thing I did not understand was why it took so long to do these things, because this was a safety issue. My company had the plane crash; I felt responsible. But out of it came the discovery of the fault and the knowledge that such a problem will never happen again. All aeroplanes worldwide got new regulations that the thrust reverser had to be designed in a different way. It is also not safe any more to continue a flight when the reverse thrust isolation valve warning light is flashing. Until this accident, it was thought to be safe. The producer of the reverse thrust always said this system was fail-safe, so the pilots could continue flying.

Money was never a problem. 500 million dollars maximum insurance. For the plane, 80 million; for the passengers 20 to 30 million. So money didn't come into it. But the human side of the tragedy was much, much more important.

The thing that really hit me was that no one seemed to understand that the first thing you have to worry about is the people who knew the people who got killed. If you lose your wife, if lose your child, whatever, you need to understand why they have gone. A human being needs an explanation. That is the point. The worst thing is if you leave these people, they will speculate because, like you, they don't know the truth and they get so confused with press issues, which they interpret in the wrong way, going forward and backwards. The damage you do to the feelings of these people is so bad that it's ridiculous.

If I tell you that your wife got killed because the thrust reverser deployed, at least you understand why she is not here any more. And this is what I told them a hundred times: you cannot leave these poor people sitting there speculating. If you know the answer, you should tell them! But nobody wanted to listen, which is why I pushed so hard.

I spoke to as many relatives as I could and told them they were always free to call me. There was one guy, who was the boyfriend of the purser on the plane. He was completely finished; said he was going to kill himself because he had nothing to live for any more. I talked him through all this. But even with all the pain and the loss, I have to say that nobody really attacked me personally. And maybe that was because, from day one, I promised that I would find out what had happened.

The whole thing was the worst experience of my life; my accident [at the Nürburgring in 1976] was nothing compared to this. The crash in the Ferrari was a different issue because I decided to take a chance of maybe killing myself: this was my decision. If I kill myself this is my own problem and nobody else's – maybe Marlene can complain, but nobody else. But to run an airline and 223 people want to go from A to B and they don't arrive, that's a different responsibility.

CHAPTER 25

Lauda Air: Final Call

I always thought it was possible to design a technical master-piece such as an aeroplane so that it is absolutely safe; so that the human controls the technique. Even today, if I look at big planes, I cannot understand why my plane came down. The technique has beaten the human genius. I never thought that this could happen.

Niki Lauda was speaking in August 1991, reflecting on the loss of Flight 004 three months before and recalling the scene of devastation he had witnessed in the Thai jungle. At this stage in the conversation, the cause had yet to be confirmed. He told Alan Henry:

Flying is still important to me; very much so. Motor racing, particularly during qualifying, was all about going over the limit and then, desperately, trying to pull yourself back from the limit. It's all about making sane and rational decisions from a totally irrational situation.

Flying is completely the opposite. It's totally logical. From the moment you start out on a flight, you know exactly where you're going, what you're going to do and where you should end up. It is a completely different discipline and, because of the way it contrasts with motor racing, it's relaxing. When I was racing, it brought me back to earth – if you know what I mean!

The Lauda Air expansion to Melbourne via Kuala Lumpur and Bali had been created thanks to Niki spotting a gap in the market as licences to the Far East had become available. Austrian Airlines may have had a strong European network but their links to Asia and Australia were limited. Lauda seized his opportunity. This had proved beneficial for the Asian economy as Phuket became a favourite with Austrian holidaymakers thanks to the connection to Vienna. There were also daily flights to Dubai, Cuba and Miami via Munich. The fleet was later expanded to include the Boeing 777 for direct flights to Melbourne from Vienna. This was handy for Formula One people following the Australian Grand Prix's move to the capital of Victoria in 1996. Helmut Zwickl said:

Because I was a qualified pilot, Niki would let me sit in the third seat on the flight deck and we would usually talk about flying rather than Formula One! He was an exceptional pilot. The chief test pilot with Boeing told me that Niki was the best pilot he ever had in the ratings school for the 777. He said he was amazing; very concentrated; very accurate. He could fly under pressure and do several things at once.

Gerhard Kuntschik of *Salzburger Nachrichten* said:

I remember I could fly three or four times a year for free with Niki. In 1985, his last year racing, he took me in his private plane to Bologna for the San Marino Grand Prix but he had to leave immediately after the race. I had to work and I found a colleague with whom I could drive home, but it was worth it, just to experience flying with Niki.

Even when he had the airline and the Australian Grand Prix was in Melbourne, you would find half the F1 paddock had been upgraded to Amadeus Class [the Lauda Air equivalent of Business Class]. I frequently saw a number of the older generation of journalists, people who Niki had known for years. He wasn't stupid. He was the best at PR and I wrote a piece for his seventieth birthday saying he was better at PR than some of the professionals.

Many times on these flights, Niki would be the captain. People who didn't know him would find it strange that the captain would appear from the flight deck wearing old jeans, a sweatshirt and the red cap we were all familiar with. But he took it very seriously. When he was captain, the crew would be on high alert. I remember seeing him come out of the cockpit, check the toilets and go back to the flight deck.

I was on a 777 flight to Australia via Kuala Lumpur and he was flying the first leg. From Kuala Lumpur to Melbourne he was sitting in the back row of Amadeus Class, in an aisle seat, across from where I was sitting. I was totally relaxed and fell asleep, waking up only when they said we were about to land in Melbourne. He leaned across and said: 'What are you doing? You should have stayed awake and enjoyed the benefits of our service, not sleep eight hours!'

Lauda's mind was perpetually working on the latest developments necessary to keep his airline flying efficiently and economically. He introduced trans-Atlantic routes after striking a deal with Lufthansa to share the schedule. The so-called codeshare started with flights to Miami via Munich, followed by a second route to Los Angeles. Lauda, aware of the importance of image – particularly the influence of his own – made much of the distinctive red double 'L' applied to the fleet's tailfins. The introduction in 1993 of an Italian subsidiary, Lauda Air Italy, had the innermost 'L' painted green. Positioned either on the fuselage or engine cowling, a gold angel carried the company's motto 'Service is our success'. With the airline's reputation not only intact but also thriving following the successful outcome of Lauda's fight with Boeing over Flight 004, two more 767–300ERs were ordered.

That was typical Niki. He wasn't afraid to take on anybody if he felt he was doing the right thing for him and his airline. For a couple of years, they had a mini-hub in Salzburg, using small aeroplanes coming from Linz and Graz to Salzburg and continuing to Brussels, London and Paris. At that time, he was in big competition because he was associated with Lufthansa, and Austrian Airlines was still with Swissair in Zurich and Sabena in Belgium. They were competing against each other and we had seven flights a day from Salzburg to Frankfurt; three times with Tyrolean, which was associated with Austrian Airlines, and four with Niki for Lufthansa. It was crazy.

Further expansion saw the introduction of routes to the emerging Baltic states along with Bali, Ho Chi Minh City and Mexico City. Meanwhile, the busy charter operation saw, starting in March 1994, the addition of Boeing 737 variants, along with eleven Bombardier CRJ100s. The Amadeus Class received a number of prestigious awards, all of the foregoing prompting Lufthansa to increase its stake from 26.47 per cent to 39.71 per cent in 1994. Three years later, a further change in structure would mark the beginning of the end for Lauda Air as Lufthansa reduced its share to 20 per cent and sold 19.74 per cent to Austrian Airlines. Niki said:

Lufthansa had been the first part-owner of Lauda Air. Then Lufthansa asked me if Austrian Airlines could be my partner. I agreed to it because, on the economy side, this was the most sensible thing to do. But my biggest mistake was that I tried to make two different cultures work; you had the state culture of Austrian Airlines trying to work with Lauda Air's private culture. This never worked out because the Austrian Airlines shit destroyed Lauda Air. In the end, they had an option to buy my shares – this was part of the original deal – so I sold them and left.

The magazine *Airliner World* revealed that an audit of Lauda Air had exposed poor decision-making and financial controls, particularly with regard to foreign exchange risks. Austrian Airlines' stake was increased as Lauda Air was integrated and eventually phased out. Lauda said:

I was blocked from being in the business for three years. Then I started a new airline. It was called Niki because I couldn't use the name Lauda any more. Within seven years, we were blowing Austrian Airlines off again. We had four million passengers in six years. It was funny because Austrian Airlines always blamed me and everybody else, but then I had the second airline and, again, I was profitable and they still lost money.

Niki was covering all of Europe. It was like an easyJet concept – but better. Low cost with quality. We were working together with Air Berlin because I needed the critical mass. We had 138 aeroplanes together with 21 in Vienna; Airbus and Embraer. I continued to fly two or three times a week, but only the Airbus.

Later on, when Air Berlin collapsed in 2017, flyNiki (as it had by then become known) formed the basis of a new airline,

Laudamotion. This began operation in 2018 and soon became part of Ryanair. The 'motion' in Laudamotion was dropped, leaving the famous surname as a timely reminder of the company's spirited founder. Gerhard Kuntschik said:

> Niki wasn't happy with having to sell to Austrian Airlines because they were a state airline that had all the benefits that came with the association with politicians. So long as Austrian Airlines was a state airline, there would always be two CEOs; one was from the Conservative Party and the other from the Social Democrats. There was always politics – and Niki hated this. But the important thing was, he knew everyone on the business pages of the newspapers and he was close with all the society pages. And he remained close with everyone involved in Formula One.

In truth, Lauda never let go of his ties with the sport, the familiar red cap turning up in several different places as its owner continued to make his mark as the millennium rolled in.

CHAPTER 26

Ferrari Facilitator

In November 1991, Luca di Montezemolo was appointed President of Ferrari. Since the glory days with Lauda and Ferrari in the 1970s, Montezemolo's continuing rise through the Fiat empire had included managing the Cinzano drinks company and Itedi, an influential publishing group. Sport had also continued to play a part in the ascendancy as the suave aristocrat managed Azzurra, Italy's America's Cup challenger, and ran the organising committee for the 1990 World Cup.

Scuderia Ferrari, meanwhile, had gone through several phases that may have brought a couple of Constructors' Championships in the early 1980s but no drivers' title since Jody Scheckter in 1979. With further disarray likely following Alain Prost's acrimonious departure before the 1991 season had ended, the Fiat board looked to Montezemolo for a speedy and effective cure. An assessment of the mixed management line-up at Maranello led Montezemolo to make his own decision about a suitable appointment in the supervisory chain. John Hogan said:

Montezemolo rang me up out of the blue one afternoon. Marlboro were, by now, heavily into sponsorship of the Ferrari team as well as personal sponsorship arrangements with drivers. Luca said he had a friend in front of him that I knew very well; someone with funny trousers and a red cap. 'He wants three million dollars. What shall I do?' asked Luca, kinda tongue in cheek.

I'm not sure who approached who but just as much as Montezemolo may have seen the need to have Lauda on board, this was Niki's way of saying he wouldn't mind being a player in F1. His initial response was to talk to Ferrari because he was smart enough to realise he wasn't going to get anything if he approached McLaren. Niki once said to me he would like to run Ferrari, the team. I told him that he should know better than anyone what Ferrari is like, and they hadn't changed – and were unlikely to change. But he went ahead anyway – as you knew he would, having weighed everything up in his usual methodical way.

'There were several factors,' said Lauda. 'Ferrari didn't work; that was my opinion. When Montezemolo came in, there was an opportunity for me that wasn't there before. I had respect for him and he had respect for me.'

It was no coincidence, perhaps, that Lauda Air was expanding at the time. Following F1 around the globe could be a useful logistical asset for Lauda when investigating the airline market, particularly when he was not tied to a rigid schedule with the team. 'Luca said from the start it was an independent role,' said Lauda. 'It was very simple. I was running an airline. I was there purely to advise; to use my experience for Ferrari's benefit. I had to watch, to stand and observe and then ask: "Why do it that way? Why not try it this way?"'

Experience as a driver and former World Champion would play its part but Lauda was not one to overplay his distinguished past, particularly as the sport had moved on from a technical standpoint. He said:

I didn't see it as a disadvantage not to have driven the latest cars. What the driver has always needed to do most is to communicate to his engineers what the car is doing. The cars can change but that remains the same; it's the key. My job was to be the interpreter; someone who pulled together everything Luca and the technical people did; to make the team work efficiently.

You can't compare the old days with the new days. You couldn't even compare the previous year's car with the new one. There had been a complete change of management; a new way to go. It was a matter of getting the right people into the right jobs and going from there. The problem for these new people was they had inherited a car that was not theirs and they had to modify it and try and get it to work. That was not going to be easy and I had to try and explain that.

It was also important that Montezemolo and I both knew how everything worked with the pressure of Italian politics, the media and so on. Luca was not going to change his ways or his mind because of that; there would be no time wasted when discussing stupid things going forward and backwards. This was good for me to know because I'd seen the damage this can do. We needed to make sure that everyone understood this would take time; that you couldn't do it overnight.

Lauda's pragmatism and knowledge provided a useful buffer between the uninformed optimism of certain branches of the media and the reality of bringing an F1 team up to speed – particularly if their 1992 car had a dual floor concept that may have seemed sound in theory but, on the track, was proving to be unpredictable and almost impossible to drive. In simple terms, having twin floors, one above the other with a small gap between the two, would produce twice the amount of downforce. More downforce would mean the car being glued to the road and cornering faster. It was fundamentally flawed and destined never to work as envisaged. It didn't even come close.

'When Niki went to Ferrari, they were totally in the shit,' said Gerhard Kuntschik. 'There was a test session at Estoril and the car was six or seven seconds off the pace. It was a disaster. But I remember Niki spoke to the Italian media and told them this would take time, but everything would turn out fine. By playing this ambassador role, he took a lot of pressure away from Ferrari.'

Looking at the bigger picture and knowing that Montezemolo's tenure might be brief, given the pace of Fiat's management escalator, Lauda could see the need to find an effective figurehead who understood racing and was capable of the necessary commitment. At the same time, Luca had come to accept that his old friend Lauda would not be with Ferrari for the long haul. Their collective gaze fell upon Jean Todt. Apart from having been a top-flight rally co-driver, the Frenchman had led Peugeot to success in the World Rally Championship, followed by the Le Mans 24-Hour classic. Lauda recommended Todt, the irony being that this would ultimately lead to Niki's parting of the way with the famous team – and much to the regret of Gerhard Berger.

Having raced for Ferrari for three years before moving to McLaren to join Ayrton Senna in 1990, Berger had found himself being persuaded to return to Ferrari two years later as Lauda acted as a facilitator. Berger said:

It was Niki, together with Luca Montezemolo, who brought me back to Ferrari. Niki played a big part in convincing me to go back and help them bring the team forward again. My first meeting to negotiate was at Montezemolo's home in Bologna – and Niki was present.

Niki was with Ferrari as a consultant, but the circumstances became difficult for him once Jean Todt had arrived.

To be fair to Jean, he was working very hard to turn Ferrari around. But he didn't want to have Niki only being there part of the time and then telling Todt what to do. Jean doesn't work like that and he effectively pushed Niki to the side.

In some ways Jean was right because Ferrari had become his baby and he was working there day and night. In some ways he was wrong because all Niki wanted to do was to give good advice. But it became a personal thing between them. I was caught in the middle because I understood both and I liked them both, but it was becoming very difficult for me to handle this and not hurt one or the other.

Jean Alesi had been with Ferrari since 1991; a dream come true for a driver with Sicilian blood – but an increasing nightmare given the car he was presented with in 1992. He said:

To be at Ferrari was, for me, the best thing in my life at the time. I loved the passion I had from the fans and the mechanics and everyone. It was unbelievable. And then, when Niki came to Ferrari, that was fantastic.

The first time I really met him was at Silverstone for the British Grand Prix in July of 1992 – and we had no warning from anyone at Ferrari that he was coming. When Niki arrived, I was impressed because, of course, he was an F1 hero, but I hadn't had the luck to meet him in person until that moment. I understood immediately why he was there because the situation in Ferrari was ... dramatic. Montezemolo was working very hard to have a team around Gerhard and I to help us, which was good. The moment Niki and I spoke for the first time is imprinted on my mind. When he asked: 'How are you?' I said, 'I am okay – but we are having a hard time.' And he said, 'Yes, I understand. At Ferrari, the food is very good – but the car is shit.'

That was the very first thing he said to me! I was absolutely paralysed because I didn't want to laugh because I had respect for Ferrari – it had always been my favourite team; the best – but this was the first time in my life I heard someone saying something like that about Ferrari! And it was true, of course.

Niki was very useful because he didn't talk about the set-up of the car or stuff like that. He just looked at all the technical assets and he was looking for adding the maximum needed to build the new car. He knew that year's championship was already over for us and he wanted to put the best engineers and people in place for the following season. His great power was that he had been a driver and understood what we were thinking. But in the meantime, he was good for us because he was very sharp, very direct and sometimes he was upsetting people. But he knew – and Gerhard and I knew – this was necessary most of the time. That's why he was so effective.

In the beginning, Niki had the green light everywhere to get things done because he had such a good relationship with President Montezemolo, and this gave him the power he needed. But, unfortunately, when Jean Todt arrived [in July 1993], they had some friction and, from then on, he was not really able to do the job he would have liked. It was a pity because Jean Todt was the choice of Niki for very good reasons, but it didn't work between them like it would do later on between Toto [Wolff] and Niki at Mercedes.

Berger and Alesi would eventually make way for Eddie Irvine and Michael Schumacher, the latter chosen by Todt in 1996. It marked the start of a partnership with Schumacher that, eventually, would bring Ferrari consistent success under the control of Ross Brawn as technical director. All of this had been closely monitored in print by Pino Allievi and his newspaper *La Gazzetta dello Sport*. Allievi said:

I always had the feeling that Niki was never fully convinced to do this job with Ferrari. He had a lot of commitments with his airline. I think it was a case of Lauda trying to help his friend Montezemolo within the limit of the time that he had available. It was never a clear and straightforward collaboration. When Montezemolo said he wanted to have Lauda full time, Niki said he couldn't because he had other business. Niki didn't like Todt as a person, but he told Montezemolo that he had to take him for the future of Ferrari. That was typical of Niki and the straightforward way he worked. No politics – which, you have to say, was very unusual for someone working for Ferrari!

Lauda was recording his progress – or lack of it – at Ferrari through regular briefings with Herbert Völker for a column in the Austrian magazine *Auto Revue*. 'The Ferrari consultancy didn't work very well at all,' said Völker. 'The situation was bad and it wasn't helped by the usual Ferrari political troubles coming eventually. It got to the stage where Niki didn't really think he could change anything. That's when he made a compromise; just take the money and let it be.'

With the new regime under the firm control of Todt, a driven man who wanted autonomy when managing such a potentially volatile team, the time was right for Lauda to quit the Scuderia in 1997. Simply 'taking the money' would never be enough for a restless spirit like Lauda. Besides, his life had become even more hectic following Lauda Air's strategic co-operation with Lufthansa. But he was not yet done with Formula One.

CHAPTER 27

Cruel for Cats

When Jaguar Racing enlisted Niki Lauda to further their Formula One ambitions, they could hardly have been blind to the public relations benefits of bringing in a man with three drivers' world championships and some truly heroic exploits to his name. But both sides knew the work involved had to be far more demanding and influential than image enhancement. Cosmetic considerations have never meant much to Lauda, not even in the immediate aftermath of a Nürburgring crash that threatened to incinerate his head.

The unmistakable prose of award-winning sports writer Hugh McIlvanney, published in the *Sunday Times* on 25 February 2001, marked the introduction to a piece on Lauda's latest challenge: a resuscitation of Jaguar Racing that, in truth, had been needed since the moment of the F1 team's birth at the end of 1999.

Purchase of Stewart Grand Prix, a team partly funded by Ford from the outset, had bought the American motor manufacturer a ready-made F1 entry, but misguided use of the racing heritage associated with their Jaguar subsidiary in the 1950s had imbued Ford with a false sense of entitlement and ambition. The return of Jaguar ran with the tag line 'The Cat's Back', a motto that brought increasing derision as the season progressed. Talk of winning straight away had been made to look silly and ill informed by a mere 4 championship points and ninth place near the bottom of the teams' league table in 2000.

As McIllvanney noted, the necessary work was more than merely cosmetic. If anyone could wield an axe through the web of misplaced optimism and inflated self-esteem, it was Niki Lauda. In one sense, the timing was right, now that he was free of major decision-making with his airline. In another, it could not have been worse since much of his laser logic would fail to penetrate the corporate shield protecting the decision-makers at Ford and their institutionalised way of working.

Lauda had been hired by Wolfgang Reitzle, a German industrialist of Lauda's acquaintance who had been made head of Ford's Premier Automotive Group overseeing the luxury brands including, among others, Jaguar and Aston Martin. Reitzle had no background in racing and the choice of Lauda seemed a logical move – in isolation.

Lauda's immediate problem was the presence of Bobby Rahal, the American having signed a three-year contract as CEO of Jaguar Racing in September 2000. Rahal, winner of the Indianapolis 500 in 1986, was a respected force in North America – but not necessarily in Europe, or in the eyes of Lauda.

Rahal did, however, have useful contacts, among them Adrian Newey with whom Rahal had worked when racing in Indycar. Rahal was using his friendship with Newey to persuade the respected designer to switch from McLaren to Jaguar; a move that almost came off until, in a last-minute intervention, Ron Dennis talked Newey into staying. Lauda said:

Reitzle had asked me if I want to run the motor-racing side. My role was very simple. The group was headed by Reitzle and the motorsport arm of this group was the Premier Performance Division. That was my responsibility. Jaguar was the only brand they had that was currently active in motorsport and my role was to bring together Jaguar Racing, Cosworth and PI [engine and electronics providers respectively; both owned by Ford] to work together properly. Contrary to the rubbish that was written, I was not in charge of Jaguar Racing; that was Rahal's job, not mine.

Basically, I was not happy with what I saw and I decided, with Reitzle, that we needed to make a leaner structure. As I say, Rahal was in charge and thanks to him we had Newey signed – which would have been a very good thing for Jaguar – but then Newey changed his mind and went back to McLaren because Ron can be very persuasive.

In the meantime, Lauda had first-hand experience of Ford's methods as he watched the company deal with a tricky problem from an unexpected source:

For the first board meeting I attended, Jackie Stewart was there; Reitzle was there; Richard Parry-Jones (a vice president within the Ford Motor Company); everybody. I was just listening to everything going on, and Jackie suddenly said we had a problem. He said we would have to sack Tomas Scheckter [a test driver on the F1 team] because he was caught with a hooker in a Jaguar car in London. They started talking about it, saying we cannot allow this because it damages the name of Jaguar: blah, blah, blah.

I said: 'Excuse me; he's a racing driver. He's twenty-one years old. I would accept this if he's quick as a driver. I understand your Jaguar problem with image and so on, but I will talk to him, give him a written fine, whatever. I would certainly not sack him.' I could see the look on Reitzle's face. He was shocked by what I was saying. They decided to fire Scheckter.

Reitzle got me on one side afterwards and said: 'Listen, you're lucky. That was close. You can't say things like that.' I told him I had given my view as someone he had hired to help run the racing team. This was the way I saw it from a racing point of view. What did he expect me to do? That was not a good start in my relationship and I began to realise what it would be like with these people.

At a subsequent press conference, Lauda was confronted by the delicate question of Scheckter's misappropriation of his company car. Gerhard Kuntschik, representing *Salzburger Nachrichten*, was in the audience. 'It was an FIA press conference at the Austrian Grand Prix,' said Kuntschik. 'We were supposed to be talking about Jaguar's chances that weekend. One journalist asked why Scheckter had been fired. Niki paused for a minute, pushed his cap back, rubbed his forehead and then said: "Well, to be honest with you, he blew himself away." It was the best quote in any FIA press conference I ever attended!'

For Lauda, that was a subtle remark compared to some of his more trenchant views. Nav Sidhu, formerly with the media relations side of the Williams F1 team, had been employed by Jaguar to handle any unfortunate fallout. He said:

I had joined Jaguar at the beginning of 2001, not long after Lauda had been appointed. I had followed racing and Niki had been one of my heroes. The perception was he could be quite an intimidating man and I wasn't looking forward to meeting him; I wasn't sure I would be up to the task.

I saw him arrive in the car park in his Jaguar S type. There was an aura around him as he walked into the building, down the corridor and into his office. After a couple of minutes, he came out and shouted: 'Nav! Where's Nav?' He didn't know who Nav was, and he certainly didn't know that Nav was an Asian. But he put his hand out straightaway and said: 'Niki . . . Come in. So, what do you want?'

We sat down and it was clear that he didn't give a toss about public relations or the media, in a sense that, he'd been doing this for long enough and the media were his friends. I wasn't going to make the car go quicker – so what did I want? When I explained that I was there to work with him, to be in support, he said that was good and he hoped we could work well together.

I finished by saying the IT guys had asked if he wanted a laptop. 'Why would I need a laptop?' When I said for emails, he pulled out his mobile and said: 'This is all I need.' It was clear in our brief conversation that here was a man who was going to do things his way. He's not compliant; not a corporate animal; not subservient to suits. You either go with him or go against him.

I nicknamed him 'The Beautiful Nightmare', because he was a lovely man – but he was a nightmare. And I say that in an endearing way. There was no point in me trying to manage the media because the relationship Niki had with the more senior motorsport journalists went back a long time. Quite often, they would know about something before I either knew or was ready to issue the press release, thanks to Niki being indiscreet in his direct way.

Sidhu had been alert to the value of persuading Lauda to return to the cockpit for the first time in 16 years and acquaint himself with the latest breed of F1 car. This was arranged at the

Valencia circuit in January 2002 during a routine test session with Jaguar's drivers Eddie Irvine and Pedro de la Rosa. Lauda completed ten laps of the Spanish circuit. Despite spinning twice, he quickly got up to speed. He said:

I spun because I braked where Pedro had told me to brake! But I was pleased that I went into the corner at the same speed as him until I spun. I would much rather have spun than be accused by Pedro and Eddie of having tiptoed around the circuit. It was an interesting experience because I wanted to learn more about the electronic systems on the car so that I could relate to the drivers' experiences when they're describing technical and computer-related issues.

I didn't want to sound like some guy stuck in the past when talking about the latest car and making comparisons. But the big thing for me was that, when I was racing, everything was in the hands of the driver – the gear changing, managing engine revs, clutch control; all these things. Having driven that car, the driver's job seemed easier. Traction control, automatic gear changes and launch control was not how I felt drivers who are seen to be the best in the world should operate. That was my immediate opinion.

Lauda's personal way of working in many things was not always in line with what was expected, as Sidhu had discovered. Sidhu recalled:

During an earlier test in Spain, Niki was standing at the back of the garage, taking stock. He reaches into his jacket, pulls out a packet of fags and he's just about to light up when I say: 'Niki! You can't do that here!' He looks at me, takes off his cap, points to his forehead, and says: 'Are you mad? What d'you think's going to happen to me? I'm used to fire!' And then he lit up. That's when it's reaffirmed that you're dealing with someone who's very much his own man with a real sense of character, a real sense of humour. But, more importantly, he's extremely charming and personable. And quite self-deprecating at times. On the day he drove the F1 car at Valencia, I jokingly said to him: 'Niki, I've not seen you for a few days. Have you done any training for this drive?' 'Ja,' he said. 'I stopped smoking this morning.'

Lauda's unorthodox approach also affected the factory at Milton Keynes and how much of it he would make available to journalists he knew and trusted. One such was Michael Schmidt, the leading F1 writer from Germany who, more than twenty years before, had sat as a youngster in the Monza grandstand and been mesmerised by Lauda's comeback following his crash at the Nürburgring. He said:

In 2002, when the Jaguar team was in crisis and nothing worked, Niki wanted to show me that the basic elements were there; that it could be okay. During the weekend of the British Grand Prix, he said that I should come to the factory, because it was at Milton Keynes, which wasn't far from Silverstone. When I said I was flying home on the Monday, he said to change my flight. I said if I was to do a story, I would need to have a photographer, but I knew teams never allow photographers inside their factories because of all the secrecy – so that would be a problem for me; I had to have pictures. He said: 'You can take any picture you want. I am the boss. I will tell them.'

And at the time, they had this Ford [Cosworth] engine. Ford were really proud of it but they were paranoid about having photographers go near it at the racetracks – so there would be no chance at the factory. Again, Niki told me not to worry; it would not be a problem.

So, we were walking with the photographer through the factory and the people there couldn't believe that Niki was allowing this. And then it came to the engine department and the guy there, Nick Hayes, got really upset and tried to insist that they couldn't show all these secrets. Niki said: 'Don't tell me about secrets. There have been pictures of the engine in the pit lane and on the grid; okay, maybe not like this, but it doesn't matter.' I thought this poor guy, Nick, was going to be physically sick! We took pictures of the wonderful engine that he wanted to keep secret for ever. Niki was unbelievable. He was so pragmatic.

Lauda's seemingly insensitive attitude towards the hard-working engineers was the product of his belief that the Ford engine was hardly a pace-setter worth copying, the entire scenario underpinned by Formula One's obsession with secrecy. More damaging was a directness that had contributed to Rahal being fired in August 2001. In May 2002, Reitzle had moved on, just as Lauda began to feel he was making progress. Lauda said:

[Eddie] Irvine finished third at Monza [September 2002], so we had started to get going. Irvine was good as a driver. He was completely mad but, on his right day, he was absolutely quick and perfect. He didn't want to work much with the technicians, but I could handle him. I gave him bullshit when he was doing a bad job and he accepted it. He was a bright guy; I liked him.

Irvine had joined Jaguar at the beginning of 2000 after winning four Grands Prix during four seasons with Ferrari. His earnings with Jaguar were reputed to be £5 million per year and his more practical values had been shaped by the prodigious work ethic driven by Jean Todt at Ferrari. It would be hard for any team, never mind Jaguar, to match the Ferrari doctrine. Irvine was ideally positioned to spot the difference and the gradual seeping of Lauda's enthusiasm. He said:

Once you're a Ferrari driver, your world profile is a lot higher; you get in the papers a lot more. Ford needed a big brand driver and I guess I was the only one available at that time. It was a good contract for me; it was for three years and it was a lot of money back then. But Ford didn't invest in the infrastructure of the team. They thought painting a car green and putting Jaguar on the side was going to be good enough. They didn't even have a wind tunnel; one was promised but it didn't happen. The whole thing fell apart because Ford just didn't understand Formula One. It was a mess from the beginning. Niki did a sensible job, but I don't think he was focused enough at times. He made some good decisions and it was going forward. And then Ford got rid of him.

According to Lauda:

We had a very good race team in the end. The people in charge, put there by Ford, were not so good. To tell you the truth, some of the English guys were useless because they didn't know anything about racing. I sacked them in the end. But I had underestimated the British way of working together. These guys [Tony Purnell and David Pitchforth; two engineers who had worked through the Ford system] then convinced Richard Parry-Jones (responsible for the F1 effort in the absence of Reitzle) that they could run the team.

I was getting ready to go to a test session at Paul Ricard when I got a call from Parry-Jones on the Sunday evening.

'Come to England. I need to talk to you.' So, on the Monday, I went to his office and he says: 'Niki, I must tell you, you did a perfect job, you did nothing wrong. I admire you. But I want British people to run the team.' When I asked if Purnell was now in charge, Parry-Jones said he was. I said: 'Good luck. For me, it isn't logical. But, fine; I have to accept this. You're the boss.'

Then he had a piece of paper which he said I needed to sign. This had been prepared by the same Ford lawyer I had worked with for two years. Whenever there was more than one possible solution, he put the second one in a different colour to the first and then you – not him – would have to decide so that you would take the blame if it went wrong. As soon as I saw it was this idiot lawyer, I was laughing to myself. I said to Parry-Jones: 'D'you think I'm stupid enough to sign this now? Let me take this with me.'

I went to see Bernie [Ecclestone] and asked if he had a good lawyer. Bernie was laughing when he read the piece of paper and put me in touch with a lawyer. Then I wrote a letter back to Ford saying, first of all, I had done nothing wrong. My contract was three or four years – I can't remember – and Richard Parry-Jones had finished it early. Fine; I have to accept this. But pay me.

After much legal wrangling, and as Lauda would say 'going forward and backwards' over the next six months, he received the money due. But not before an experience summing up a footling bureaucracy that would contribute to the eventual demise of Jaguar Racing. Lauda recalled:

On the day when I started working there, the finance guy called me over. He said: 'I have to give you this book. This is the Ford Compliance Rules.' When I asked him what this meant, he said: 'It means that whatever you do, it has to comply with these rules.' When I asked for an example, he said: 'When, say, you are in a hotel and you take a water with soda from the minibar, you have to pay for it. But if you take one out without soda, you don't have to pay for it.'

I said: 'Are you serious?' When he said yes, I told him to keep the book. 'Niki,' he said, 'you must take this. You don't want to make any mistakes.' I told him I didn't want to know. I said I would pay for everything myself from my own money; there would not be any expenses from me. Very simple. So, when everything ended between me and Ford, suddenly there were people from Ford America, coming all the way over to Jaguar and asking to see my account. The guy at Jaguar Racing said there was no account for Niki Lauda. 'What do you mean? He must have expenses. Where's his account?' Can you imagine? They were looking for this bloody mineral water with soda!

Lauda would also experience Ford's short-sighted and inflexible methods at a level more significant than the settling of a minibar bill. Lauda said:

I knew that budget was always a problem. At one stage, I went to Richard Parry-Jones and said I had this guy, [Dietrich] Mateschitz, who wants to go into the American market. I said Mr Mateschitz owns Red Bull and he would be interested in sponsoring the team; maybe investing in half of it. Richard agreed to see him. Mateschitz flew to England and we showed Parry-Jones the proposal. Richard said he would have to think about it. Then he called me and said Ford could never accept having a drink like Red Bull on the car. These people would rather close down the team than have an energy drink on their car.

In an effort to cut its losses across the board by $1 billion, the Ford Motor Company decided in November 2004 to end its involvement with the beleaguered Jaguar Racing team and save an estimated $50 million per annum. Within days it was announced that Jaguar Racing would be sold to Red Bull. Five years later, the team from Milton Keynes would be poised to win the World Championship for four seasons in succession.

CHAPTER 28

Anniversary of the Ear

My crash, here at the Nürburgring? They ask me about it all the time – but that's okay. I was recording something just now for television with RTL and they showed the accident. I said: 'Why the fuck are you showing this again? Do I have to cry, or what?' I could see from the shocked look on their faces, they thought I was being serious!

Standing a ten-minute drive from the scene of the fiery accident that had almost consumed him, Lauda was in a whimsical mood. He went on to explain that each time the Grand Prix visited the New Nürburgring, someone would wish to remind him of events on the old circuit, the start of which could be seen winding its way into the nearby forest at the beginning of its tortuous journey through the Eifel mountains.

We were talking in 2011, 35 years after the infamous crash on the Nordschleife. If anything, the passage of time had further enhanced a story that had already reached a remarkable conclusion, not least because Lauda was there to recount it – or the bits he could remember. Never one to look back, Niki had nonetheless been persuaded ten years before to mark the 25th anniversary by visiting the accident site – but with a typically playful proviso. Apart from anything else, it would offer a break from his increasingly difficult travails with Jaguar Racing. The only unfortunate part was that Lauda had failed to communicate his intentions with Nav Sidhu, the team's press officer. Sidhu recalled:

It was a Thursday; press briefing day at the beginning of the 2001 German Grand Prix weekend. We had set up an interview slot with Niki for about 3 p.m. It was open door; journalists could come in, sit down with Niki, have a coffee and get race preview material. It was pouring with rain.

At about five to three, Niki came marching out of the motorhome, jacket zipped up, carrying a brolly. When I asked him where he was going, he'd clearly forgotten about the press call. I reminded him this was the German Grand Prix and people were coming to meet him. He said, sorry, but I'd have to cancel it because he had to go. Some of the press guys had already arrived and they were looking at me, as if to say: 'What's going on?' I wasn't sure whether to stay put or run after him.

I looked down the paddock and saw Niki disappearing through the turnstile and heading for the car park with Bernard Ecclestone and Karl-Heinz Zimmermann. This was clearly something that had been planned. I had no idea what was happening but, from the way they were behaving, I could only think they were up to no good!

Karl-Heinz Zimmermann had a reputation for mischief-making. This had been evident, almost from the moment of his first connection with Formula One in 1977 through a new Grand Prix team owned by Austrian-born Canadian Walter Wolf. Zimmermann said:

Walter had invited members of his team – Peter Warr, Harvey Postlethwaite, Jody Scheckter – to my brother's hotel in Lech [an Austrian ski-resort]. Then, all of a sudden, Niki turned up with his best mate Bertl Wimmer – I was good friends with Bertl before that. We had really funny times in those days. Niki enjoyed it because he could see the difference between living in Vienna and coming to Lech to ski during the day and then party at night!

Zimmermann used these contacts to establish himself as a caterer for various F1 teams, including McLaren-Mercedes. On his visits to the races, Lauda would gravitate to the hospitality unit run by Karl-Heinz on behalf of Lauda's former team. Zimmermann said:

Niki enjoyed being with us. When his family – Marlene, Lukas and Mathias – came to a race with him, they could always join us. I knew them very well by this time because the family would often come to Lech for skiing. Niki would also use our hospitality area if he was doing an interview – but usually only with journalists he knew. If you wanted an interview, he would say: 'I have breakfast tomorrow at 7.30; come and see me.' They could sit next to him while he was eating his eggs and, if he trusted the journalist, then you could see from the way the conversation went that it was a good interview; that Niki was telling it like it is! The journalists liked it because, to see a driver nowadays, you have to ask three weeks in advance and they tell you from 11.42 to 11.44. 'You have two minutes – and don't talk about this or that.' It wasn't like that with Niki.

Zimmermann got to know many of Lauda's personal traits, one of which was being careful with his money:

I think 'careful with his money' is being far too polite! He was tight! And not just with us, but also with his boys. I loved his sons; Lukas and Mathias are really good guys. On one occasion, he came to Barcelona with his boys and I said to Niki: 'Listen, because you are so tight with your sons, you're going to have to pay when you come into my motorhome for food and everything.' This was at the beginning of the weekend, on the Friday. I said: 'Seeing as it's you, Niki, I'll make a special price; a cheap price; a hundred euros.' He gave me a hundred euros – and I slipped it to Mathias when they left and said this was for him and his brother.

Next day, Mathias said to me: 'Listen, you won't believe this. He must have seen what you did with the hundred euros because, on the way back to Barcelona, he asked if I got the money from you. When I said I had, he asked me to give it back to him.'

As soon as I heard this, I thought: 'You wait, you bastard. You'll pay for this.' When he arrived at the next race, I made him pay a hundred euros straight away – even if he was only going to have a coffee! He wasn't happy about this and went away, saying he wasn't going to come back. But then he found he had nowhere else to go! All of a sudden, he came back again.

I told the girls working for me to make sure he paid a hundred euros. They would go over to him: 'Good morning, Niki. What would you like?' 'I'll have an espresso.' 'That's a hundred euros, please.' He paid. After that, it became normal. When he arrived at the start of a weekend, he would already have the money in his hand, put it on the table, sit down and have a coffee or breakfast or whatever. He paid a hundred euros every weekend. I kept the money and, at some stage, I would manage to give it to the boys. Everybody who came in knew about this hundred euro payment. It became a big joke with everyone; we had a lot of laughs together.

Although Zimmermann had arrived in F1 a few years after Lauda's accident at Bergwerk, he was aware of both its significance in his friend's life and the landmark date when they returned to the Nürburgring in 2001. Zimmermann said:

I was joking with Niki on that weekend and said if we went out to Bergwerk, we should take a good look and maybe find his ear! When Niki said this was not a bad idea, I said I would arrange something.

While shopping for supplies in Adenau, I went to the butcher and asked if I could have two pig ears. The guy said: 'What do you need pig ears for?' I said: 'Do you have some or not?' He said: 'Yeah, but tell me why you need them.' I replied that we were having a barbecue and some people liked pig ears. The guy wasn't a hundred per cent sure and he kept asking me why I wanted them but, when I threatened to take our business somewhere else, he said he would have them ready for the Saturday morning.

I then said to Niki that, for sure, there would be television people and journalists there. I explained that I was going to put an ear in the grass and show him where. Then, when he was explaining how the accident happened, how he had been badly burned and lost his right ear, all of a sudden he would find one in the grass! Niki was very happy to do this.

When Bernie, Niki and myself drove to Bergwerk on the Thursday afternoon, the RTL TV crew and various people were already there. And also Arturo Merzario, one of the drivers who had pulled Niki out of the burning Ferrari. Niki began to explain to the TV cameras that this is the corner where I came round and something broke on the car. I hit the wall over there and this is where the car stopped and Arturo pulled me out. Then he went off to the side, bent down and said: 'Bloody Hell! Look what I found!' He picked up the pig's ear and said:

'That's my ear!' and held it on the right-hand side of his head. Everybody was laughing. 'Bloody Lauda!' they said. 'Only he could do something like this with a pig's ear!'

But then it started. A lot of people – Germans who don't have a sense of humour – saw this on television, called in and said it was revolting; we were taking the piss out of this poor guy with no ear. But Niki loved it; he was always up for that sort of thing. The humour could not be black enough for him. He couldn't have given a damn about whether this was politically correct or not. We had the schnapps and beers I had taken to Bergwerk and toasted twenty-five years of his survival. It was bloody good fun.

Lauda recalled:

That was such a crazy thing. Typical of Karl-Heinz to do something like this. But the really funny part was, when we were out there, six Germans happened to be cycling by and they saw me. 'Oh, Mr Lauda!' they said. 'What are you doing here?' When Karl-Heinz came into the middle of this group and said 'We're looking for his ear!' these people were so upset, they nearly hit him! 'You cannot do this to Mr Lauda!' they said. Then Karl-Heinz produced the pig's ear and they suddenly understood it was a joke.

Nav Sidhu was hard-pressed to see the funny side of coping with a room full of journalists and having no star attraction to answer their questions:

After a while Niki, Bernie and Karl-Heinz came back laughing and giggling; all in good spirits. Niki saw me standing there and said sorry he had caused a problem with the press conference but this was something that had to be done. At which point, Karl-Heinz explained what had been going on, the story of the ear and so on – and they all start giggling again.

I got to meet Karl-Heinz again at the next race, which was the French Grand Prix at Magny-Cours. Normally, the motorhomes were all in a line and, being Jaguar at the bottom end of the row, we would be nowhere near Bernie and Karl-Heinz's hospitality area, which was always alongside Bernie's bus. At Magny-Cours, however, the paddock was square-shaped and we happened to be across from Karl-Heinz's area. This was a very forbidding place for most people. The awning was always zipped up on all sides; you could never see what was going on in there because, if anyone went in and out, they always made sure the entrance was kept zipped shut. It was all very secret.

The French Grand Prix was a relatively quiet race from a sponsorship and media point of view. By four or five o'clock, you could be done. I was sat in the motorhome, working away, when Niki walked past and asked if I needed any more from him. When I said we were done, he said: 'Good; come with me. We go to Karl-Heinz and we have a drink.' I didn't know what to make of that because I had no idea what went on in that hospitality area; it looked like the Tardis.

Once inside, I was a bit intimidated by the company sitting there; Bernie Ecclestone and [drivers] Michael Schumacher [Ferrari], Ralf Schumacher [Williams], Juan Pablo Montoya [Williams] and a couple of other paddock faces. They've all got big fat cigars and some schnapps. No one's drunk; it's just a traditional get-together.

Niki introduced me – and it was nice because he never introduced me as his PR guy or press officer or whatever; it was always 'This is Nav.' I wasn't asked if I would like a schnapps; that's not the way it worked with Karl-Heinz. It felt like some sort of initiation. He put one in front of me and said: 'Drink! It's good!' They were talking in German and I chatted with Montoya. After a while, I didn't think I could sit there and drink any more schnapps, so I said thanks very much; I had to get back to work.

Just as I was leaving, there was a mighty 'Boom!' It was like three double-barrel shotguns going off at once. Really deafening. Apparently, this was one of Karl-Heinz's traditions, started way back in his Lotus days with Peter Warr. He had a small cannon and he would fire the thing out the back of his motorhome without warning. I mean, it was terrifying, particularly if you weren't expecting it. I was really quite shaken. I said to Niki: 'What the fuck was that all about?' He said: 'What do you mean? There's nothing else to bang here this weekend!'

Lauda's impish sense of humour had become more pronounced in direct proportion to the increasing absence of pressure at the racetrack. A profound knowledge of the sport – and a unique and direct way of expressing it – made him popular among the members of the media. Journalists who did not know him well frequently found difficulty in deciding whether or not a contentious statement boarding on the outrageous was driven by fact or a sharp sense of humour; often it was an engaging mix of both. A common theme was blistering common sense based on unparalleled experience. Despite Lauda's seemingly laid-back approach, the gradual demise of Lauda Air in its various final guises made it seem only a matter of time before someone in F1 snapped up his services again.

CHAPTER 29

Mercedes Marriage

It's very simple. I made a deal to be chairman – but my contract makes clear that Mercedes did not want me to be the sort of chairman who has a board meeting three times a year. Certain points in my contract make clear the areas where I need to be informed, where I can get straight in and do things. In other words, I'm a chairman who is also part of the team.

Niki Lauda's characteristically uncomplicated description of his responsibility within the Mercedes–AMG Petronas F1 team summed up a role that would turn out to be as successful and productive as his managerial associations with Ferrari and Jaguar had largely been unrewarding. When he signed a contract to be non-executive director in September 2012, however, the future of the team looked far from rosy – which was why Lauda had been approached in the first place by the board of Daimler AG, the parent company of Mercedes.

Fifty-five years after withdrawing from motor racing fol-lowing the death of more than eighty people during the 1955

Le Mans 24-Hours, Mercedes had returned to F1 with its own team – as opposed to simply supplying engines to McLaren and others. The purchase of 75.1 per cent of Brawn GP, the 2009 World Champions, had given Mercedes a ready-made entry for their so-called Silver Arrows, the story taking on additional interest as Michael Schumacher also chose to return after a three-year sabbatical.

As he explained in an interview with Nigel Roebuck for *Motor Sport*, Lauda arrived at the former headquarters of the Brawn team in Brackley, Northamptonshire, to find he was dealing with Ross Brawn and Nick Fry, directors of Brawn's eponymous team who remained a part of the new set-up under Mercedes. Lauda said:

> When I came to Brackley for the first time in my new position, Ross Brawn and Nick Fry were there. I said good morning, asked them questions about things I had no idea about, and then Fry asked me how often I was intending to come to England. I said: 'Why do you ask?' And it turned out that Norbert Haug [formerly the long-time competitions director of Mercedes] was only at the factory three times a year. I said: 'Well, I can tell you that I will come as long as it takes to be competitive.'

Even allowing time for a new team to find its feet, the first three years had been disappointing. The Daimler board had become restless, particularly in the light of an increasingly difficult relationship with Bernie Ecclestone and F1's majority shareholders, CVC Capital Partners. With financial terms at stake, Daimler had asked Lauda to use his relationship with Ecclestone to help broker a more favourable deal. That done, Lauda's influence was about to have an even more significant effect. He said:

I attended my first board meeting as a guest in 2012. When I asked who was going to drive in 2013, Haug seemed to think it was a stupid question and replied 'Schumacher and [Nico] Rosberg.' I replied, 'Yes, but what if Michael wants to retire?' I was assured he wouldn't, but he didn't have to let the team know until October – by which time all the main drives would be settled. I didn't think it was a good idea to wait and I made my feelings known. I got permission to talk to Lewis [Hamilton] because I knew he was the only big name that might be free. I knew he still had to commit to McLaren [after six seasons with the British-based team and winning the title in 2008].

In his interview with *Motor Sport*, Lauda explained what happened next: 'After the race in Singapore I went to see Lewis, and then the whole thing started. The first time was at two o'clock in the morning in his hotel room – I have to say I'd never before been with a man in a hotel room at two in the morning – and I didn't know him at all. From the beginning, though, we seemed to have a good understanding of each other, and this was the start of trying to convince him to come to Mercedes.'

'I got this call from Niki,' said Hamilton. 'We'd never really spoken before and he was on the phone saying, "You should come to Mercedes. This is where you need to be." That was the start of it. The first thing he said when we sat down together was: "Listen, you're a racer, just like me." From then on, our relationship just got better and better. I talked to other people about Mercedes, but Niki was the one who brought it across the line.'

Lauda said:

I made it very simple for Lewis. I told him: 'If you stay for ever with McLaren, that's very nice – but where's the challenge in your life? I changed from one team to another – people do that, and don't get bored. It's very simple.' He understood that, but still it was difficult to explain to him why he should leave McLaren, a winning team, and drive for us.

Lewis said to me: 'Would you change?' I said, 'No – honestly, no. But if we get things together, if it works out . . .' I said to him, 'If you could be World Champion in a Mercedes – a works team – can you imagine what this would do for your image?' It's like me winning with Ferrari. Why am I known? Because I burned my ear off, and drove Ferraris, and won championships, right?

I said: 'I think that Ross [Brawn] has put the right people in the right places.' There had been some encouraging changes in the technical group, which I explained to him. I made some promises to him at a time when I didn't know if they were going to happen. At the time, McLaren was trying like you do not believe to persuade him to stay.

A year later, Jonathan McEvoy, writing in the *Daily Mail*, would reveal that Dennis had flown to Stuttgart to meet Dieter Zetsche, chairman of Daimler AG. 'Dennis is understood to have made a series of claims which can only have shown Hamilton in an unflattering light,' wrote McEvoy. 'Some have interpreted that as an attempt to dissuade Zetsche from signing the Briton.' McEvoy went on to say that Dennis had relayed a story, previously reported in the *Sun* newspaper, about Hamilton's alleged energetic partying in London.

Writing in his book covering the Brawn GP era, Nick Fry claimed Dennis's clumsy efforts to keep Hamilton on board actually had the reverse effect. Following the visit by the McLaren boss, Zetsche had called Brawn, who in turn spoke to Fry and prompted a phone call to Simon Fuller, Hamilton's agent at the time. If anything, Dennis's reported behaviour hardened Hamilton's resolve to leave McLaren although, according to Fry, Lauda then came close to derailing the entire negotiation at the eleventh hour thanks to jumping the gun during one particularly blunt communication with Fuller. Lauda took it upon himself to tell Fuller the deal was done when, in fact, important loose ends were in need of tying up. Lauda may have been cutting to the chase but he had stomped all over the agent's toes in the process. Fry wrote that a furious Fuller called from Los Angeles to say the deal was off thanks to the actions of a former World Champion whom Fuller summed up with a four-letter word. Sensitivities were eventually soothed and the negotiation completed.

In the meantime, Eddie Jordan blew the story wide open in his role as pundit for Channel 4's F1 TV coverage in Britain. Many people thought the garrulous Irishman was taking a wild punt – but he was on the money. Jordan said:

I got a lot of stick for that. People just didn't believe it, saying it was a load of Irish baloney from Jordan. But, as we now know, it was perfectly true. The reason I knew about it was because Niki had made contact with Lewis, who had been thinking about the move but couldn't decide. Niki asked me to speak to Lewis and reassure him that going to Mercedes would make a lot of sense because they were a hundred per cent professional and would give him the full support and loyalty he would appreciate. Niki and Lewis did get together but, since I knew all about it, I thought I would break the story before anything was officially announced. People got very upset – but not Niki; he couldn't give a shit about that! Mercedes had Lewis and that's all that mattered.

'Lewis won at Budapest in our first year together [2013],' said Lauda. 'He had some pole positions and the team moved from fifth to second in the Constructors' Championship. That was the start of it.'

In January 2013, Toto Wolff had arrived as executive director of the Mercedes F1 team; too late to be involved in the Hamilton negotiation, but scarcely surprised at the outcome, particularly knowing that Lauda had been involved. According to Wolff:

> It was a very good strategy between Dieter Zetsche, who committed the budgets, Ross Brawn, who brought credibility, and Niki's persistence in not giving up trying to get Lewis. It wasn't very clear if Michael would continue and the team wasn't very decisive in what to do next. Using his driver's intuition when working out what Michael might do, Niki, like always, went full steam ahead and dealt with Dieter, hired Lewis and got the deal across the line, helped by Ross doing a really good job in making sure Lewis believed in the team.
>
> Niki's presence was very important at the time when Lewis was finding his way and building up relationships within the team. He was not a person who trusted easily. But the one thing he could trust straightaway was Niki being a three-time World Champion; he was one of his kind. Lewis knew that Niki had been through what Lewis was going through; that relationship was very important at the beginning of our journey.

Wolff also noted that, initially, Lauda had not visited the team's headquarters very often. 'I see everybody at the races anyway, so there's plenty of time to discuss things, if necessary,' explained Lauda. 'And before the season started, I was at the tests and I went to England – backwards and forwards. I thought I should understand more technical things – because of my own experience I like to know how these modern cars work, and what the drivers are doing compared with what I was doing in the past.'

Lauda refuted the suggestion in the media that he had a particular responsibility for the drivers. He said:

Except for being chairman of the board, I have no responsibility – but, if Toto or Paddy [Lowe, technical director] asks me, I have knowledge of certain things, and then I give them my input. I only do something when we three all agree that maybe now I should speak to Nico and Lewis.

To give you a simple example; when the drivers are discussing good or bad news, then Toto is there to remind them that they're driving for Mercedes, okay? This is a company with 300,000 people, and he is very strict on this: 'Hey guys, watch it – we are representing Mercedes.' Sometimes, though, the drivers – how do I say this politely? – don't understand this nice way of talking to them, and in that situation I think I have an advantage because, when I talk to Lewis or Nico, we are speaking on the same level. Okay, they're five generations or whatever ahead of me, but I was a driver, too, and I can be very straightforward with them because I know the words, I know what their brains are fighting about. Toto is happy to leave this to me.

Wolff may have been an Austrian but his awareness of Lauda went beyond a predictable sporting appreciation. He said:

Niki was a second cousin to my first wife. When I met my girlfriend back in 1996/1997, she said we were going to have dinner with Niki and his girlfriend at the time. Having followed racing and begun competing myself, I obviously knew all about Niki Lauda; how could you not as an Austrian? We went to the cinema, the four of us, and he said to me: 'I've already got the tickets. You owe me fifty schillings.' He was forty-seven and I was twenty-four. After that, we went to an Italian restaurant and it was awkward because he wasn't particularly interested in a lot of conversation.

But when he did talk, he had the ability to find interesting topics; he didn't like to make small talk. At the time, I was building a business in Poland and commuting regularly between Vienna and Warsaw. So, Niki was very interested in finding out whether the planes were full, which airline did I use, what the service was like, was the morning flight more full than the evening flight – and so on.

Because Vienna is a small community, our paths would cross at dinners, parties and functions; our relationship was always very friendly, but far away from being close. In 2000, when my motorsport was becoming more of a business rather than a hobby, I told him I wanted to beat the record for GT cars on the Nürburgring Nordschleife – 'Oh, and by the way, Niki, I'm going to beat your outright record [six minutes 58.6 seconds] as well!' He said: 'You're such an idiot; why would you want to do this? It's much too dangerous and no one cares if you beat an old bloody record.'

I went for it, did a 7.01 on a warm-up lap and I thought: 'I'm going to do this one lap, even though I know there's something not quite right with the car.' Going into the Fuchsröhre, I had a puncture at 268 kph; impact at the guard-rail was 27G. While I was in the ambulance going to Adenau, I had pain in my legs and wasn't sure if I was paralysed. Then they flew me to the neurology department in Frankfurt. They didn't know what was going on and they flew at low altitude to avoid creating pressure on my brain. I broke some vertebrae, damaged my nerves for taste and smell and had heavy concussion. I couldn't sleep flat for months; I had to sit.

I thought: 'Niki's right. Who cares? I hurt myself for some random mid-life crisis record.' I called him a few days later and told him what had happened. He said: 'I told you! You are such a stupid wanker. Why did you do this? That record is a hundred years old!'

Contact between the two increased in 2009 when Wolff, as an investor in the Williams F1 team, began to attend races as a non-executive director. Wolff said:

We flew together and Niki said if I wanted to keep flying with him, I would have to pay fifty per cent! Then I was asked by someone on the Mercedes board for my opinion on why their team was not competitive. I did this and they made me an offer to become a shareholder and run the team.

They said I needed to tell Niki because, as non-executive chairman, he needed to know this and it would be better coming from me. In Brazil, at the end of 2012, I said I had to talk to him and suggested we go out to dinner. He said: 'No, no. Let's sit down now. What is it?' When I insisted it would be better to talk over dinner, he said: 'Tell me! What is it?' I told him I was buying 40 per cent of the Mercedes team and I thought I was going to become chief executive officer. He said: 'What! Why didn't they tell me?' I said I was the envoy sent to tell him. I really wanted to do this and I thought we should be doing this together. He said he wanted to think about it for twenty-four hours.

Two hours later, he shows up in Williams hospitality and asks if I have a minute to talk. He says: 'I'm up for it. Let's do it together. I think we can achieve our targets quicker together than me alone – but there's one condition. I think you are a clever business person. I'm taking 10 per cent of your deal [with Mercedes].' And off he went.

Wolff did not necessarily criticise Lauda for being frugal to the point of parsimony:

I think he didn't want to be abused. He always had the feeling that he worked hard for everything he had achieved and he worked hard to be a personality; a brand. He didn't like it if he felt you were taking advantage. But in a private environment, he was generous.

When we negotiated the Mercedes deal, we had a massive legal bill and I told him, since he was taking his 10 per cent, he owed me 25 per cent of this legal bill. 'No, no,' he said. 'That's not agreed. I have another idea. You pay the whole legal bill and you can fly with me for ever to the races. I'm not taking anyone else; just you.' We agreed on that.

Mutual agreement was not always forthcoming during the first six months as Wolff and Lauda worked together. Wolff said:

It was very difficult at first because we had both been running our own businesses and making our own decisions. There had never been anybody else saying 'This is what you need to do.' Suddenly, Daimler had thrown us in the project together. Niki didn't really understand that he was a non-executive chairman; he felt more of an executive chairman. We would sometimes pull in different directions. It was almost like a fight over who was the most competent to make decisions.

It came to a head in May 2013 over a tyre test session in Barcelona. Ross had an idea that we could test tyres with the current car because, in his view, the regulations allowed it. I said he would need to get permission from Charlie [Whiting; F1's race director and general 'go to' person for decisions on technical matters]. I was sitting next to Ross when he did this and Charlie said we could do it. So, we went testing immediately after the Spanish Grand Prix – and got protested by Red Bull and Ferrari and we then got called to an International Tribunal.

Niki said: 'What a mess! I'm going to sort this out.' He went to see Bernie, who told Niki that if Ross, as team principal, wrote a letter saying he was in breach of the regulations and apologised, then, in Bernie's words, that would get us off the hook. Ross and I said we were not going to do that because we had a verbal okay from Charlie. We were not prepared to admit to any breach. We would go to court because we believed we were in the right. Niki completely disagreed. He said we had to admit fault. I was upset about it because I thought Niki was interfering in what was Ross's and my business. It ended up in a big conflict between Niki and I.

We were called before the Daimler board. On the day, we both arrived from different directions; me from Oxford, Niki from Vienna. Before we went to see the board, he said we had to talk. He said he thought we could still achieve our targets together – but we had to stop this disagreement. I said okay. There were three board members in the room. One said that Niki was not an executive chairman and he shouldn't get involved in the business. Another board member asked us about the detail of the tyre test and the protest – by which time we had won the court case when it was agreed we had not been in the wrong.

Then Niki, in his usual pragmatic way, said: 'It all started between Toto and me. We've discussed it and, from now on, we're going to do everything together. Right?' As he said this, he looked straight at me – and put his hand out. I had to make the decision about whether to let him down and say it was not sorted and I wanted to clarify it; or whether I would give it a try. I grabbed his hand. And that was to be the proper beginning of a wonderful adventure together.

CHAPTER 30

Loose Cannon in a Red Cap

Bradley Lord, as communications director for the Mercedes-AMG Petronas F1 team said: 'We had our moments with Niki. He was a loose cannon; a semi-guided missile. There were certain things that we, as a team, wanted to say in public – but couldn't. Niki would go ahead and say them.'

Lord had his work cut out making good any damage caused by the political fallout from Lauda's forthright comments. These would frequently be broadcast on air as Lauda fulfilled his role as pundit for RTL. Florian König was presenter of the German TV channel's live F1 broadcasts. König said:

When we met for the first time in 1997, I was very young and fresh to Formula One. I was quite nervous about meeting this icon of the sport, but it only took some minutes before he said to me: 'Listen, Florian; this is how we've got to do this. You ask the questions and I give the answers. I don't give a shit about what you ask but you don't interfere with my business. I'm the expert; I'm the pundit; please leave that to me.' And that's how we did it for more than twenty years. Sometimes I was tempted to show that I also knew something about F1, but he always gave me a hard time for a couple of minutes – and that would be that!

He was a fantastic person to work with – and not just because of his knowledge and presence as the former World Champion in the famous red cap. Many people are concerned about what they can say when interviewed. They act like diplomats. Niki was totally different right from the start. It was a dream come true for us – and for me especially – because you could ask him any question and get an honest answer. He had his opinions. They were wrong sometimes, but he never had any doubt about whether or not he should say them. He was very outspoken and that, of course, is a dream for a broadcaster because nowadays people are very politically correct and it's difficult to really get to know the essence of that person. But not with Niki.

Lauda, given his contacts and experience gained during fifteen years in F1, could literally open doors for König and the RTL team. König said:

If I wanted to know something from Bernie [Ecclestone], Niki would say 'Come on, let's go!' and take me straight in. It was the same with [Luca] Montezemolo at Ferrari; with the Mercedes guys; with everybody in F1. He could also help me a lot with things that were going on in the paddock. There's a lot of bullshit talked and he would say: 'Don't pay any attention to what that guy is saying. It's not correct. It's not important.' He was my compass. We had no secrets. There was no PR assistance; no manager; nothing. I had his mobile and I could call him whenever I wanted to know something. He always took the calls. It was never a problem.

As an F1 reporter, König was not alone in being grateful for Lauda's grasp of the sport's current affairs. Unlike some retired champions, Niki remained hands-on thanks to his role with Mercedes. König said:

There was a time when people thought his best days were over because, after he retired, he wasn't following F1 as closely as he had done before. But I was so happy for him that he then had those years with Mercedes. Everybody could see that he and Toto Wolff had built a team that was so dominant.

Of course, when he started with Mercedes, we recognised his position and said: 'Okay, Niki, do whatever you want with Mercedes but, when you're with us, with RTL, if you say the word "us", it means RTL.' But, being Niki, when he said 'us' it was clear he meant Mercedes. As a result, some people said he was no longer impartial. But the thing about Niki was that he wasn't shy of criticising Mercedes when he felt it was deserved. There was no holding back. There were times when the Mercedes board members came to him and said: 'You can't do that!' And he would reply: 'I am Niki Lauda; I have to do that; I will always do that.' So, for me, it was not a problem – any more than it seemed to be a problem for him.

It was definitely not a problem for König and RTL when Lauda would be indiscreet about strategies the Mercedes team wished to keep close to their collective chest on race day. According to König:

When I arrived on Sunday morning and we had a coffee, Niki would say: 'I was in the strategy meeting. We are going to stop on lap 18 and then for the second stop, lap 42.' He would say it without hesitation. During the race, when he and I were off air, he would be listening to the Mercedes radio. He would suddenly say: 'Lewis is coming in. They're pitting him two laps early.' I'd take my walkie-talkie and tell our producer: 'Don't go to the commercial break. Tell the guys Hamilton is coming in early.' I really don't know what Mercedes thought of this!

Wolff may have been busy running his race but, once it was over and his team radio headset had been removed, he would soon receive word of his non-executive chairman's latest supposedly confidential disclosure. Wolff said:

Niki never saw these things as we did; he just wasn't aware. He had no filter. He would go from an internal meeting and, sometimes, go on air soon after and tell the story about what we had been discussing. Bradley and I would say: 'Niki! You *can't* say that!' He would say: 'I know, I know ... but it's not very critical.' 'It is, Niki – and you just can't say that!'

In the later years, however, that happened much less. Niki had such an ability to learn, and to improve. There was a situation when I was flying into Nagoya with him for the Japanese Grand Prix. We were going through a thunderstorm and the plane was shaking in all directions. We're sitting just beyond the cockpit. Suddenly Niki heard a noise, got up, went into the cockpit and gave the two pilots a mega bollocking. He came back and sat down. 'Idiots,' he said. 'They pumped fuel from left to right; on the approach you don't need to do this. If you are in bad weather, first you fly the aeroplane, then you do the rest.'

When I asked him if going into the cockpit while the pilots were wrestling with the weather and the aircraft was the right thing to do, he said: 'Well, what else would you do?' I said I would write it down and, once we had landed, debrief the pilots and tell them they shouldn't have balanced the fuel out while approaching in the bad weather. 'No,' he said, 'that doesn't function for me. I need to offload it immediately.'

Six months later, we were flying somewhere and I could see him taking out a little notepad with a little pen – so he must have organised it – and writing stuff down. When I asked what he was doing, he said: 'Writing down what I want to tell the pilots later.' I said: 'You are unbelievable! At sixty-eight or sixty-nine years old, you're still able to learn.' He agreed!

Lauda may have been in his late sixties but, as Florian König discovered, Niki treated his advancing years as an irrelevance. König said:

On a personal, private level he was just a very, very nice guy. You could have so much fun with him; you could see the little boy in him still. He was always looking for somebody to play jokes on. When, for example, Nelson [Piquet] and Niki were watching a race together, it was hilarious; we should have broadcast that, not the race!

But there was also the serious side when necessary. You could be sitting with him watching practice and he would receive a call from the Chancellor of Austria. Or maybe the CEO of Embraer [Brazilian aerospace company]. Or he might be selling the shares of some company or dealing with another and arranging to fly back and forth.

Every time we met for the first time, after saying hello, he would always ask the same question: 'When can I go?' That was not meant to be rude; it was just him trying to be as effective as possible. He didn't want to waste any time. For example, if the broadcast ended at 16.20, he could call the captain [of his private aircraft], have a slot at 16.45, be in Vienna at 18.00 and have his next meeting at 18.30 or whatever. He was like that all the time; his batteries never seemed to run down. He had amazing energy. I often wondered how he could do that because I like to have my days off when I can be lazy; do nothing. But that was not how he worked; Niki never had time off. His mind was always thinking and he would never give up easily. He was incredibly determined.

Wolff would have first-hand experience of Lauda's stubborn resolve in the air as well as on the ground:

The safest I have ever felt when flying was with Niki. He did everything absolutely by the book. His attention to detail was unbelievable. We had a situation when we were flying back to Europe from the race in Shanghai. So, it was the usual story after a race weekend; it's early evening and everyone is tired. Niki would always have two pilots; he would take off and land, and they would fly the rest of the way. But if he was tired, he would say so and let them do the work; he was always conscious of his own state of mind.

We had a Global Express [a large business jet made by Bombardier] and, when we arrived, the pilots said it would not start up; there was a bug in the electronics. Niki went into the cockpit and asked them to explain what they had done. Then they tried again, but nothing happened. He went through the handbook and said: 'Okay. Different start-up procedure. Do this, do this, do this.' It didn't start up. By this stage, I was preparing to jump on a commercial flight.

Then Niki said to switch everything off, take the auxiliary power off, shut the whole plane down; lights in the cabin, everything off. Then he came into the cabin and said we need to wait until the last piece of electronics had shut down and gone to sleep. After ten minutes, he stood up, had the umbilical chord [auxiliary power] reconnected, the plane became alive again – and it started up. We were in the most complicated and sophisticated long-range aeroplane you can have, and no one was capable of starting it up. It took Niki an hour, but he wouldn't give up.

Lauda would frequently fly into Oxford and travel the 20 miles from Kidlington airport to the team's headquarters at Brackley, where he would meet key personnel, among them, in the early years of Niki's tenure, the technical director Paddy Lowe who had previously been the technical director at McLaren. Lowe said:

Niki employed me to come and join Toto in 2013. I can't remember where I first met him but that was my first dealing with him. He was so matter of fact and probably the most unsentimental bloke I've ever met. On one occasion, he came to my office in Brackley and I had a Christmas card for him from Lewis. He opened it, read it – and put it in the bin. 'Niki, don't you want to take it home?' No, he didn't!

Being aware of Lauda's unemotional attitude, Lowe sensed trouble when he heard about commemorative trophies being made by the team's engine partner, Mercedes-AMG High Performance Powertrains (HPP), situated at Brixworth, 30 miles north of Brackley. He said:

In 2014, HPP began a tradition of making a championship trophy for their staff and for a few of us at Brackley. In my view, they made a mistake by numbering them. Andy Cowell (boss of HPP) brought one for Niki by hand all the way to the Canadian Grand Prix in Montreal. I was in our little office with Toto and Niki when Andy presented this trophy. When Niki opened it and saw that he was only number two, you can imagine the conversation! When we were tidying up the office at the end of the weekend, the trophy was still there; Niki didn't take it with him. Andy was obviously unaware of Niki's history with trophies – as in, he never kept any!

In the 1970s, Lauda tried to use one winner's cup as a dog bowl but the unusual appreciation of such an award was lost when decorations on the trophy prevented the dog from devouring the last scraps of meat. Lauda had explained his attitude to trophies during a television interview in 1979:

Trophies are the saddest thing in the world. First of all, they are ugly; there's not one trophy which looks nice. They are all some kind of a funny thing, which I don't like at all. The other thing is, what have you got with a trophy? You can look at it, but it's not worth anything to me because the memory of something is worth much more than the trophy. But there are people who like my trophies. The guy running my local petrol station asked me one day if he could have the trophies on display. So he put them up there, cleans them every day and has two dogs to watch them. From his point of view, he likes having them. So why not? He gives me a free car wash every now and then, so we're both happy.

Most of the time, Lowe found he was more than happy with the former World Champion:

This lack of sentimentality had its positive side. As Toto and I worked with Niki as our chairman, it was valuable to get his advice and perspective on things because his views were so straightforward: 'No bullshit' was how he put it. So, you'd always get a clear opinion which you either took or ignored, depending on whether it made sense. It usually did.

It's a great skill. It's something I've learned over the years as an engineer when trying to be better at my job. Engineers tend not to be quite as bad as lawyers, but they're not far off when it comes to complicating things beyond necessity. So, having someone like Niki who would cut through all the bullshit and say 'this is what we're going to do'; that's just what you want in a team. His clarity of thought would usually take you in the right direction – sometimes, not – but it was good to have the view of a proper racer; someone who was proper old school.

In Lauda's case, such old-school methodology did not necessarily understand – never mind embrace – the usefulness of therapy and the acceptance of emotion in the workplace. Wolff said:

At the beginning of our relationship at Mercedes, Niki did not come to Brackley so often. But in the last few years, if he felt he was not doing enough, I would say that having him come to the factories in Brackley and Brixworth, and just walk around, was the most powerful thing. His sheer presence was the biggest factor for the team. But at first, I needed to tell him this. I would say: 'Niki, people look up to you so much. Your energy is positive.' He always felt he had to be proactive and he eventually found his peace with this role, providing real performance for the team by being Niki Lauda. He was so important in that respect.

Lauda's presence took on a different dimension within the team in 2015 and 2016 when the rivalry between Lewis Hamilton and Nico Rosberg became increasingly intense. Wolff said:

Niki was a sparring partner. I would do the main download of events immediately after the race or at the factory with Paddy or James [Allison, who succeeded Lowe as technical director] and the engineers. But, in the immediate aftermath, I would use Niki as a sounding board. I would ask him: 'What was most important for a driver in that situation?' He could see things from a driver's point of view and say to me: 'Look, he was thinking this, or he would have been thinking that.' He told me what I needed to bear in mind when speaking to the drivers about whatever it was that had happened. He could see things very clearly; explain it in a very straightforward way.

There were, however, occasions away from the racetrack when Lauda's pragmatism could startle Wolff. He recalled:

We were in Shanghai. Niki really enjoyed having dinners together – either the two of us, or a small group of friends – but, on this occasion, I said: 'We're having a sponsorship pitch tonight. It's a big sponsor; important people from the company will be there. You need to be present.' Niki didn't want to know. I said: 'We've got to do this, Niki.' 'Okay,' he said. 'How much?' 'Ten million, over three years – but please, Niki, don't mention it.' 'Okay.'

We get there that evening. Waiting in a private room is the chief executive officer for the company, the chief executive officer for Asia, the chief marketing officer and another guy from the agency. Niki goes round them all and shakes hands: 'Niki Lauda ... Niki Lauda ... Niki Lauda ... ' One guy is into aviation and asks a question about Lauda Air. We chat for about ten minutes then I say we should sit down.

As we sat down – we hadn't even ordered drinks – Niki looked across at the chief executive officer and said: 'So, are we doing the sponsorship or not? Ten million is our offer.' I couldn't believe he was ruining our whole game plan. The man looked at him. There was silence. Then he said: 'Yes, that's okay. Ten million. Three years.' We shook hands.

When we eventually left in the taxi, I said to Niki I couldn't believe what he had done. 'It's very simple,' he said. 'You make it too complicated.' He may have been too extreme the other way – but you couldn't help but laugh about it. He was quite incredible. If you put some of the things he did in a movie, people would say it's too far-fetched.

CHAPTER 31

Rush

Lauda remembered:

Ron Howard, the guy who made the film *Apollo 13*, and Peter Morgan, who writes film scripts, came with me to the British Grand Prix in 2012. They wanted to see what F1 was like and Bernie [Ecclestone] gave them tickets. After they'd looked around the paddock, they said: 'There's something wrong here. You've got these huge monsters of motorhomes – but there's no life, there's no atmosphere, there's no emotions. Has it always been like this?' I said: 'No, it hasn't. Look at my time in F1. That's why you're going to do this movie.'

Howard and Morgan had both been intrigued by the 1976 season with Niki Lauda and James Hunt, two vastly different characters, going neck-and-neck through a year filled with every conceivable kind of drama. As Morgan noted: 'There's no need to embellish the script, as you normally would for a movie. If anything, you have to tone things down with this one.' But first, he needed Lauda's approval. With Hunt having died in 1993, it was essential to explain their plans to Niki. Lauda said:

I'd never been in this type of operation before. Peter Morgan called and asked if he could talk. He said he had this idea for a movie. 'But,' he said, 'I tell you now: you won't like it.' Why would I not like it? 'Because I write the script. I'm in charge and I know.' I thought, 'Well, he won a Golden Globe or whatever, so he should know what he's doing.' Then he started asking me questions, questions, questions. I met with him seven or eight times, but when he started asking funny questions, stupid questions, I got a little bit worried.

So, I asked him to read something to me, to show how the movie is going to be. He opened his laptop and said: 'Okay, you jumped in the Ferrari, you put the seat belts on, you turned the key and off you went.' I said: 'Are you nuts? There's no bloody key in a Ferrari racing car; there's a button. And I can't put the seat belts on myself. If you're going to make a movie like this; you've got to stop. This is a movie where not even the least important things are in order.' After that, Peter got a little worried and he began asking me all these technical questions very carefully, to make sure it was right.

Having gradually gained Lauda's confidence, the next vital step for Howard and Morgan was to find someone suitable to play such an iconic character. In the eyes of many film directors, a German actor playing an Austrian would be ruled out immediately, given the crucial and easily identified variation in accent and the latent animosity between the two nations. There would be even less of a chance if the actor in question was typecast as only suitable for playing a German in Second World War movies.

As an American, however, Howard had no such European film industry baggage. He immediately saw Daniel Brühl as a likely candidate. The man from Cologne, in turn, jumped at the chance even though it presented several potential difficulties; not least having to play a feisty, living legend. Brühl said:

I knew about Niki's bluntness. You only had to listen to any interview or see him on television. I said to Ron and Peter that I really needed to get in touch with him. But I didn't know if Niki would be willing to do that or, indeed, if he was really that fond of the project or the idea that I would portray him. He was Austrian and I'm German; they don't like us that much – and vice versa. Anyway, I didn't want to disturb him knowing what a busy man he is. So I said to give him my number, because I didn't dare to call him.

One day at 6 a.m. – of course! – the phone rang and I saw the number was +43, so I knew it was Austria. I answered and, in his very unique Niki style, he told me to come to Vienna – but it would be a good idea if I just travelled with hand luggage in case we did not get on with each other, so then I could, in his words, piss off right away. I took hand baggage. Fortunately, the first day in Vienna was longer than expected. And at the end of it he said: 'Well, yeah; actually you're a likeable guy; we can spend some more time together.' So I went out and bought a new shirt.

From that moment on, the ice broke. Actually, it had begun to break after about fifteen minutes. I could feel something very interesting within me; I lost all of my nervousness and fear about dealing with such an impressive man like Niki. He made me feel very relaxed. It was remarkable how this man who, from the outside, could seem cold and calculating, could open up so much emotionally as he did with me. We talked about all sorts of things; fears and death; vanity and vulnerability. He would always answer my questions – and I'm deeply thankful for that.

His ability to answer a question with a straight answer was fantastic – especially in my world as an actor. You don't find that attitude – and I include myself – in the movie industry. Some call it diplomacy, and every now and then that can be helpful. Others call it lying, not being straightforward, trying to avoid conflict by avoiding honesty. Niki was the opposite in every respect.

I'd never come across a man quite like him. That's what I deeply admired about him. This was more than his courage and bravery when coping with the effects of the accident – which already was unbelievable. But dealing with other people in such an honest way is something that I find very, very brave. That impressed me. No matter how tricky the subject, if it was something painful that had to be said in front of someone – he would do it, no matter how uncomfortable the situation. He would tell you the truth to your face and often it would be paired with his Austrian sense of humour; sometimes a very dark sense of humour.

There were times when I could not believe what I was hearing and seeing. He did a live interview and he was asked by a young woman interviewer what he had done for our film. He said he had done nothing for the film; he had just organised the barbecue – and then, straight to camera, showed his face. Unbelievable. I thought it was such a healthy way of dealing with what had happened to him. This incredible sense of humour was one of his weapons.

I had to confront him with so many tricky questions concerning our movie that I didn't want to dig any further into the rest of his life; I really didn't need to know much more about that. During conversations, he would tell me a lot about his airline. And the fascinating thing was he would let me be there during quite tough and interesting business meetings. He didn't care that I was around. Afterwards, he would say to me: 'He's an idiot' or 'That one is a fool; he doesn't know anything.' It was fun to be there and witness a big negotiation for, I forget how much, but a lot of money when he sold his company.

Because of his idiosyncratic clipped accent when speaking English, Lauda was one of the most imitated drivers in the F1 paddock. Since *Rush* would be in English, it seemed logical to assume that Brühl would wish to converse with Lauda in English when they were together. Daniel said:

No. We always spoke in German. Ultimately, I knew I would have to dub myself in German and I found this much harder because people from Austria would hear subtleties more than when I played Niki in English. Interestingly, I found it easier to believe that I was him when I was speaking in English. Being a German, I didn't feel as much a non-Austrian in the English version as I did in the German version.

I got some harsh reactions in Austria. In Vienna, when people already knew that I would play him, they used a not very nice word in German. It was like: 'You foreigner, you German; you want to play our national hero. It's not gonna work.' So that was not very helpful. But the dialect coach I had was amazing; she got me there. For English, I listened to Niki's interviews and watched documentaries. The way he spoke also defined the way he thought and the way he was. In the Austrian accent, there's a certain amount of arrogance and sense of humour but also a directness that I wanted to hit just right because it helped me in understanding him and portraying him.

Part of the portrayal would come from observing Lauda's mannerisms. Brühl went on:

His short, quick walk; I noticed that. It was like when Andre Agassi walked across the tennis court; those purposeful steps. I wanted to get the physicality right. It was very important to show the big differences between him and James Hunt in that respect. Chris [Hemsworth, who played Hunt] and I studied both guys so well; we wanted to show all the differences accurately; even the most subtle ones. Also Niki had a specific way of moving his hands, particularly when he was explaining something; he moved them quite a lot. Then there was that little smile; slightly mean at times.

Brühl had to work his way through shooting of the film not knowing what Lauda would make of it and hoping it would be good enough to satisfy someone so precise. Brühl said:

I thought, if this guy is not happy with my performance then, I'm really ... I'm fucked! That was obviously the most important thing for me to achieve. It was comforting that every now and then he would visit the set – although he got bored after about two minutes! But there were little moments when he would notice something in costume or whatever. When he made very subtle compliments, I could by then understand that he was confident and happy with it. But ultimately you never know until you see the whole picture. Will he be happy with the film? Will he be happy with the performance?

Lauda said:

When they were shooting Daniel called me and asked if I put on the crash helmet first or the gloves. I explained that I put the helmet on first because I have to do up the chinstrap without gloves and then I put the gloves on. So this was an ongoing situation and Daniel was working very hard to get this right, which impressed me.

When I saw the movie for the first time, they showed it to me without music; without the cuts; just the raw movie. When I looked at it I thought: 'Pah! I must have really been an asshole in the past. The way he played me and the way I said yes and no and always negative and forward and backwards. I really was worried. I was not happy, to be honest. I said to Peter: 'Okay, you made your movie, as you said you would. But I don't think I was that bad.'

Then I went to the premiere of the movie in London. I was worried going in there; all the people watching it for the first time. Now I was seeing it with the music and it already started to look a bit different to me. I looked around to see how everyone reacted: I saw them laughing; I saw them crying; there was a lot of emotion.

By accident, Ecclestone was sitting next to me. When it was over, Bernie said to me: 'That was good. I want to see the movie again right away.' I thought: this is a good start! And everybody applauded. My thinking in the beginning had been too hard. The film is eighty per cent right when showing what happened that year. There's a little bit of Hollywood in there, which is logical. But I have to say, especially seeing the acceptance of the people watching it, I really like it. I thought the job Daniel did was incredible. The only sad thing for me was that James is not here any more. If he had been with me, I would have been really happy.

If Lauda was anxious at the premiere, Brühl's feelings can be imagined when he saw the film for the first time in Lauda's company:

The first time I really sat with him, sat next to him, was in Vienna. I was extra nervous because his family was there; and some of his friends – who, of course, were Austrian. After the performance, he said: 'Thank you for making me less of an asshole than I actually was!' I guess that was his way of expressing his happiness.

As I had discovered in my conversations with him, he had tried not to think too much about the accident in 1976 and the moments after that because it was just too tough to be reminded of the whole horror. So, for Niki to watch a film that told the story quite accurately and was very well shot and scripted, he was deeply moved; I could tell. His eyes were wet. To achieve that – in Niki, who was not so easy to be moved – was a very important moment for me; for all of us. Being German, to get a compliment from an Austrian, is really quite something! It's a film that has made me feel most proud. Niki Lauda was one of the most fascinating human beings I've ever met.

Rush was widely acclaimed – significantly, by F1 fans known for their statistical and technical exactitude. There were, as Lauda put it, elements of Hollywood to help the story along. The Grand Prix calendar as portrayed did not follow the actual 1976 schedule; James Hunt would never have used premeditated physical force on a journalist; Willi Dungl was not mentioned. Objections to these quirks by one or two fanatics missed the point. *Rush* delivered a sensitive and, when it mattered, accurate portrayal of two drivers engaged in one of the most captivating duels in the history of the sport. In Lauda's case, the film also brought home the truly remarkable make-up of a man many outside F1 had previously known nothing about. It gave the wider world a flavour of someone the motorsport fraternity regarded with enormous affection and respect.

CHAPTER 32

It's Very Simple

Niki Lauda was the 'go to' voice of reason for the motorsport media. In the frequent event of a controversy kicking off in the Formula One paddock, politics and self-interest would generate statements and responses to the point of confusion and contradiction. Lauda would effortlessly provide a clarity flavoured with humour and, when necessary, waspish comment. As a foretaste of the practical judgement to follow, he would inevitably begin with: 'It's very simple . . . ' And then go on to deconstruct the unnecessarily complex argument being put forward. He was a breath of fresh air, a bastion of common sense in a red cap.

As F1 reporter for *Motor Sport* magazine and the *Sunday Times* newspaper, Mark Hughes witnessed Lauda's direct approach from many angles. One in particular stood out. He recalled:

I was walking down the Montreal pit lane moments after the race had finished – and walking towards me was just the man I needed to talk to: Ron Dennis. This was 2005, the race where McLaren had been running 1–2, [Juan Pablo] Montoya leading [Kimi] Räikkönen. This was a bit awkward for McLaren because Kimi was the team's title contender and

Montoya was nowhere, as he'd had his motorbike/tennis shoulder injury earlier in the year. But then came an opportunity just around the pit stop window as there was a safety car for [Jenson] Button's accident in the Wall of Champions.

McLaren somehow contrived to leave Montoya out there for another lap but bring Räikkönen in – which of course won Räikkönen the race. It seemed a bit hard on Montoya, but had it really been as deliberate and cynical as that? Had they really screwed over one of their drivers to help the other one? If that's what had happened, it could only have been Ron Dennis's call as the boss – the race team wouldn't have been empowered to make such a call. But maybe there was another explanation. So, I asked Ron what had happened.

He seemed very uncomfortable with the question and continued walking and said something like, 'Oh there was a radio communication problem. We will be making a statement later.' So, I pressed him further, but just then Niki – who was working as a TV pundit – appeared with a big grin on his face, clearly delighted at Ron being in an uncomfortable situation (those old wounds from '85 were still there). 'Hey, Ron, that was lucky, huh? The safety car allowed you to screw Montoya over, huh?' Big toothy grin.

Ron, with me the journalist alongside him, couldn't really answer Lauda as he probably wanted to. 'Er, no there was a radio communication problem,' he said, now really uncomfortable.

'Bullshit!' said Niki with a huge grin, winked at me – and then left. Just so him. Wonderful.

Mathias Brunner, F1 writer for the Swiss publication *Speedweek*, had an early encounter with Lauda that set the tone for an association stretching across three decades. He said:

It makes me cringe the way somebody is hailed as a star or even a legend these days. Every third-class actor in a quirky soap opera or in a stupid reality show is a star. It's ridiculous. Call me old fashioned, but a star is a person known worldwide and someone who's really achieved something outstanding. For me, Niki Lauda was more than a star, he was a legend.

People like to tell stories about his unrivalled will to live, particularly after that life-threatening accident at the Nürburgring. Many will also remember him for his no-bullshit attitude. He didn't suffer fools gladly, always spoke his mind and more often than not this truth could hurt. But there was another side of Lauda which, for me, was demonstrated by a personal moment.

In the early '80s, I was a young journalist, sent to an F1 test for the first time. Talk about being star-struck! It felt simply unreal to be in an F1 paddock among drivers I had admired on television and in magazines. Of course, these were completely different times. In a modern F1 test week, drivers sort of evaporate. You only get a glimpse of them when they move from the pits to their motorhomes. Usually, the single chance to speak to them is in pre-scheduled media events. In the past, if let's say his engine had blown up, a driver leisurely stood at the pit wall to have a look at the competition, or to have a chat with whomever was around. They were approachable, candid – normal.

My plan was to speak to McLaren drivers Alain Prost and Niki Lauda. So, Prost was standing around with obviously not too much to do. I humbly introduced myself and asked when we could speak for ten minutes or so. Prost icily replied: 'Oh, I'm very busy now. I have a meeting with my engineers soon. Maybe you come back later.'

I thought: 'All right, he's certainly got bigger fish to fry than speaking to a young journo; that's fair enough.' Half an hour later, I went around a corner and discovered all about

Prost's very important meeting; he was having a grand time playing cards with some friends under the tent of a camper (no temple-lookalike motorhomes then). You can't imagine how disappointed I felt. I made a mental note regarding Prost's character.

A little later, Niki Lauda strolled by. I approached him with the same question. 'Well, I'm on my way to the pits, but come back in 30 minutes.' Being Swiss, I was back in 20 minutes. Lauda came out of the pits at the exact time he said he would. We sat down and you cannot imagine how patiently and kindly he answered all my questions, many of them perhaps not the brightest candles on the cake! He was honest, in-depth, funny; he threw in some anecdotes. In the end, we sat for almost an hour. Then a mechanic literally had to drag him away to drive again. Prost was still playing cards – and I noticed he looked over every once in a while. I was immensely impressed by Niki's openness and how much time he invested in a young man he did not know. I have been an admirer ever since.

Formula One is an environment in which you are forgotten very quickly. Either you decide to leave in order to do something else, or your time on earth is up. But rarely is there time to reflect and to truly treasure the memories of people having left this strange, little circus called F1. But Niki Lauda is someone we shall never forget. He really was larger-than-life.

The author's first interview with Lauda took place sooner than expected. Having been introduced to Niki by Alan Henry between practice sessions in Detroit in 1982, the immediate goal was to arrange an appointment for later. Lauda short-circuited that by immediately saying: 'Okay, do it now. Start!'

It was a typical examination of the questioner's competence.

Having been warned by Alan that this might happen, and despite the less than satisfactory environment of a noisy pit lane, I had my questions and cassette recorder ready. With this first test dealt with to his satisfaction, Niki's answers were full and frank, a wonderful foretaste of many interviews to come.

Michael Schmidt, having witnessed as a youngster the moment of Lauda's return at Monza in 1976, had a similar experience after becoming a journalist and facing his hero on a professional footing for the first time. Schmidt said:

It was at the French Grand Prix at Paul Ricard in 1982. I wanted to interview him and thought I would have to arrange something. I went to Niki and said: 'Mr Lauda, would you have time over the weekend? Can you give me five minutes?' And he said: 'Let's do it now.'

Shit! We were standing in the pit lane and he was putting me immediately under pressure because, obviously, I was not prepared; not at all. I thought he might say tomorrow, or whenever, and then I would have time to write down some questions. So, there was a bit of panic! Fortunately, I had been following everything very closely and I was able to think of questions straightaway. They were obvious, for sure, and not the best questions but, right from the beginning, his answers were clear and precise.

He was always black and white. He would never give you an answer that actually said nothing at all. He used very few words but there was always something in what he said. By giving short answers, he was also increasing the pressure, because you had no time to think about the next question. But you had the feeling that he enjoyed it; just to see how you dealt with this; to see if you were professional because that's what he expected of everyone he worked with. Once you knew that, then there was never a problem.

First impressions were startling for Tim Collings when covering the 1987 Austrian Grand Prix during his first year in F1, working for Reuters. He said:

> I walked into the paddock at the Österreichring and the very first person I saw was Niki Lauda. I thought: 'This is a good start; I'll see if I can speak to him.' I introduced myself, said I was from Reuters, and asked if I could interview him at some point during the weekend. He said: 'Reuters? This is good. Let's do it now.'
>
> Then he asked if I was English and, when I confirmed that I was, he said he hoped I had a sense of humour because he had a joke for me. Without further ado – and, don't forget, I'd never met the man before – Niki asked: 'Has your wife ever caught you wanking behind the kitchen door?' When I replied: 'No!' he nodded and said in mock seriousness: 'Safe place, eh?' And then that little laugh. It was so instantaneous and typically abrupt. He always nodded at me and smiled for many years thereafter. And we did go on from there to have an interview!

It mattered little to Lauda which branch of the media he was dealing with; provided the question or request was reasonable, the response would be immediate. Having worked as an international sports cameraman for more than twenty-five years, and in all branches of motor racing, Jean Michel Tibi has come into contact with many and varied sports stars on the other side of his lens. He said:

> I'm French and I really supported Alain Prost back in the '80s. So when Alain went from Renault to McLaren, he was with Niki Lauda and this was interesting for me because Lauda was like a legend; the man with the red cap and the

burns on his face. For me Lauda was someone like [Ayrton] Senna; someone who seemed superhuman; someone beyond the normal. I had worked with Senna but, to be honest, I preferred working with Niki because he was a man of passion, who really loved the sport. I always got the feeling that he understood exactly what we were trying to do. He was like a normal person, working alongside you. He never was rude or told you to take your camera and get out; he realised you respected privacy and would do a professional job.

In the garage, he always looked like a quietly confident and knowledgeable person who had been around thirty or forty years and seen it all. There was a calmness about him that was very reassuring. If something went wrong, you would see people in the garage looking at Niki to see how he would react. It was as if, with all his experience, he would have the solution – and that solution would be right.

Each time we met, he would always look straight at me and say 'Bonjour' – always. He spoke very good French, although he obviously spoke with a different, slightly harsh accent! I saw him in St Tropez few years ago. We were having lunch and he was very kind; he came to my table and spoke with my family. 'The famous red cap man is coming to our table to say hello.' My father-in-law was very impressed! Of course, I tried to play it down as if this happens all the time. I was a bit overwhelmed, to be honest. Usually you go to your hero but, here, the hero had come to my table. And he was as polite and straightforward as ever. For me, that moment summed him up as a person.

Lauda's ready acceptance of others also applied to an easy acknowledgement of his own condition and looks, evident from the moment of his first public appearance following the destructive accident at the Nürburgring. His summary 'You have to look at me; if you don't like it, that's your problem, not mine' became a leitmotif that turned into a marketable trademark as time went by. F1 photographers had no worries about causing offence should the portraits of Lauda highlight his blemishes. Darren Heath's creative work as photographer for F1 sponsors and leading sports publications led to a typical reaction from his subject in the familiar red cap. Heath said:

> I was working for *F1 Racing* magazine and Jaguar at the time. I did a side portrait of Niki showing the back of his head, his right ear and the red cap. He didn't know I was taking it. *F1 Racing* ran the image as a DPS [double page spread]. When he saw me at the next race, Niki said: 'Huh. Didn't know what the side of my head looked like. My ear looks bloody terrible!' Then he nodded, the way he always did when everything was okay, and moved on. I thought: 'That'll do! I assume you don't much like the subject but, typically, you're not making a big thing about it; just saying it like it is.'

Herbert Völker continued his relationship with Lauda long after Niki had stopped racing:

> As editor of *Auto Revue*, I had to have contact with him. We had a regular column which we kept alive for many years after his withdrawal from racing. We would discuss everything and I met him every three weeks or so in the Imperial Hotel cafe, which he liked so much. Meeting at 07.15 was very early for me! Fortunately, I live very close to the hotel. We were close friends, so it was more than merely a journalist working with a driver. We had a lot of laughs. During working time, he was as precise as always. He would want to read through anything I had done, but it was very easy because he never ever wanted anything corrected and also because we had such a good time.

Giorgio Piola's main brief was the production of technical drawings to illustrate the latest developments on F1 cars. Often, he would need to write a description to accompany his artwork, a task that would require contact with the drivers, particularly post-race. If a driver retired for technical reasons, Piola would need to know what had gone wrong with the car. Piola said:

In 1982, Lauda was disqualified from third place in the Belgian Grand Prix because his McLaren was found to be under weight. I was a journalist with *La Gazzetta dello Sport*, so I had to speak to him after the race. When I asked Niki what had happened, he said very simply: 'My team is shit. I was stupid; driving an illegal car.' Usually, when something like this happens, the driver will say: 'It's not fair. I drove for 68 laps. I risked my life for nothing. I didn't know anything about the car being like this.' Here was Niki saying the team was shit and, as a result, he drove an illegal car, but there was nothing more to be said. Fantastic; he didn't make any excuses at all.

Another example of his honesty came in China in 2017, when Lauda was working for RTL, the television company. [Sebastian] Vettel had won the previous race for Ferrari in Australia. I was chatting with Niki about this and he said: 'Giorgio, last year when [Nico] Rosberg won the same race with Mercedes, this was a driver with a German passport, driving a Mercedes, which is the symbol of Germany – and RTL had 3,800,000 viewers. This year, Vettel wins the same race and they have 4,600,000 viewers; 800,000 more. What does it mean? It means with Mercedes – nobody cares. Me? When Ferrari wins, my heart does like this [thumping his chest to represent fast-beating heart]. I care about this. But I have to think of the money – so don't write this!' He repeated that two or three times: 'Don't write it! Don't write that Ferrari is making emotion; Mercedes – nothing.'

The thing is, when he came first into F1, Niki was ten times worse than Schumi [Michael Schumacher] when it came to showing no emotion. He was just a computer; no words, no explanation, nothing. After his accident [in 1976], it was like there was another Niki Lauda. Totally different man; much more open; more fun. It was also different because of his girlfriends. The first girl he brought to the races was really like a piece of stone. But the second one, Marlene, was a wonderful woman; very interesting. For me, he was a completely changed man. He was so much fun and always good to talk to – even if you couldn't write some of the things he said! In the end, I always had a very good interview; very straightforward. For television, it was fun when he was talking in Italian; his Italian was simple but, at times, very rude! He was saying these bad words – which made people laugh! For me, he was a fantastic man.

There was never the impression that Lauda's mannerisms had been deliberately fashioned. To him, dealing with people in this way was second nature; it made sense. Why bring unnecessary complications through devious or political methods? Life was too brief for such nonsense; a straightforward view that had been sharpened by the shocking reality of coming close to having that life cut short. The world around him would be the better for it thanks to respective experiences and memories that would have no equal.

CHAPTER 33

Memories

Gerhard Kuntschik

When Niki was racing, I visited him once or twice at his home in Hof for interviews. This was before mobile telephones. He had a secret number, which was a message service. You would leave a message and ask him to call back. He always called back. Of course, this being Austria, it was easy to keep the few F1 journalists updated. It was totally different to Germany where [Michael] Schumacher created a sort of F1 euphoria and it was difficult to keep fifty or fifty journalists happy. In Austria, it was six or seven of us. As soon as mobiles were introduced we had his number.

Each time he retired from racing, I stayed in touch – especially in 1981 when there were rumours of his comeback. My newspaper [*Salzburger Nachrichten*] used my contacts with Niki for the business section, particularly in connection with Lauda Air. He was known and respected by so many people.

Before the start of each season, when Niki was with Mercedes, we would meet in Vienna. His favourite place was the coffee shop in the Imperial Hotel, where he had breakfast, always in the same seat, behind a screen. When I was due to meet him in 2017, we had an arrangement for 9.15 a.m. He said he had another guy to talk to before me and, if he wasn't finished, I could wait just outside. When I got there, he was on the phone and this guy had gone.

It turned out this had been Sebastian Kurz, the young guy who was then the Foreign Minister and, at the end of that year, would become Chancellor of Austria. Niki said Kurz had asked him for a meeting to exchange opinion. He respected Niki on a business level and he was very interested in having guidelines on some political issues. They obviously found a lot of common ground. Niki said he was very impressed by Kurz and, even though Niki wasn't normally into the political side of things, he said he would support Kurz – and he later made this support public.

That was the only interview I ever had with Niki where I didn't have to pay the bill. With Niki, he would say if you want something from me then you have to pay the bill. He would have an egg in a glass, white bread with butter and jam and a cappuccino; only small things. It would be twenty-five euro or something like that and I would always pay. On this occasion, when I asked the waiter for the bill, he said the gentleman before me had paid for everything; breakfast had been on the Austrian Foreign Minister!

Max Mosley

Had Niki gone into motorsport management, he'd have been brilliant. The respect for his experience as a three-time World Champion would have been a terrific asset, not to mention his method of getting things done. In fact, when I was president of the FIA, I had tried to involve Gerhard Berger, another Austrian who is really clever. Between the two, I would say Gerhard would probably have been better to run the FIA because Niki's personal skills were not quite as good as Gerhard's. Niki was a bit too precise: 'Okay, now we do it! Let's go!' But he would have been effective nonetheless.

He was the ultimate 'No bullshit' person, which is very attractive. He was such an interesting character. It's generally true in sport that people who get to the top – even if they're running 100 metres, which is about as simple as it gets – they're always exceptional in some way or another. Niki was a fine example of that. Another asset was his willingness to accept reality. A classic example was his acceptance of [Alain] Prost being quicker when they were together at McLaren. Most drivers never admit that: they'll say, 'The car's wrong; the tyres are wrong; the engine's got no power.' It's very, very unusual for a driver still at the top to admit there are other drivers who are quicker.

Alain Prost

I never had a single problem with Niki. We had a lot of fun together. At one stage, I think in the winter of 1984/85, we had a press conference in Vienna. We had a suite in a hotel and the press conference was to be at 8.00 in the morning. So, the night before, we went for dinner and then he wanted to show me Vienna – which, obviously, he knew very well. We went to nightclubs – I don't want to go into details of that! – and then we went back to the suite and had a few more drinks. Niki was very relaxed. He wasn't wearing his usual red cap and the next thing I know, he has appeared wearing a shower cap! We had an evening like you can't believe. We did not sleep at all and, when we went to the press conference, we were completely drunk. We couldn't stop laughing. I can't remember if we answered a single question without breaking out laughing. At the time, there were no mobile phones or social media, or whatever. Which was just as well because if that had happened today, we would have been posted everywhere within minutes and we would have been in big trouble.

I remember Niki as a person who had a little bit of everything; super professional; serious but fun; easy going but tough at the same time. When you got to know him well, he was someone exceptional. Very different.

Eddie Jordan

My first memory of Niki is back in the late 1970s, early '80s. I was part of the Marlboro World Championship Team, racing in Formula Atlantic and Formula Three. Marlboro used me to help promote their Raffles brand. I had got to know James Hunt and, along the way, I met Niki. He came across as such a smart guy – and brutally honest. Everything was black and white with him; no grey areas at all. Niki noticed that I liked doing deals and was very comfortable in the business world. It was Niki who suggested that the time was right to start a business in racing and I took his advice. I was already managing drivers, but I started a F3 team and, as we know, that led to Formula One in 1991. It was Niki who sowed the seed – and he was right.

In 1993, the last two races of the F1 season were a fortnight apart in Japan and Australia. I was staying over at the Sheraton Mirage in Cairns and arrived at five o'clock in the morning. As I checked in, I noticed some people in the pool at that hour. It was the tail-end of an all-night party. As I looked closer, I could see one of them was Niki. I didn't recognise the bald head at first because, of course, he wasn't wearing his familiar red cap! There were a few air hostesses in the pool and this had something to do with the celebration of an inaugural flight as Lauda Air expanded its routes to Australia. Niki could be a real party animal and there he was, in that pool, partying as hard as the rest of them as the sun came up.

Gerhard Berger

I have to say, I didn't know Niki very well in the beginning. When I was younger, Niki wasn't the image of a racing driver you dream of. I liked the wild, Jochen Rindt style of driving and I wasn't a big fan of Niki. Even when I was racing, he didn't attract me too much. It was only much later that I started to think: 'Shit! He's won three World Championships and I've won none; he must be bloody good!' I began to think about how this guy could take pole position at the old Nürburgring; if you don't have super big balls, no way can you do anything there.

When I stopped racing [end of 1997], I had a 45-metre boat and sold half of it to Niki. He was saying that maybe he would like a boat so I said, okay, let's do this together. We started to take our families on the boat and have holidays together; we became very good friends. That's when I got to know him much, much better.

I began to study Niki very carefully and I became a big fan of him and what he had achieved. I realised he was an unbelievable package; a lot of brain, a lot of discipline. We began to do business together and he was always the same; on the point, clear and fair, super nice – and funny!

He had this image that he never paid for anything – but it's not true. Yes, he was careful; he wasn't a money spender – except when it came to aeroplanes because that was his big passion. He had a good sense for business; a good balance. If you were in trouble, he would help. For some reason, he built up this image of being mean – and he enjoyed that! But the reality was, he was normal; when we went out, sometimes he would pay, sometimes I would pay. In business, he calculated strongly, but it was always okay and fair. He was just normal.

Saying that, the way he dealt with the plane crash in Thailand was unbelievable. I talked to him a lot about this and studied what he did. He dealt with the relatives in an excellent way, and also in the way he managed the media. He has a plane crash with 232 people dead and he has sympathy from everybody, including the families of people who died. Quite incredible how he did that.

All of this took up even more of his time than when he was racing. He was always there for Marlene, and two great boys, Lukas and Mathias. But he was so busy with his life that he had very little time. When we got the boat together, however, he brought the little twins, Max and Mia, and his second wife, Birgit. [Niki and Marlene divorced in 1991. In 2008 he married Birgit Wetzinger, a flight attendant for his airline. Birgit had donated a kidney to Lauda following a failure in 1997.] He enjoyed the twins very much and he started again to increase the contact with Mathias and Lukas. He suddenly became a family man for all his children. He was very happy and had a good relationship with all of them.

Florian Koenig

We would meet from time to time away from the races, but not too much. We called each other on birthdays. It was a professional friendship as TV presenters working together; not a deep personal relationship. He always said he didn't have friends. But he had many friends of course, and he had many people he liked or he loved. He was loved by so many people, and that was nice to see.

In later years, he got a little bit softer with his young family and he was enjoying fatherhood because previously he had been racing, racing, racing. It was nice to see that he had something new for him in his later years. In the end it was what you might call a perfect patchwork family. He once told me one of his biggest successes or victories was that he had united his family. It was a typically honest summary from a very nice guy. He was one-of-a-kind.

Lewis Hamilton

Niki never talked to me about driving. As racing drivers, we don't really do that necessarily. He hired me to do a job. He didn't hire me to then tell me how to do the job. He was just, for me, a massive part of my journey. Obviously I wouldn't have joined Mercedes if it wasn't for Niki. And then, along the way, just understanding how he was a racer and his approach and how he pushed the people around him to help extract more from the team. I definitely learnt that sort of thing from him. I could see that from him all the time, so I've definitely incorporated that in how I manoeuvre throughout my year. In terms of driving, that's all been trial and error through myself really, but as I said, I wouldn't have had the platform to develop as a driver; I wouldn't have the platform I currently have without Niki.

Toto Wolff

Every single day Niki and I spoke. We had so many topics in common; we would share our family lives, family problems, gossip, F1 politics. We would holiday together. He would ask: 'Where are we going on holiday?' I would say I didn't know where he was going, but I was going to Sardinia. It became comic. I would wake up on the first day of the holiday and, at eight o'clock, I would see on WhatsApp: 'I'm sitting in the breakfast area. Where are you?'

He had this boat in later years. When I said I was going to Sardinia again, Niki said he would think about what to do. I flew in with my family and, when I pulled the curtains up, there was Niki's boat, right at the front of the beach. This was where he parked it and stayed for two weeks; we spent the whole holiday together.

At the very end we were very close, I felt that somehow he knew that things were not so good with his health. After we won the last championship in Abu Dhabi before he got ill in 2017, we were flying back and we had dinner. I looked at him and said: 'Niki! Do you have a tear in your eye?'

'No!' he said. 'I would never have a tear in my eye.' Then he repeated what he had always said about having no real friends – which, of course, was absolutely not true – and talked about having no one to call if he was lying in the ditch at two o'clock in the morning. And then he looked up and said: 'But if there is something like a half friend, you are half friend.'

I said: 'Niki, I cannot believe you just said that! Are you getting emotional in your old age?' He denied it, of course. But in that moment, you could see a small but significant change in him; as if he knew something was happening.

CHAPTER 34

Last Lap

Gerhard Berger said:

The Monaco Grand Prix in 2018; that was the beginning of his illness. Niki was on his boat in the harbour. I got a telephone call from him saying he was in bad shape and asking if I could find him a doctor. When I asked what had happened, he said he had a lung infection and he was having difficulty breathing. I went to the boat to see him; he looked very bad.

I called the right-hand man of Prince Albert [reigning monarch of the Principality of Monaco] and asked for his help. They brought Niki into hospital and he got antibiotics, injections and all the things they do. I said to Niki that he should either stay in hospital or go back to Vienna.

Next morning, I was walking through the paddock and I saw Niki in a corner, standing in the shade. 'Niki! You're crazy! What are you doing here?' 'No, no,' he said. 'It's better; I have to work.' What can you say to this guy? It was typical Niki. But he didn't look good.

That was a view shared by the German journalist, Michael Schmidt:

Niki was missing on the first day at Monaco, which was a bit strange. Normally, he never missed anything but, on this occasion, he stayed on his boat. He appeared on Saturday and some of his friends said he would have been better if he'd stayed on the boat and given himself a rest. But he wouldn't do that. He didn't look well.

He looked better at the next race in Canada, but when we went to the French Grand Prix in Paul Ricard, you could see on the Sunday that it had come back really bad. I was sitting with him and a few others around the table in the motorhome and you could see from the way he was sitting that he was suffering. I thought: 'Okay, it's the flu. He'll spend a week in bed and then it's done.' But by the time we got to the British Grand Prix in July, he looked really miserable.

Lauda would, however, have enough energy for what would turn out to be one last push with his three best mates: Attila Doğudan, Toto Wolff and Gernot Schaffler, a close friend of long standing. Wolff said:

The four of us had agreed that, once a year, we would spend three days together somewhere, just being silly boys, spending time as friends. All of us had families and we had had a tragic incident where a friend of ours had committed suicide; so, we wanted to be close to each other. We agreed that, after Silverstone, we would spend three days on Niki's boat in Ibiza.

I flew on Monday night to Ibiza and we all had dinner on the boat. Niki's cough was okay – but it was still there. We had the most amazing evening. At two o'clock in the morning, Niki said: 'Let's go to Pacha!' It's a very famous nightclub in Ibiza, known for its Flower Power theme from the 1970s. We had plenty of drinks; a massive night out behaving like young boys. It was as if Niki again had this ... how do I say ... sixth sense that I referred to before. That he knew what was coming.

The next day, he said he didn't feel too well. There was a big football match on the television that night, but Niki went to bed early. The following morning, he said he was feeling really bad and we needed to get him back to Vienna. The four of us flew back in my plane and Gernot took him to the hospital. We were told his lungs only had 10 per cent function left. This stupid virus had attacked the lungs. The next thing we knew, he had a lung transplant.

Given all that Lauda had been through following his crash during the 1976 German Grand Prix, it was easy to believe that he would deal with a lung transplant forty-two years later with the same sense of almost impertinent irritation. That seemed to be the way of it, judging by subsequent medical reports saying he was expected to make a full recovery.

Lauda had suffered from so-called hemorrhagic alveolitis, an inflammation inside his lungs, which was accompanied by bleeding into the respiratory tract. When acute lung disease followed, a period in intensive care showed further deterioration and quickly led to the startling pronouncement of a life expectancy lasting only a few more days.

Following an urgent transplant, the improvement was dramatic, the outcome of the operation being described by surgeons as 'a very, very gratifying development. We can state that the patient survived it excellently and could already be extubated after twenty-four hours. That means the tube in the lung could be removed and the patient could breathe spontaneously. This is extremely important for us and the entire healing process as well. We can see that he is fully conscious and all the institutions are functioning properly.' It was anticipated that Lauda could return to a life 'that is normal for him'.

That would mean a typically realistic assessment of the operation and aftermath when talking to his friend Pino Allievi on 23 December 2018. The F1 correspondent for *La Gazzetta dello Sport* flew from Milan to Ibiza and recorded what would turn out to be one of the last interviews with Lauda. 'I knew it would be hard, very hard,' Lauda told Allievi. 'In such conditions I could only do one thing: fight. I was never afraid. I was in the hands of specialists.'

Lauda explained that he had been particularly touched by a handwritten letter reccived from four-time World Champion Sebastian Vettel who was now driving for Ferrari:

One of the things that most pleased me was the letter that Sebastian sent me, written in his own hand, full of fine words and affectionate considerations. I didn't expect it. Usually drivers don't do these things; they just drive. But he's a good person.

I didn't miss a single Grand Prix. I phoned the garage during the weekends; they always told me what was happening. It was like being together with the others at the side of the track. I must say that I discovered once more the warmth of the people with whom I've been working for years; all good, all worried.

Lauda told Allievi he planned to spend Christmas with his family in Ibiza, adding that he was accompanied by two full-time trainers and intended to do six hours training each day. The clear intention was to return to the races in 2019 and carry on as before. Then, just over a week later, Lauda was admitted to hospital with flu, the effects of which would be exacerbated by his existing condition. He would later be transferred to the University Hospital of Zurich to enable dialysis treatment.

'I think I was one of the few who was able to visit him in hospital,' said Gerhard Berger. 'I came very close to his family. I have to say Lukas was unbelievable. He was there, every day, in the hospital even though this was in Zurich and Lukas's family was in Barcelona. He stayed the whole time next to his father's bed and took care of him. He couldn't have been better. If you have a vision of how a dream son should be, in my opinion, that would be Lukas.'

After four long months in hospital, and with close family by his bedside, Niki died in his sleep on 20 May 2019, twelve weeks after his seventieth birthday.

CHAPTER 35

Sons of the Father

Lukas Lauda was born in 1979, three years after the accident that almost killed his father and in the same year Niki retired from racing for the first time. By the time Mathias was born in January 1981, thoughts of a comeback had yet to surface but Lauda Senior's mind was fully occupied with the development of his airline. Either way, Lukas and Mathias would not see much of a father who, to the boys, was a regular dad despite his fame as a racing driver and the scars he carried as a result. Lukas said:

> My brother and I grew up in Ibiza. We lived in the countryside so, for me, although I knew my father was a racing driver, I was living on the land and my friends were, typically, the son of a carpenter and so on. As far as Mathias and I were concerned, my father had a normal job like, say, a farmer.
>
> When he became World Champion at Estoril in 1984, I watched it on television. I remember this because my mother was not at home; she had left in the morning and then we saw her on television, standing on the podium at Estoril with my father. It all seemed very strange. When he arrived back in

Ibiza, we went to the airport and they had organised music and celebration and so on. Otherwise, I don't remember much, apart from playing around at home with his crash helmet and overalls.

I only began to realise how famous he was when we moved to Austria in 1988. I was only nine years old, so this was a bit of a shock for me as a kid. The thing that struck me was the reaction of people when we walked in the city. People would turn around, take a good look at him and ask for autographs. For me, as a little kid, it was maybe a bit annoying; a bit much to understand. I had never seen this when living in Ibiza.

People would be curious about his looks. For us, it was normal. My mother could never watch scenes from the accident. But Mathias and I had seen it since we were small. We'd only known our father since after the accident so, for us, the way he looked was completely normal. We only began to realise it was maybe different for other people when you'd sometimes see them looking at his right ear. It was strange for us to see pictures of him as a kid before the accident; that was actually stranger for me than seeing him as he was.

Strolling through the streets of Vienna would be an oasis of comparative calm compared to the scene confronting Niki and his sons when they attended the Italian Grand Prix. Lukas said:

The first time I went to a Formula One race was Monza after my father had retired. We went with my brother and my father's friend, Bertl Wimmer. It was really crowded, tifosi everywhere. It was massive; really impressive. That's when I began to realise how big he was in F1. We had to walk from the paddock to the heliport through the crowds and it was, like, Whoa! People wanted to touch him; it was an amazing experience.

He was always nice with his fans. He would never say 'No' to anyone. When he was in Ibiza, we would go to a little village for breakfast and, because we were always with him, we would see people ask for an autograph, a picture, or whatever. He always said 'Yes' and he would be very patient with people, take his time and talk to them. He told us often as kids that this is part of being a sportsman and being famous; you have to give it back again. He always really respected that, which I thought was really, really nice. He felt it was part of how we should be very well educated in this and other things in life. This was always very important to him.

Niki's priorities would be shifted dramatically in the aftermath of Flight 004's crash in Thailand. Lukas said:

I was with my mother when we saw the banner headline on the news. Many things go through your mind at a moment like that, particularly for the poor people on the aeroplane. But we knew it would be a very difficult time for my father. I didn't see him for one year, he was so busy flying every-where. I remember particularly that he said if the crash was his fault, or a mistake by the pilots or the airline, then he would have no hesitation in closing the company. He said that right from the beginning, and I thought that took a lot of balls. But he was soon convinced there was another problem and he really worked hard on finding out what that was. He lost a lot of weight during this time. He was very sad with this; it was the biggest shock; the hardest punch he ever had. He was such a perfectionist with every detail; that was so important with everything he worked on. He just kept fighting.

Even without this terrible crash, he was always very, very busy and not at home very often – which is normal. But, very important for us, he was always there if we needed him; there was never any question about that. I only bothered him if it was an emergency but, when the need arose, he would be there. It was the same with his good friends; if they needed a favour he would respond immediately. That was a strong side of him.

Of course, he used to say that he had no friends. He actually had lots of friends but saying he had none was just a strategy. It meant he didn't feel he had to call people for no reason, or that they wouldn't get annoyed if they didn't see him. The truth was, he never liked to be alone. He liked to be surrounded by people – but only with the right people and when the time was right. Saying he had no friends gave him the freedom to do his own thing.

Communication with their father became tricky in the initial stages of Mathias realising he wished to race. Lukas said:

Even the thought or discussion about going racing was completely forbidden at home. It didn't affect me because I never really wanted to do that; I'm too big; too heavy. I loved riding and racing motorbikes. When I was six, my father gave me a KTM 50 [a bike for young riders]. I loved it. I did some motocross racing as a hobby and I'm still riding them. I'm also into Land Rovers; I like the adventure stuff.

It was different for Mathias. When he was in his late teens, he drove like an idiot on the road. He said he would like a test because he was always racing on the street and he needed to do something to find a release for all this adrenalin. We went to Marc Piedade, the son of Domingos Piedade, the boss of AMG-Mercedes. He organised a test with a Formula Ford and a Porsche. Mathias did really, really well, but it had to be kept a secret.

When we eventually told our father, he didn't like it. At that time, he was the head of Jaguar Racing. He spoke to Trevor Carlin, who ran an F3 team. When Mathias went to Pembrey [racetrack in Wales] for a test with Carlin, my father flew in by helicopter from Jaguar. It was raining and Trevor said if Mathias did a certain time, then that would be really good. My father said: 'Okay, now you have a goal. If you reach it, you can race.' When Mathias got below the time, Carlin was impressed. My father said that was okay but now Mathias had to do this on his own – which was good.

In the beginning, he didn't support us much. But later, yes, he did. I took care of the sponsorship but when we eventually had trouble getting the whole budget together, then my father made some deals with sponsors. I remember one was connected with the sponsor on his cap at that time. But the main thing was that he was always there for Mathias.

Mathias started racing really late compared to the young guys you see today. His goal was never to get to Formula One. Mathias reminds me a bit of the old-school racers in that he's quick in a car that's badly set up but, after that, he's perhaps missing that last little bit. My father would always encourage us to be realistic about these things but, at the same time, he was always there for us.

Looking back, I'd say our relationship was not so much father–son; more like two friends together. We had a lot of fun. We went out together; we laughed a lot. He always liked going out with the boys, having a drink and doing stupid things.

A child/parent relationship can become even stronger and more intense during times of personal difficulty; the Lauda family bond would be no exception. Lukas said:

The day they called me and said my father had a problem, I took a plane the next day and I stayed with him at the hospital for nine months. I was always there from the beginning to the end. It was very complicated; a lot of bad luck with the bacteria he got from somewhere on the lung. There were some good days, but I always knew they were unlikely to find a cure because of the problems, particularly with his age and the various complications. The whole situation was very, very difficult. After the lung transplant, he was so weak; it was difficult to get him in shape again. Moving his arms and legs; it was really, really hard for him.

Because of the circumstances, I was spending more time with him than I had ever spent before; we got to know each so much better as result. He needed me there; it was good to be there. I'd like to think I helped him a lot in this time and that it meant a lot to us both.

CHAPTER 36

Saying Goodbye

It was raining solidly on the morning of Wednesday 29 May 2019 but that did not deter thousands from coming to pay their respects. The bell, high in the North Tower of St Stephen's Cathedral, beat a mellow, mournful rhythm across central Vienna. Six solemn pallbearers, dressed in grey from head to foot, slowly carried the coffin through the Giant's Door and gently eased it onto a catafalque lined on either side by three tall candles.

Lukas and Mathias Lauda stepped forward and placed the familiar red helmet on top and surrounded it with a simple laurel wreath. The service within the imposing nave of the cathedral, more commonly known by its German title 'Stephansdom' or 'Dom', was ready to begin. The last goodbyes to Andreas Nikolaus Lauda were about to be said.

There were Formula One drivers from the present – Lewis Hamilton and Valtteri Bottas – but mainly names from the past: Gerhard Berger, Jean Alesi, Sir Jackie Stewart (accompanied by Lady Helen Stewart in a wheelchair), Nelson Piquet, Nigel Mansell, Damon Hill, Pedro de la Rosa, Nico Rosberg – and Arturo Merzario, the driver who, at the Nürburgring in 1976, had played such a significant part in allowing Niki Lauda to live for another forty-three years.

Lewis Hamilton, looked thoughtful in a dark suit and trilby hat. 'I will miss our conversations, our laughs, the big hugs after winning races together,' said Hamilton. 'I am struggling to believe you are gone. God rest your soul. Thank you for being a bright light in my life. I will always be here for your family should ever they need me. Love you man.'

For Lukas and Mathias, however, one of the most unexpected emotions was the silent respect being displayed by people Niki had never met, but for whom he clearly meant so much. Lukas said:

I was really, really surprised. We were staying at Attila Doğudan's hotel next to the Dom. With so much on my mind concerning the day ahead, I woke up early and decided to be there at 7 a.m. It was raining like crazy and there were people waiting to go in. The queue was never-ending. People came from Russia, from all round the world, to say goodbye; it was so moving.

We never expected so many people and so much emotion. There were all sorts; all ages. There were former stewardesses from the days of Lauda Air and they were wearing their old uniforms. It was amazing; so very, very nice. And when we went to the grave after the service, the policemen there were crying like little boys. I went to talk to them; it was really emotional.

The Lauda family had asked Gerhard Berger to speak during the church service. He later said:

I was very close to the family and this was a great privilege. This was not what I would call a normal funeral. It was like a state funeral because it was clear that Niki had the respect of all Austria. People were outside the church all day long, just waiting, wanting to pay their respects and say 'Bye Bye'. I would say this was comparable with Ayrton's [Senna] funeral. Brazil is a bigger country but, by comparison, it was similar in mood and feeling.

Seeing this reminded me that Niki was absolutely a one-off; no question about it. He had proved it again and again in different ways: three times World Champion in motor racing; raced for Ferrari, which is always special; a fantastic entrepreneur; the way he managed the plane crash; the way he was in the media. He always had a clean image; in the whole of his life, there was never anything about Niki being dirty or corrupt. He was just an outstanding personality and we were all reminded of it on this day.

Gerhard Kuntschik was among the reporters writing about the man they had worked closely with for the best part of four decades:

When Niki died, it was at the top of the news in every radio and TV station. They immediately pulled out all their archive material. They ran two documentaries. There was a live discussion on ORF [Austria's national broadcaster] with [F1 journalist] Helmut Zwickl and a lung specialist, who explained how difficult it had been for Niki to recover from his last illness; how even the mildest infection had been totally critical for him.

It was the end of an era in many ways. I always stayed in touch with Bertl Wimmer; he'd got to know Niki in their early days and they remained very close friends. Bertl's birthday was 10 May and I called him this year. His voice was very weak. He said he appreciated the call but he was not in good health. Ten days later, Niki passed away. Six weeks after that, Bertl went too.

Niki was a national hero in Austria; the newspapers were full of stories about him. In the past there had been some critical journalists in the business sections who had reported some Lauda Air employees saying Niki didn't like union representatives and things like that. But the truth was, he talked to everybody and his arguments were always precise. You couldn't claim that anything he said was deceitful or bad. All I know is that there were always people applying for jobs because they wanted to fly with Niki. And many, many people who had worked for him were at the funeral. You only had to look at them to see how upset they were. There was just so much affection and emotion that day.

Herbert Völker was of a similar view as he reflected on the man he worked with closely when writing books together:

The funeral was incredible; I've never seen anything like it. The only mistake was that the family underestimated the public reaction. There were thousands outside the cathedral. They waited for hours, in the rain. It would have been fantastic if the ceremony inside the cathedral could have been transmitted to the people outside but nobody had known beforehand that the response would be so high. None of us expected that.

If there was to be disappointment, it was felt by Jean Alesi as he scanned the congregation. He said:

I was very happy to see Lewis [Hamilton] and Valtteri [Bottas] there because they were the only two of the current F1 drivers who took the trouble to attend. I later wrote a letter to [French motorsport magazine] *Auto Hebdo* saying I had not been happy to see so few of the present drivers pay their respects to a legend who had done so much for the safety of drivers in motorsport, right up until the end. I said that instead of changing the rules to make F1 more interesting or whatever, I thought it was important for the drivers to change their attitude and become more interesting for the public by showing respect for someone who was an incredible character; an incredible man. A funeral is never nice but I have to say that the funeral of Niki was fantastic – if that's the right word.

John Hogan agreed:

It was an impressive occasion. The cathedral was full. The management company, or whoever was organising it, did a brilliant job, the way they arranged who you sat with and where. It was a nice funeral in so far as, for oldies like me, people were coming up and saying: 'Do you remember so and so?' Or, 'D'you remember when Niki did this or he did that?' I saw people from all walks of his life; from the drivers and familiar F1 people to a pilot who had flown with Niki, almost from the start of his flying days. You really got a feel for the depth of his achievement in so many ways.

Lauda's final achievement had been his work with the Mercedes F1 team. For Toto Wolff, however, this represented far more than paying tribute to a colleague. He said:

The Austrian President [Alexander van der Bellen] was at the funeral. But it was appropriate that Arnold Schwarzenegger was there because he and Niki were the two most prominent Austrians of recent years. We Austrians look up to anyone who has proven themselves in a competitive international environment; Niki had certainly done that – and against many challenges.

I remember reading about something Gianni Agnelli once saying that life was more than simply thriving for your fifteen minutes of fame, as per Andy Warhol; it's about staying relevant for the whole of your life. And Niki did that. He was a racing driver and then he reinvented himself; came back to the sport as team principal, then as a long-term expert with RTL television, then the Mercedes door opened. It was continuous.

My recollection as a child was that he was everywhere and doing extraordinary things. The red cap was omnipresent in Austrian media. It seemed that, no matter what the topic, people would call Niki and his opinion would be widely quoted in the media. Everything he said always made sense in a very straightforward way.

He spoke the truth and, for him, that came before how you might feel when you heard this. There was always that element of realism. When Mercedes won our sixth championship [in October 2019], had he been there, Niki would have said: 'Congratulations on the sixth one. Now you have a problem doing it again next year!'

We would have flown back together from that race in Japan and talked things through. He had been such a part of our success over the years. It's been very difficult, because I miss him; we all do. I think about him every day. It feels so surreal that he's not here because he was larger than life. When faced with making a difficult decision, I find myself asking: 'What would Niki think? What would he do?' But that doesn't compensate for the loss of such a very special person.

EPILOGUE

When Ken Tyrrell became terminally ill in 2001, the legendary team owner placed several phone calls to friends, associates and former drivers. He talked to each at length. This was unusual.

Telephone conversations with Tyrrell tended to be direct and frequently abrupt, almost to the point of being rude. When calling Ken it was essential to know exactly what needed to be said, and then to spit it out immediately. Otherwise, he would terminate the conversation with the minimum of formality.

On this occasion, however, the opposite was true. Tyrrell was ready to chat at length while engaging in personal talk that previously would have been ruled out by the need to get on and run his F1 team. Each recipient came away with more or less the same thought: 'Really nice to talk – but what was that all about?' In most cases, it would be the last words they would ever have with Ken. He passed away a few weeks later.

I had, to a lesser degree, a similar feeling after an incident in Abu Dhabi in November 2017. While chatting with Anthony Rowlinson, then the editor of *F1 Racing* magazine, I spotted Niki Lauda sauntering through the Yas Marina paddock. Hands deep in his pockets, he wandered over and began to chat. This, too, was unusual. Normally I would approach him, and only if I had something specific to say or ask. It was never the other way round.

The protocol had been established in my mind after many years as a journalist working with a World Champion who did not suffer fools gladly and had little time for idle chat. That said, Lauda was never dismissive or unprofessional during the subsequent conversations. Quite the reverse, in fact; each discussion being peppered with quality and frequently priceless opinion, often delivered in salty language. But gossip and personal exchanges were never on the agenda – unlike this curious encounter in Abu Dhabi.

Unprompted, and in keeping with the relaxed mood, Anthony pulled out his cell phone and asked us to pose for a photo. Not only did Niki agree, to my surprise he stuck his arm round my shoulder. Job done, he gave his familiar crisp nod of the head and continued on his way. Anthony and I had exactly the same thought: 'What was that all about?'

The reason only began to become clear during interviews for this book, particularly when Toto Wolff gave his illuminating view on Niki's mindset during their return flight from that very race in Abu Dhabi. Being a realist, Lauda would have understood and accepted the long-term consequences of his advancing illness.

After more than forty years of F1 coverage, my schedule of Grand Prix visits had been reduced. I never had the opportunity to speak to Lauda again. But that conversation in Abu Dhabi came immediately to mind when news of Niki's death was announced in May 2019. It was one of many memories of an outstanding individual and a master of his art.

When the question is raised about who deserves to be considered the greatest racing driver of all time, Lauda's name is scarcely mentioned. Possibly that's because of the unobtrusive manner of his driving; the absence of drama surrounding most of his twenty-five Grand Prix victories. Whatever the reason, none of it mattered to the man himself.

Despite his accomplishments, Lauda remained modest and devoid of arrogance. He knew what he had achieved and was completely satisfied if, in his view, he had got there with integrity and the maximum of application and effort. All of which contributed to the fact that he remains respected as much for his character as for his achievements.

Niki Lauda was much, much more than a highly successful racing driver. Hopefully, the preceding pages have explained why he was an extraordinary human being; the rare and precise definition of a hero – almost because he never saw it that way. I was clearly not alone in admiring him enormously.

BIBLIOGRAPHY

Books

Autocourse Grand Prix Annual (Hazleton Publishing. Icon Publishing).

Brabham: The Grand Prix Cars, Alan Henry (Hazleton Publishing).

Flat-12: The Racing Career of Ferrari's 3-litre Grand Prix and Sports Cars, Alan Henry (Hazleton Publishing).

Formula 1: The Knowledge, David Hayhoe (David Hayhoe Publications).

Formula One and Beyond: The Autobiography, Max Mosley (Simon & Schuster).

Grand Prix Season 1976: Hunt v Lauda, David Benson (Daily Express).

Grand Prix Who's Who, Steve Small (Icon Publishing).

March: The Grand Prix & Indy Cars, Alan Henry (Hazleton Publishing).

McLaren: 50 Years of Racing, Maurice Hamilton (Prestel).

McLaren: The Grand Prix CanAm and Indy Cars, Doug Nye (Hazleton Publishing).

My Greatest Defeat, Will Buxton (Evro).

Niki Lauda: For the Record, Niki Lauda with Herbert Völker (William Kimber).

Survive. Drive. Win., Nick Fry with Ed Gorman (Atlantic Books).

The Perfect Car: The Biography of John Barnard, Nick Skeens (Evro).
To Hell and Back: An Autobiography, Niki Lauda with Herbert
    Völker (Stanley Paul).

Magazines

Airliner World
Autosport
F1 Racing
Motoring News
Motor Sport

Newspapers

The Advertiser (Adelaide)
Daily Express
Daily Mail
Detroit Free Press
OM Magazine
Sunday Telegraph Magazine
The Guardian
The Independent
The Observer
Sunday Times

LIST OF ILLUSTRATIONS

Lauda at Monza in 1978 (© Getty Images); Lauda, Nelson Piquet and Gordon Murray (© McKlein Photography)

11. Long Beach Grand Prix in 1982 (© Shutterstock); Lauda and John Watson (© PA Images); Lauda and Alain Prost (© McKlein Photography)

12. Lauda and Nigel Mansell (© McKlein Photography); Lauda and Florian König (© Getty Images); Lauda and Daniel Brühl (© Getty Images)

13. Lauda with the Fokker F27 (© Rex Features); Lauda at the scene of the Lauda Air Boeing 767 (© Getty Images); Lauda in the cockpit (© McKlein Photography)

14. Lauda and Eddie Irvine (© Getty Images); Mercedes team celebrating (© Getty Images); Lauda and Toto Wolff (© Getty Images); Lauda and Lewis Hamilton (© PA Images)

15. Lauda and his sons (© Getty Images); Lauda commemorating the 25th anniversary of his crash (courtesy of Karl-Heinz Zimmermann); Lauda's funeral (© Getty Images)

16. Niki Lauda (© Getty Images)

INDEX